Rural–Urban Relationships in the Nineteenth Century

The nineteenth century saw rapid urbanisation in many locations around the world as agriculture became increasingly mechanised and rural workers moved to towns, following the spread of new centres of manufacture and trade. As a result of this urbanisation, key sites across the UK, the US and Europe saw increased conflict and found themselves in the midst of compromises and negotiations with their neighbours.

Rural–Urban Relationships in the Nineteenth Century is a collection of 12 new essays, presented in four sections which highlight key examples of these rural–urban encounters. They explore the changing working practices, the impact of modernity and different perceptions of social mobility, and examine how rural–urban negotiations were enacted in a range of different regional locations. This volume includes work by both established and emerging specialists from a wide range of disciplines, including literary studies, cultural history and social science. They draw upon a variety of methodological approaches and archival sources, including census records, newspapers, memoirs, contemporary illustrations, literature and private correspondence.

This book reveals how, in addition to conflict and cultural anxiety, in some cases social change created welcome new practices and facilitated the formation of positive and enabling relationships, whilst in others tension was always more evident than cooperation. In so doing, the book demonstrates the contribution specific and nuanced micro-historical approaches can make to national cultural histories. This text is of interest to those who study economic history, urban studies and social history.

Mary Hammond is Associate Professor of Nineteenth-Century Literature and Culture at the University of Southampton, UK, and founding Director of the Southampton Centre for Nineteenth-Century Research.

Barry Sloan is Professor of English at the University of Southampton and a member of the Southampton Centre for Nineteenth-Century Research.

Perspectives in Economic and Social History
Series Editors: Andrew August and Jari Eloranta

For a complete list of titles in this series, please visit www.routledge.com.

Rural–Urban Relationships in the Nineteenth Century

Uneasy neighbours?

Edited by
Mary Hammond and Barry Sloan

Routledge
Taylor & Francis Group

LONDON AND NEW YORK

First published 2016
by Routledge

2 Park Square, Milton Park, Abingdon, Oxfordshire OX14 4RN
52 Vanderbilt Avenue, New York, NY 10017

Routledge is an imprint of the Taylor & Francis Group, an informa business

First issued in paperback 2019

British Library Cataloguing in Publication Data
A catalogue record for this book is available from the British Library

Library of Congress Cataloging in Publication Data
Names: Hammond, Mary, 1960- editor. | Sloan, Barry, editor.
Title: Rural-urban relationships in the nineteenth century : uneasy neighbours? / edited by Mary Hammond and Barry Sloan.
Description: Abingdon, Oxon ; New York, NY : Routledge, 2016.
Identifiers: LCCN 2016000885 | ISBN 9781781447536 (hardback) | ISBN 9781315545820 (ebook)
Subjects: LCSH: Rural-urban relations--History--19th century.
Classification: LCC HT361 .R875 2016 | DDC 307.2/409034--dc23
LC record available at http://lccn.loc.gov/2016000885

ISBN: 978-1-8489-3552-5 (hbk)
ISBN: 978-0-367-87603-6 (pbk)

Typeset in Times New Roman
by Saxon Graphics Ltd, Derby

Contents

Illustrations

Figures

Tables

Contributors

Michelle Deininger currently teaches courses in nineteenth- and twentieth-century literature at Cardiff University, UK, as well as preparing mature students for undergraduate study through Cardiff's Pathways to a Degree scheme. She completed her AHRC funded doctoral thesis at Cardiff University in 2013, which mapped a tradition of the female-authored short story in Wales. She has published articles on the novelist Bernice Rubens and the New Woman in Wales. Forthcoming publications include an exploration of ecofeminism in 1970s short fiction.

Michael Edgar obtained his PhD from the University of Southampton, UK, in 2008. His thesis was a study of the social, economic and demographic history of the Isle of Purbeck in Dorset during the nineteenth century.

Christopher Ferguson is Assistant Professor of History at Auburn University, Alabama, USA. His book analysing the life and ideas of James Carter, *An Artisan Intellectual: James Carter and the Rise of Modern Britain, 1792–1853* will be published in autumn 2016. He is currently writing a book about the idea of the city in nineteenth-century Britain.

Reagan Grimsley is an Assistant Professor and Archival Studies Program Officer at Auburn University in Auburn, Alabama, USA. His research interests include the long nineteenth century and archival studies.

Mary Hammond is Associate Professor of Nineteenth-Century Literature and Culture at the University of Southampton, UK, and founding Director of the Southampton Centre for Nineteenth-Century Research. She is the author of a number of works on nineteenth-century literature, reading and publishing history, including *Reading, Publishing and the Formation of Literary Taste in England, 1880–1914* (2006) and *Charles Dickens's Great Expectations: A Cultural Life, 1860–2012* (2015).

Andrew Hinde is Senior Lecturer in Population Studies at the University of Southampton, UK, and a member of Southampton Statistical Sciences Research Institute. He is the author of *England's Population: a History since the Domesday Survey* (London: Arnold, 2003) and of more than 30 articles on various aspects of the population history of England. He is a member of the Editorial Board of *Local Population Studies*, the only British journal dedicated to population history.

Sarah Holland is a lecturer in history at the University of Nottingham, UK. Her research focuses on rural identity and regional variation, the dynamic relationships between town and countryside, and knowledge networks. She is also engaged in projects that explore the relationship between history, health and wellbeing. Recent publications include 'The Evolution of a Northern Corn Market: Doncaster 1843–1873' in *Northern History.*

John A. Macaulay received his PhD in American History from the University of South Carolina and has served as Assistant Professor of History at Erskine College, Research Associate with the Papers of Abraham Lincoln, and is now Senior Training and Communications Specialist at the State Department. He is the author of *Unitarianism in the Antebellum South: The Other Invisible Institution* (University of Alabama Press, 2001). His recent publications include 'Tree Stump or "Treason"?: Unitarians Debate the Role of the Pulpit in the Age of Reform' in *Journal of Church and State*, and '"Quaker" Gun vs Balloon' in *Astride Two Worlds: Technology and the Civil War* (Smithsonian Press, 2016).

Jakub Machek lectures in the Department of Media Studies at the Metropolitan University, Prague, Czech Republic, and is a research fellow at Charles University, Prague, in the Faculty of Arts Institute of Czech and Comparative Literature and Literary Theory. He is currently finishing a project on 'The Emergence of Popular Culture in Czech Lands' supported by a post-doctoral grant from the Czech Science Foundation.

Julia Neville is an honorary research fellow in the Department of History at Exeter University, UK. Her principal area of research is the history of social change in the late nineteenth and early twentieth centuries, and she has published recently on issues related to politics in local government, hospital development and the changing role of women in public life. She is also actively involved in promoting engagement by local history societies in planning and undertaking research.

Barry Sloan is Professor of English at the University of Southampton, UK, and a member of the Southampton Centre for Nineteenth-Century Research. He is the author of two books on Irish literature, *The Pioneers of Anglo-Irish Fiction 1800–1850* (1986) and *Writers and Protestantism in the North of Ireland* (2000), and of over 20 articles and chapters on nineteenth- and twentieth-century English and Irish literature.

Andrew Walker is Vice Principal at Rose Bruford College of Theatre and Performance, Kent, UK. His recent published work includes editing *Lincoln's City Centre: North of the River Witham*, Survey of Lincoln (Lincoln, 2015), in which he contributed a chapter on the city's butchery; and 'English Historical Perspectives on Rurality: viewing the country from the city' in Gary Bosworth and Peter Somerville (eds), *Interpreting Rurality: Multidisciplinary Approaches*

(Routledge, 2014). He has also co-edited, with Shirley Brook and Rob Wheeler, *Lincoln Connections: Aspects of City and Country since 1700. A Tribute to Dennis Mills*, Society for Lincolnshire History and Archaeology (Lincoln, 2011).

Guy Woolnough is a Teaching Fellow in Criminology at Keele University, UK. His research focuses on policing in Victorian England and problematises conceptions of policing by deconstructing the role of the police through an examination of discretionary policing, public expectations of the police and the functioning of police bureaucracy with particular emphasis on petty crime, vagrancy and the policing of plebeian culture.

Introduction

Mary Hammond and Barry Sloan

'God made the country, and man made the town.'
William Cowper, 'The Sofa', *The Task* (Book 1), 1785

Change is, perhaps, the most universal theme in accounts of the 'long' nineteenth century, usually taken to stretch from the start of the French revolution in 1789 to the outbreak of war in 1914; although – as the epigraph above by Cowper demonstrates – inexorable change and its resultant sets of social, geographical and moral oppositions were being recognised even earlier. That the idea of change came to characterise the nineteenth century in particular is, however, unsurprising in a period which saw an unprecedented expansion of urbanisation and industrialisation, the development of new kinds of work and ways of working, the dissolving and reforming of national and regional boundaries and the radical transformation of communications. It was also a time of enormous population movement, with unprecedented numbers of people departing from traditional occupations on the land to seek new lives in the towns and cities or overseas, or being forcibly removed from their places of origin. These phenomena increasingly affected more societies as the century progressed: Britain may have been not only the first industrial but also the first urban nation, as Alun Howkins has noted, but similar developments soon followed in many European countries and in the United States, and in each context they highlighted the changing relationships between town and country.[1]

The inseparable connection between change in its many forms and the movement of people, particularly from rural to urban environments, and the consequences that followed, underlie the chapters in this book, as, indeed, they engaged the attention of contemporary writers. Raymond Williams opened *The Country and the City* by asserting that '"Country and "city" are very powerful words, and this is not surprising when we remember how much they seem to stand for in the experience of human communities.'[2] His exploration of the truth of this proposition centred on readings of literary texts which exemplified the contested relationship between country and city since classical times, and how this assumed particular prominence in nineteenth-century English writing. So, for example, in the early part of the period, William Cobbett made a swingeing attack on the poverty he saw on his *Rural Rides*, undertaken between 1822 and 1826, which resulted from a combination of the economic depression of the post-Napoleonic War years and its exacerbation by Londoners' insatiable demand for food, and the malpractices he alleged against the urban-based government. The young William Wordsworth evoked his bewilderment and disorientation on first experiencing the noise, crowds and endless motion of the capital in Book vii of *The Prelude*, 'Residence in London' (1798), and contrasted these with the rural space and peacefulness of the Lake District.[3] In fiction, Charles Dickens represented the trauma of Sissy Jupe when she was forced to give up the nomadic freedom of a country circus for the regimented schooling and life of industrial Coketown in *Hard Times* (1854), and the cultural confusion and unhappiness of Pip when he departed from rural Kent to pursue his 'great expectations' in London (1860–1). More positively, Elizabeth Gaskell's *North and South* (1855) showed how Margaret Hale's move from the pastoral tranquillity of the New Forest to the pollution and ceaseless activity of the industrial town of Milton Northern precipitated her re-evaluation and more complex understanding of both her rural origins and the new urban home to which she eventually commits herself through marriage. Conversely, in characters like Clym Yeobright in *The Return of the Native* (1878) and Grace Melbury in *The Woodlanders* (1887), Thomas Hardy explored the displacement experienced by individuals coming back to their rural communities after exposure to the wider horizons and opportunities of urban life which have changed both them and their relationship to their past. And in non-fiction books and articles, writers such as Richard Jefferies, Henry Rider Haggard and George Sturt discussed contemporary evidence of the recasting of relationships between rural and urban communities, and speculated on the larger implications of social upheaval – a theme which was also pursued in the columns of periodicals such as *Cornhill Magazine*, *Fraser's Magazine* and *Longman's Magazine*, as well as other less well-known publications.

Across the Atlantic, the interaction between emerging cities and rural communities was, perhaps, less sharply visible than in England, although industrialisation and urbanisation have again been identified as principal agents in 'the deep changes in the quality of American life which seriously tested older value systems and behavioural patterns', especially between 1880 and World War 1.[4] In the thirty years from 1880, the number of urban dwellers grew from just over 14 million to almost 42 million, or 44 per cent of the total population, many of whom were housed in cities that had literally come into existence as 'thousands of sleepy little townships … were transformed' and where 'the sense of rural to urban change must have appeared most challenging and, to some, most traumatic'.[5] Yet despite these changes, or perhaps because of them, Michael Bunce has described how 'By the second quarter of the nineteenth century agrarianism had become for most Americans a romanticised image of farms and farming communities populated by simple, decent country folk living in harmony with nature, the land and each other.'[6] With its origins in the ante-bellum poetry of Bryant, Whittier, Longfellow and Cole, and the fiction and journalism of Sarah Hale, 'the literary mythology of agrarian simplicity came to dominate American attitudes to the countryside throughout the nineteenth and indeed well into the twentieth century', and was sustained by a constant stream of popular fiction, some of which achieved enormous commercial success.[7] In American art, too, as Sarah Burns has argued, the 'cultivated middle landscape or landscape of equilibrium' became 'an emblem of welcome progress, largely uncomplicated by gnawing doubts and regrets'.[8] Whereas 'the sanctification of the wilderness was a romantic literary and artistic idea that served as a vehicle for potent spiritual metaphors', untamed land was an obstacle to farmers who found the greatest beauty in terrain that was 'cleared, tilled, and productive', and artists and writers found that 'this kind of landscape was as richly stocked with ideas as with nature's bounty, and as fertile a ground for metaphor as mountain sublimity or forest fastness'.[9] But while positive images projected country life as the seedbed of sturdy individualism, family life, hard work, thrift and democracy, they commonly ignored the increasingly significant changes both facilitating and resulting from the growth of agricultural capitalism. There were also negative representations of what Marx and Engels termed 'the idiocy of rural life' centred on 'negative stereotypes … which indirectly reflect the shiftings of power and its aggrandizement in the urban sphere of capitalism, industry and commerce'.[10] Whereas the farmer had been the very type of the worthy yeoman in the ante-bellum period, as the influence of urban cultural values spread, he became 'a comic figure on the stage, dressed in overalls and sporting a goatee'.[11] On the other hand, there was also disillusionment with city life and its debilitating effects. This is implicit in texts such as George Lippard's *The Empire City* (1850), Henry David Thoreau's *Walden* (1854), Herman Melville's 'Bartleby' (1856), Matthew Hale's *Sunshine and Shadow in New York* (1868) and, in a different way, in Edward Bellamy's best-selling fantasy of a utopian city of the future, *Looking Backward* (1888). Equally, the celebration of Nature promoted by Ralph Waldo Emerson and the anti-urbanism of Charles Eliot Norton are grounded in unease and concern about the future health and development of a society increasingly attracted to materialism and urban values. As in England, longing for a lost rural past and a simpler way of life are also evident, whether in the work of writers like Sarah Orne Jewett and Hamlin Garland, or in the nostalgic sentiment of James Whitcomb Riley's popular verse.

Commentators have pointed out that the origins of this cultural history of the valorisation of the rural over the urban extend back to classical times, but as Michael Woods has noted, the reproduction of the pastoral myth in Western societies over centuries also had the effect of reinforcing 'the dissonance of the sign and the referent'.[12] As a result, this not only 'disguised the exploitation and oppression of the countryside, first through the brutality of feudalism and later through the appropriation of the rural land for capitalist production in the agrarian revolution'; it also – and even more significantly for the focus of this book – 'disguised the scale and connections between the city and the country, with the dynamics of rural localities and the everyday practices of rural life already heavily inscribed with more prosaic urban renderings of the rural: as a source of food, fuel and building materials, as hunting ground and as a defensive buffer'.[13] And, we might add, as an increasingly indispensable source of people to service and develop the industries and businesses of the expanding cities.

Furthermore, if many writers seem principally exercised by the social and cultural losses they associated with change, it was the new possibilities that accompanied it which fuelled the ambitions and aspirations of countless millions in Europe and North America who were ready to exchange rural for city life, or to move opportunistically between the two environments. Thus, for example, Nicholas Marshall concludes from his microhistory of two families in ante-bellum America that the 'most striking feature' is the way in which individual family members 'crisscrossed the ... North, sometimes living in rural areas, sometimes in urban', and switched to and fro between manual and white-collar work according to necessity and chance, but always in search of material and social improvement.[14] Several of the chapters below provide examples from other contexts and locations which show similar fluidity of movement between the country and the city, both by individuals and by occupation groups.

We see, therefore, that while both in Britain and in North America in the nineteenth century, contemporary writers and thinkers recognised that the advance of modernity was affecting people's relationships with the country and the town, and that while this may often have appeared to them as potentially more problematic than beneficial, the dynamic was clearly far more complicated than the simplistic binary of Cowper's God-man poetic formulation implies. As Donald MacRaild and David Martin observe: 'The distinction between urban and rural areas became increasingly hazy as the century progressed', so that in Britain 'it has been argued that very few genuinely rural districts existed in the early twentieth century away from the south-west of England, central Wales, the northern Pennines area, the Lake District and northern Scotland'.[15] Furthermore, the countryside itself became increasingly 'man-made' with the application of scientific approaches to ever more aspects of agricultural production and the expanding use of technology and machinery, which impacted upon traditional methods of production and the number of labourers required to do the work. Paradoxically, as farms became larger, to save costs farmers preferred to rely more on seasonal rather than long-term employees, and this both encouraged the movement of rural labourers to the towns, and helped to create the shortage of skilled agricultural workers so often mentioned in late nineteenth-century writings.

But if the country was becoming industrialised and urbanised, in a complementary way, city authorities took initiatives to ameliorate the built environment with developments such as Victoria Park in London's East End (opened in 1845) and Birkenhead Park in Liverpool (opened in 1847), which reinstated rural elements into densely populated areas. The example of Birkenhead Park greatly influenced the American F.L. Olmsted, whose projects in New York, San Francisco, Philadelphia, Chicago, and elsewhere ensured that 'in the North American city in the second half of the nineteenth century ... the large pastoral urban park achieved its full potential'.[16] These instances show how in very practical ways both the rural and the urban environments were evolving and influencing each other throughout the period.

It should be remembered, too, that although allusions to nineteenth-century cities inevitably call to mind the great metropolitan centres such as London,

Liverpool, and Manchester in England, New York, Chicago and Boston in the United States, and Paris and Berlin in Europe, the majority of towns and cities were relatively small and followed 'regionally distinct patterns of development' which were directly influenced by their relationship with their hinterlands and by the particular migrants who settled in them.[17] Rather than disappearing into urban anonymity, in some circumstances the incoming migrant population 'encouraged an outgrowth, a diffusion from a core, of local customs and practices' which 'helped to enforce local identities, and some types of customary behaviour, rather than destroying them'.[18] Unsurprisingly, this dynamic occurred most readily when migrants with a shared background settled in specific urban areas, which was – and remains – a familiar pattern.

These cultural and factual contexts underlie the chapters in this book, which demonstrate that the effects of change and population movement are neither simple nor monochrome: the accounts of anxiety, insecurity, estrangement and loss must be set against the solutions and compromises that were sometimes reached to enable life to continue in new circumstances. The characteristics of some of these negotiations may be understood with greater clarity by looking in detail at the interface between rural–urban relationships in particular communities. Here one can see how changes resulted in the erosion or modification of many deeply established customs and practices, altered the balance between relative economies, led numerous erstwhile country workers and dwellers into urban employment and housing, and, in the longer term, produced rising numbers of affluent city folk looking for rural properties and estates as retreats from the pressures of their lives and environments. But there were, equally, entrepreneurial country tradesmen to whom urbanisation meant new or enlarged market opportunities and a welcome incentive to extend and develop their existing trading practices. Examining individual responses to such changes in memoirs, journalism and literature reveals varying degrees of successful adaptation as well as of alienation; and sometimes both, even within the lifetime of single individuals. It soon becomes apparent that the history of the impact of industrial progress on rural–urban relations and identities is as fluid and multifarious as it is inexorable.

It is these sorts of nuance which we try to capture here. This book's origins lie in a conference held at the University of Southampton, UK, in 2013 which invited consideration of these dynamics of change in the critical period when agriculture and related work was ceasing to be the principal source of employment for the majority of people in much of Europe and America, and when rural populations were diminishing. Many of the contributors to the conference – scholars from diverse locations including various parts of Europe, North America and Japan – considered how these broad changes manifested themselves in practical detail at the local level in various national contexts, the questions they raised for specific communities and individuals, and the outcomes that followed. We attempt to reproduce some of the diversity of these responses. Ian Dyck has claimed that 'Town–country anxieties are, in many societies, a permanent feature of human relations', and the chapters that follow implicitly both explore and interrogate the perception of what we characterise – with full cognisance of its potential contentiousness – as 'uneasy neighbours'.[19] In particular, the chapters in this book resist the model of a simple town–country binary and complicate the notion that rural–urban relationships followed predictable trajectories or were necessarily determined by the same factors. On the contrary, as a number of the writers show, the state of established regional business practices and of pre-existing links between rural communities and their local town or conurbation, the emergence of new economic opportunities and the geography of specific locations all played their part in influencing how changes were encountered, just as much or more than the mutual suspicions of town and country residents. In short, as Alison Light has put it, 'A rural or an urban way of life did not exist in sealed compartments' in the nineteenth century, and our contributors explore how this impacted on the lives of individuals.[20]

The book is organised in four sections, each with a distinctive focus for thinking about rural–urban relationships, and the writers draw on a variety of disciplinary perspectives, including social, cultural and political history, literary studies, criminology, book history and demographics, to inform their arguments. Although a majority of the chapters is centred on England, those on Wales, the American deep south and late nineteenth-century Prague enlarge the scope of the discussions, suggesting the widespread nature of change in the period, and invite comparisons and contrasts with the English examples. One of the advantages of studies such as these, based on relatively small communities or regions where rural and urban interests are finely balanced, is that the needs, aspirations and anxieties of each party can be highlighted and usefully compared. Here, the case studies, such as those based on Lincoln, Doncaster and Exeter, or the Piney Woods region of Mississippi, are illuminated and nuanced by the use of exemplary detail showing in some depth how specific changes affected particular interests or occupation groups. Thus, for example, by considering the outcomes contingent upon the choice of site for a new market hall, or the consequences for a town bypassed by the railway, or how the problem of accommodating a long-established animal fair in the principal streets of a town aspiring to develop shop-based commerce was handled, it is possible to gain a sense of how uneasy or otherwise particular rural–urban relationships really were, and of the key factors affecting each situation. Apart from their own inherent interest, these microhistories employ a wide range of resources, including contemporary newspapers and journals, census details, police records, council minutes and reports, literary texts and autobiography, and suggest the potential of a variety of methodological approaches for understanding and interpreting the dynamics of rural-urban relationships.

In the opening chapters of the first section, *Sites of Rural–Urban Encounter*, Andrew Walker and Guy Woolnough demonstrate that, while they share certain similarities, the April Fair in the English town of Lincoln provides some striking contrasts with Brough Hill Fair in the county of Cumbria. Walker analyses the very different ways in which the growing cathedral city of Lincoln, situated in one of the least urbanised regions in the country, renegotiated the management of its April animal fair in the second half of the nineteenth and early years of the twentieth centuries. He considers how the economic advantages the fair brought to Lincoln were increasingly weighed against objections to the accompanying disruption, dirt, noise and anxiety about the influx of outsiders, particularly from Ireland, whose intentions were regarded with suspicion. Walker makes particular use of local newspapers to demonstrate the shifting balance between the interests of the businesses which increasingly dominated the regulated and feminised space of the High Street and the promoters of the fair, and to map the eventual ascendency of retail and commerce. Paradoxically, the very features of the fair which made it exciting – disorderliness, the presence of large numbers of animals and of strangers, bad language and intoxication on the streets – led to its curtailment as urban priorities prevailed over an event in which the country had annually invaded the town.

In contrast, Brough Hill Fair was held in a rural location far from any urban centres, but Woolnough argues that it was a magnet not only for the local population but for traders from beyond the region, and especially for outsiders from the Yorkshire industrial cities who travelled to the area by rail and were of particular interest to the police supervising the event. Unlike the situation in Lincoln, here it was the city dwellers who were regarded as a potential threat to the order and decency of rural Cumbria, importing various kinds of fraudulent crime, even though drunkenness, petty crime and general unruliness had always been associated with the fair. Woolnough uses police records of arrests and prosecutions to suggest how policing policy at the fair became more focused in the later years of the nineteenth century, and was predicated upon the cultural attitudes and particular views of a force consisting largely of local recruits. This, he contends, is reflected in the number and nature of the prosecutions brought against outsiders, and substantiates the view that the police regarded protection of the supposed integrity of the region, and regulation of negative urban influences which they believed might threaten it, as an integral part of their public duty at the fair.

In the third chapter in this section, John Macaulay charts the course of another kind of unease and eventual accommodation observed in the southern states of antebellum America where rural–urban differences were compounded by differences in religious beliefs. Here the established landowning planter elite, who subscribed to the Trinitarian doctrine, was faced with the increasing influence of urbanised Unitarian church members, many of whom held professional positions that gave them access to a disproportionate number of public offices. As Macaulay shows, the apparent irreconcilability of the two religious positions did not prevent a mutually self-interested strategic alliance between the rural Trinitarians and the urban Unitarians, more especially as the latter group became increasingly polarised from their co-religionists in the north over the issue of slavery. In this instance, the site of rural–urban encounter was broadly based and recurred in a number of locations across the southern states, rather than being limited to a specific community, and the way in which relationships were reshaped was not solely dependent on local circumstances but also on the tensions within the Unitarian Church on a national scale. The relevance of religious difference as an aggravating feature here is also a reminder that this is not unique to the southern states of America but was also a significant polarising factor in rural–urban relationships in parts of Europe.

In the first of the detailed case studies in section two, *The Changing World of Work*, Julia Neville shows how the well-established trade of country butchers who raised and slaughtered their own animals, and sold their meat at the market in Exeter, the county town of Devon in the west of England, fell victim to evolving urban business standards and practices in the later years of the nineteenth century. Legislative changes to improve the cleanliness and streamline the management of the market tended to squeeze the country butchers, who had relied on more informal pre-existing arrangements, and to bolster the position of established retail meat traders. Their difficulties were also reinforced by the growing fashion for the butcher to call at clients' houses for their orders rather than the customer frequenting the market. Again, this favoured the urban shops and marginalised the country butchers. Neville uses the records of individual country butchers' families to demonstrate the decline in their fortunes and, in several cases, their abandonment of the butchery trade as an unsustainable mode of business in the face of urban domination of the market.

By way of contrast, Sarah Holland's examination of Doncaster in the English north-eastern county of Yorkshire reveals much more creative and mutually supportive dynamics at work between the civic authorities and the local agricultural producers. Neville indicates that the coming of the railway to the Exe valley in the middle years of the century was an additional factor which affected the way in which meat was bought and sold in the Exeter area. In Doncaster, too, the arrival of the railway impacted on the transportation of goods to and from the town, but Holland is able to show how the relocation of the new Corn Exchange to a site close to the railway and away from the wharves, which had previously been crucial to distribution, typified the progressive thinking of the decision makers. This raises the question whether, unlike Exeter, nineteenth-century Doncaster's apparent self-consciousness of its position in a region of ambitious and expanding towns and cities, and the aspirational culture of its leaders reflected in local newspaper reports and civic records, encouraged the reciprocity between town and country that Holland reconstructs in her chapter.

Andrew Hinde and Michael Edgar's chapter complements the Exeter and Doncaster studies by placing the focus on the adaptability shown by a specific occupational group – the stone workers of the Isle of Purbeck, located in the English south-western county of Dorset – in responding to the vicissitudes in their trade. The Purbeck stone quarries had a long history of providing more regular employment than agriculture, the other principal source of work in the area, and migration rates among stone workers were relatively low. However, unlike employees whose skills were bound up with the countryside or limited to a particular location, the stone workers were also experienced masons who could equally well practise their trade in city locations where Purbeck stone was widely used. Hinde and Edgar draw on census enumerators' books and parish records to trace the migration patterns of these workers between 1841 and 1881, to show how they relocated strategically to areas with historical links to the Purbeck stone trade, and to demonstrate their tendency to resettle close to one another. Their evidence also challenges perceptions of migration as a one-way passage from the country to the city, and presents a different model of a reciprocal relationship between the two: for these workers migration was not necessarily permanent, and was commonly followed by a return to the Isle of Purbeck when conditions again became favourable.

While the nineteenth-century city is conventionally understood as the most visible hub of change, the third section of the book takes *The Impact of Modernity on Rural Life* as its theme with each chapter approaching it from a different perspective and cultural situation. Michelle Deininger makes extensive use of the recently available and currently expanding materials accessible through Welsh Newspapers Online to advance her argument that newspapers provide an invaluable aid in developing greater understanding of nineteenth-century Welsh rural life as it was seen and reported within the country. The newspaper columns complicate, and often contrast with, the hostile or exoticised representations of Wales and the Welsh by outsiders found in previously better-known texts such as government reports and literary and travel narratives. Deininger shows, furthermore, how the Welsh press not only spoke increasingly to an internal audience of better-educated readers who were curious to find out about the wider world and the changes taking place in it, and who were often disillusioned with village life, but on occasion it also posed as the arbiter of acceptable urban moral and social standards.

If much of the Welsh press addressed a rural readership that was increasingly looking to the towns, the principal audience for the popular press in late nineteenth-century Prague consisted of the large number of incomers to the city from the countryside. Jakub Machek identifies how the Czech popular press, following developments seen earlier in the century in Britain and the USA, positioned itself to serve its readers in two key ways. First, since city life was inimical to the oral networks of communication which had been the norm in rural communities, Machek contends that the popular press aimed to provide a substitute for its readers by reporting very specific local news in detail, functioning as a textual replication of village talk. However, as well as catering in this way for the rural origins and culture of many of its readers, the press also sought to mediate their transfer into urban life and their new environment with its less conservative moral values. In contrast, therefore, to the illiberalism displayed in some elements of the provincial Welsh press, the Prague sensational press represented the freedoms and opportunities for the individual in the city.

In the last chapter of this section, Reagan Grimsley's study of rural and urban change in the south Mississippi region of the Piney Woods between 1865 and 1910, modernity is represented by the railway. The presence and importance of railway connections and networks are alluded to in a number of places in this book, and it is evident that the extraordinary development and spread of construction technology and engineering skills are directly implicated in many other changes. 'What did not exist in 1848, outside England, was anything like a railway network,' observed Eric Hobsbawm.[21] But he follows this by pointing out the scale and rapidity of what followed: 'By 1855 there were lines in all five continents', and 'by 1875 the world possessed 62,000 locomotives, 112,000

carriages and almost half a million goods wagons, carrying between them ...
1,371 million passengers and 715 million tons of goods.'[22] In North America
alone, there were over 100,000 miles of track by 1880.[23] One spectacular example
of the transformative impact of this exponential growth of the railway on
employment is illustrated by the fact that 'in 1824 there was not a single
railwayman in Britain, but by 1847 there were 47,000 permanent staff; by the
1870s, 275,000'.[24] But railways not only created a whole new field of employment
in themselves; they also precipitated cultural changes in how other work was
done, in how business was conducted, in where people went to work and in the
fortunes of individual communities. Thus, commenting on what he calls 'the
teleology of second creation' in the great spaces of the United States, David E.
Nye notes how: 'As the new railway lines went into operation, Americans began
to realize that, just as commerce could be made to flow through man-made
channels, a town could be invented on any spot where a railroad chose to plant
one.' He adds: 'It followed logically that these new artificial lines of commerce
could concentrate the industry, wealth, and economic life of newly settled regions
at a few nodal points.'[25]

Grimsley shows aspects of this in his case study of the transformation of an area
previously characterised by small, scattered, largely agricultural communities into a
regional centre for lumber production. This resulted from the vision and determination
of one man, William Harris Hardy, to create a rail distribution network which not
only radically altered the region's communications but led to an equally far-reaching
reconfiguration of its centres of influence. Thus, where Gainesville had formerly
been a town of some consequence in the local economy, it went into decline when
the railroad bypassed it, whereas the new settlement of Hattiesburg built at the heart
of the network quickly established itself as a key location, and came to be known as
'The Hub' in the early twentieth century. This examination reveals how a crucial
agent of modernity – the railway – not only changed rural–urban relationships in the
Piney Woods region but determined the future of the towns and cities themselves.
Its methodology is also suggestive of how the dynamics of rural–urban relationships
may be illuminated by an approach which takes account of the geographical and
environmental features of a particular region.

As has been indicated, the first three sections of the book provide selected
examples of ways in which modernity impacted on the interface between the
country and the city in different parts of the world, precipitating new forms of
exchange and more frequent movements of people between them. However, as is
well known, changes on the scale seen in the nineteenth century also inevitably
generated uncertainties, fears and a keen sense of loss or displacement among those
faced with living through them. Drawing on autobiography, literature, journalism
and social commentary, the chapters in the final section, *Social Mobility and
Anxiety*, engage with this aspect of 'uneasiness' in rural–urban relationships.

Christopher Ferguson uses the autobiography of James Carter, a native of
Colchester in the south-eastern English county of Essex and a tailor by trade, who
migrated several times between his home town and London before finally settling
in the capital, to suggest how his life story is illustrative of the wider phenomenon

of individuals whose identities became ambiguously divided between their place of origin and their adopted home. As a countryman in early nineteenth-century London, Carter was an outsider, but as a resident there, he felt estranged from his Colchester background which he regarded as rural – although Ferguson questions the extent to which this was actually the case. Carter's repeated change of location, combined with the fact that even after London became his home he still hankered after the country, suggest his enduring sense of marginalisation and incomplete belonging in a city which was effectively unknowable because of its rapid and relentless growth and change. His initial mobility, like that of some of the Isle of Purbeck stone workers, shows that migration was not necessarily assumed to be permanent, but his autobiography makes it clear that its effects upon him were indelible, and in this, too, his experience is representative.

The migration of Philip Pirrip ('Pip') from the Kent countryside to London in *Great Expectations* is the fictional creation of Charles Dickens, but Mary Hammond, in her examination of the very different responses offered by urban and local newspaper reviewers towards his representation of the character's journey from country boy to city gentleman, opens up larger questions about rural–urban perceptions and prejudices. By demonstrating how the city reviewers' hostility towards Dickens's unflattering portrayal of the urban upper classes contrasts with the much more sympathetic stance taken in local newspapers, which also reproduced pirated extracts selected to highlight the rural characters and interests in the novel, she shows how the reception history of the text points directly to a significant animus and rivalry in rural–urban perceptions. This contest is further developed in later illustrated editions of the novel where the artwork is ideologically influenced by cultural perceptions of the supposedly 'intrinsic' relative moral features of its urban and rural settings and characters which are, as Hammond shows, nonetheless remarkably unstable. Her methodology also points to the value of studying changing urban and regional responses to a literary work over time to enhance understanding of how relationships between the rural and the urban and the regional and national were perceived by contemporaries.

The so-called 'flight from the land', or migration of agricultural labourers to the English cities, preoccupied many late nineteenth-century social commentators, some of whom were not only alarmed at the consequences for food production but also feared that urban life diminished manliness. In the book's final chapter, Barry Sloan examines the paradox whereby workers who had often been treated with contempt and regarded as a lesser species were subsequently valorised as the residuum of authentic English manhood – a shifting paradox which, as the previous chapters in the section demonstrate, was felt deeply by James Carter, and picked up on by Dickens and generations of his novel's reviewers and illustrators. Drawing on a range of contemporary periodical journalism, parliamentary reports, investigative studies and literary works, Sloan considers the key social and ideological interests and prejudices that informed these rival views and shows how the agricultural labourer became the unlikely focus for middle-class anxieties about change and the consequences of urbanisation. In doing so, he sums up the intricate mutability of urban–rural relations, demonstrated in various ways in previous sections.

Taken as a whole, the chapters in this book present a wide-ranging and diverse series of insights into some of the conflicts, compromises and consequences which affected rural–urban relationships in the nineteenth and early twentieth centuries. Specific detail is balanced against broader assumptions, often complicating these or calling them into question. Particular regional experiences are compared against each other or are situated against contemporary events in other parts of the world. The different disciplinary approaches and sources of evidence used by the writers create a map of changing relationships that are strikingly complex and varied – sometimes uneasy, sometimes enabling, always posing challenges for traditional views of the rural–urban binary which have often been characterised (both by Victorians and Edwardians themselves and by many contemporary scholars since) in terms of discourses of relative progress. Through examining specific and sometimes quite local or regional examples, our contributors add nuances to and demonstrate the complexity of a set of issues which are too often characterised by unreflexive teleological assumptions. This approach has the advantage of illuminating shared cross-cultural concerns and compromises as well as divergent national and regional particularities in a unique period in history during which the impacts of modernity and social mobility were as varied as their contexts.

Notes

1 Alun Howkins, 'Rurality and English Identity' in David Morely and Kevin Robbins (eds), *British Cultural Studies: Geography, Nationality, and Identity* (Oxford: OUP, 2001), p. 146.
2 Raymond Williams, *The Country and the City* (London: Chatto and Windus, 1973), p. 1.
3 It is worth noting that in the first version of *The Prelude*, written between 1798 and 1805, Wordsworth's initial urban impressions are much more strongly and graphically expressed than in the substantially revised text published in 1850 which conveys rather less of the impact of the new environment on the young countryman.
4 Brian Lee and Robert Reinders, 'The Loss of Innocence: 1880–1914' in Malcolm Bradbury and Howard Temperley (eds), *Introduction to American Studies* (London: Longman, 1981; 3rd ed. 1998), p. 178.
5 Lee and Reinders, p. 180 and p. 181.
6 Michael Bunce, *The Countryside Ideal* (London: Routledge, 1994), p. 57.
7 Bunce, p. 57, and see also pp. 57–60.
8 Sarah Burns, *Pastoral Inventions: Rural Life in Nineteenth-Century American Life and Culture* (Philadelphia: Temple University Press, 1989), p. 6.
9 Burns, p. 6.
10 Burns, pp. 6–7, and Karl Marx and Friedrich Engels, *The Manifesto of the Communist Party* (1848) at https://www.marxists.org/archive/marx/works/download/pdf/Manifesto. pdf, p. 17 [accessed 28 September 2015].
11 Lee and Reinders, p. 188.
12 Michael Woods, *Rural* (London: Routledge, 2011), p. 18.
13 Woods, p. 18.
14 Nicholas Marshall, 'Rural Experience and the Development of the Middle Class: The Power of Culture and Tangible Improvements', *American Nineteenth Century History*, 8:1 (2007), pp. 1–25 (p. 18).
15 Donald M. MacRaild and David E. Martin, *Labour in British Society, 1830–1914* (London: Palgrave Macmillan, 2000), p. 76.

16 Bunce, p. 145. See also pp. 141–151 for a more detailed discussion of the history of British and American urban parks.

17 MacRaild and Martin, p. 63.

18 MacRaild and Martin, p. 63. They also allude to J. Langton, 'The Industrial Revolution and the Regional Geography of England', *Transactions of the Institute of British Geographers*, 9 (1984), p. 157.

19 Ian Dyck, 'The Town and Country Divide in English History', in Malcolm Chase and Ian Dyck (eds), *Living and Learning: Essays in Honour of J.F.C. Harrison* (Aldershot: Scolar Press, 1996), p. 83.

20 Alison Light, *Common People* (London: Penguin Books, 2014), p. 38.

21 Eric Hobsbawm, *The Age of Capital 1848-1875* (London: Weidenfeld and Nicolson, 1975), p. 53.

22 Hobsbawm, pp. 54–55.

23 Hobsbawn, p. 54.

24 Light, p. 36.

25 David E. Nye, *America as Second Creation* (Cambridge, MA : MIT Press, 2004), p. 156.

Part I

Sites of rural–urban encounter

1 Lincoln's April Fair

Renegotiating rural and urban relations in a small city, c.1820–1914

Andrew Walker

During the later nineteenth century, the city of Lincoln, for many years an urban centre in relative decline, began to prosper following the development of its agricultural engineering industry. As the city grew, its links with its rural hinterland were subject to renegotiation. This chapter examines the way in which Lincoln's authorities managed one set-piece annual urban–rural encounter on the city's streets: the April fair, at which substantial numbers of traders with horses, sheep and cattle descended upon the city.

The chapter examines the increasingly uneasy relationship the urban authorities had with rural visitors, who were accommodated and regulated at this key moment in the city's annual calendar. At a time when romanticised notions of the rural impacted upon much urban cultural activity, the chapter examines how and why social and cultural exchange between representatives of urban and rural life became increasingly problematic.

Much has been written about the romanticisation of rural England. Jeremy Burchardt's work, *Paradise Lost: Rural Idyll and Social Change Since 1800*, plots the changing meanings associated with the romantic representations of the rural in Britain over the last two centuries and examines how the attitudes of townspeople to the countryside have changed over time from, for instance, a sense of romantic affiliation to feelings of patriotism and regretful nostalgia.[1] Martin Wiener's contentious work, *English Culture and the Decline of the Industrial Spirit*, asserted that the seeds of Britain's long-term economic decline, from the later nineteenth century, lay in the idealised soils of the English countryside.[2] In much of this work stress is placed upon the metropolitan consumption of rural imagery. According to Wiener, among those entrepreneurs seeking to establish country estates were many industrialists located in the large urban centres of the manufacturing north.[3] Morris and Company's range of bucolic patterned textiles and wallpapers were bought from its London premises by the metropolitan middle classes; and the work of the Pre-Raphaelites found many of its patrons based in large urban centres such as Manchester and Birmingham, as well as in the capital.[4]

However, within much of England the boundaries between the rural and the urban, the agricultural and industrial, were much less clear-cut than romanticised representations suggest, as Barry Reay makes evident in his book *Rural Englands*.[5] Reay points to the 14,000 agricultural labourers enumerated as town dwellers in

1871: in Maidstone, for instance, in the 1860s over 700 agricultural labourers worked in the surrounding farms.[6] Thomas Hardy's evocation of Casterbridge, based on mid-nineteenth-century Dorchester, emphasises clearly the links between the rural and the urban that were characteristic of many small to medium-sized towns at the time. Hardy wrote that Casterbridge:

> was a place deposited in the block upon a corn-field ... The farmer's boy could sit under his barley-mow and pitch a stone into the office-window of the town-clerk ... and at executions the waiting crowd stood in a meadow immediately before the drop, out of which the cows had been temporarily driven to give the spectators room.[7]

While much of the romanticisation of the rural appears to have been driven by the inhabitants of large urban centres disillusioned by the persistence of stubborn urban problems, especially those associated with health, poverty and law and order, in many ways more commonplace tangible relationships between the rural and urban were regularly experienced in the streets of the country's small and medium-sized towns. The relationship between urban and rural sensibilities in these more regular points of intersection in areas marked by smaller urban centres have tended to be overlooked by historians, just as, it is claimed, life in nineteenth-century country towns has been.[8] It is notable that in order to evoke life in a nineteenth-century country town, at the beginning of his historiographical review Stephen Royle has to employ the work of a contemporary author, Anthony Trollope.[9] Little recent work seems to have been undertaken on how nineteenth-century agricultural workers were represented in such small urban centres.

During the nineteenth century, as today, Lincolnshire was one of England's least urbanised counties. For much of the nineteenth and early twentieth centuries, the county's towns were in the main quite small and, necessarily, the edges between the rural and the urban were blurred. In 1801, of the eleven settlements in the county with populations of over 2,000 inhabitants, only three had more than 5,000 living within their urban boundaries. Equivalent figures in 1901 were thirty-five and twelve respectively.[10] During the nineteenth century, Lincoln's population increased from 7,197 in 1801 to 17,536 in 1851.[11] With the growth of the city's agricultural engineering industries in the second half of the nineteenth century, the population then grew steadily to 48,784 in 1901.[12] In Lincoln, the firm Clayton and Shuttleworth's, for instance, employed 2,300 workers in 1885, and Ruston's had a workforce of 700 in 1870.[13] Lincoln and its surrounding district, therefore, seems to be an appropriate one in which to explore rural and urban relations during the nineteenth century, where the fortunes of the urban were so closely connected to the rural.

In some ways, it seems notions of the urban polluting and infecting the rural were also present in Lincolnshire, as well as in rural districts more likely to be threatened by the advance of the large city. The late nineteenth-century flight from the land, which was acutely experienced in Lincolnshire, saw many agricultural labourers and their families leaving agriculture in order to find more secure and better-paid work elsewhere, either in Britain or overseas, most particularly Canada and Australia. Rural commentators sought cultural explanations for this movement. A Lincolnshire medical officer of health, Mr T. B. F. Eminson of Gainsborough, commented to Rider Haggard in 1902 that 'towns offered more excitement – more life as it was called – and shorter hours of work'. Eminson associated this 'unhealthy craving for excitement' with

> an inordinate love of pleasure and self-indulgence which became the chief aim of existence to the neglect of duty and home life and ended, in too many cases, in young men becoming damaged members of society, without energy or brain, perhaps drunkards also, or the devotees of gambling ... and finally the fathers of unhealthy children.[14]

Conspicuous differences between urban dwellers and rural visitors, even in population centres closely connected to the rural world, such as Lincoln, prompted comment in the pages of the local press by the end of the nineteenth century. The 'otherness' of rural inhabitants is clearly represented in the reports of the annual hiring fairs of agricultural servants, which took place in the county town – as in other urban centres in Lincolnshire and other parts of the east of England – throughout much of the nineteenth century. The *Lincolnshire Echo*, a relatively new title catering particularly to readers in the city of Lincoln, described vividly how to identify a rural visitor to the city in 1894:

> there is still a rural mind and the young men of the villages don't yet babble of the latest charmer on the music hall stage ... This week, distinctly rural sights are to be seen in the streets of Lincoln for our country cousins appear before us 'in character' ... The costumes affected by many of the males – the young 'dandies' we suppose of rural life – are calculated to send a fashionable tailor off his head. Who has not beheld with wonder and amazement the vari-coloured waistcoats here and there sported? Verily the patchwork quilt must have been robbed to provide the material. There is no mistaking our visitors from the country districts: their attire is as distinct from that of the artisan population as if they still donned the old smock frocks ... Coat and waistcoat unbuttoned, billy-cork hat with a peacock's feather stuck in the riband, a gaudy neckcloth, hands in pocket, slouching along, puffing a short clay pipe – these are the present day characteristics of Young Hodge.[15]

The Hodge stereotype was employed here in the *Lincolnshire Echo*, as in many other publications, to represent the agricultural worker as ignorant and behind the times; a trope that – as Barry Sloan's chapter in this volume attests – already had a long history.[16]

The remainder of this chapter will focus on Lincoln's April Fair, which will allow an analysis of the interactions between the rural and urban through the lens of key set-piece economic transactional sites, encapsulated in the staging of annual markets for horses, sheep and cattle within the city during the last full week in April. The April Fair in Lincoln was of long standing and was described in many newspaper reports during the nineteenth century as variously having a history 'extending over centuries'[17] and dating 'from the time of the Plantagenets'.[18] The colourful and detailed reports contained within the pages of the county's local press, together with consideration of council minutes and police records, provide illuminating information about how perceptions of the April Fair and its various components altered over time, and shed light upon relations between the urban authorities and rural visitors. On occasion, rural–urban interactions at other set-piece Lincoln calendrical events such as hiring fairs will also be considered in order to contextualise the analysis of the April Fair. These customary events, as historians Bob Bushaway, E.P. Thompson and others have shown, offer opportunities to explore the operations of social and cultural, as well as economic, relations within local society.[19]

The market would seem to present the opportunity for the harmonious bringing together of economic interests of both urban and rural societies. Yet consideration of Lincoln's beast market reveals significant friction caused by the interaction of the urban and the rural during the second half of the nineteenth century. Markets and fairs have been the subject of considerable research by writers such as Patrick Joyce and James Schmiechen.[20] Specific focus is directed towards the symbolic significance of the market and its location within the townscape. Both writers emphasise the liminality of the market and the challenges later nineteenth-century corporations confronted in dealing with them. Joyce describes markets as being intermediary spaces, locations of transition which occupy a place on a boundary, marking off buyers and sellers, and particularly the country and the town.[21] Recent work by architectural historians on the nineteenth-century market hall has highlighted how these sites of interaction between the rural and urban were constructed by municipalities partly in order 'to bring the social and moral behaviour of citizens under their control through the creation of centralized covered market spaces'.[22]

As the pace of urbanisation accelerated in nineteenth-century Britain, increasing attention was paid to the regulation of public space. In many ways, early-Victorian Lincoln continued to be pre-industrial in its urban composition, with members of the various social classes living close together in the older parts of the city. However, some spatial reordering did start to take place in the mid-nineteenth century and the construction of a new market place in Lincoln during this period needs to be seen in this context, where the relationship of the city with the surrounding rural districts can also be seen as becoming restructured.

Before 1848, Lincoln's weekly cattle markets and many fairs, including the April Fair, were held in St Swithin's Square, off Broad Street, an open and consequently difficult-to-control space near to the centre of the city. This location was increasingly viewed as being unsatisfactory. In 1844, for instance, the *Stamford Mercury* considered the possible benefits associated with the removal of the market from the city's thoroughfares: 'the high roads and streets of the city would then be left free and the pushing and driving and swearing now so prevalent would be prevented'.[23]

Though disapproval was voiced both by rural and urban interests, it was the desire to order and regulate that prompted the market to be relocated to the eastern edge of the town, a site north of Monks Lane, which was open by 1849. This reduced the opportunities for the urban population to become exposed to the untamed ways of the market.

As the nineteenth century advanced, even within towns closely associated with agriculture it seems that the presence of farm animals in the urban streets became less tolerated. Even some country folk commented critically upon the co-existence of urban and rural traffic. In 1857, Edward Peacock, a farmer, wrote disapprovingly of 'the numerous droves of ... cattle [which] pass daily through the streets [of Lincoln] leaving behind the unmistakeable traces of their presence'.[24]

An event which brought together the urban and rural in particularly problematic fashion was Lincoln's annual horse fair. This formed a key component of the April Fair. At the conclusion of the horse fair, according to one commentator, 'the city's streets looked and smelt like a farm yard'.[25] The horse fair, though, was less easily marginalised than the cattle market. For much of the nineteenth century, the horse fair brought in a considerable amount of revenue to Lincoln, particularly through the business conducted in the city's inns and hotels. During its heyday Lincoln's horse fair also had a significant international dimension, which was much emphasised in local newspaper accounts. Early nineteenth-century reports of the event refer to the 'many foreigners' who attended and 'bought freely'.[26] In 1842, for instance, local newspapers reported on 'agents of the French cavalry' being present in order to purchase 'noted animals'.[27] In April 1848, the *Lincolnshire Chronicle* reported that the horse fair was a 'dull affair'. Its account explained that: 'Owing to the revolutions abroad we had but few foreigners and a great decline in price was a necessary consequence of want of demand.'[28] By 1852, however, the international element associated with the horse fair was again worthy of comment, with references made to the presence of German and French buyers as well as purchases undertaken on behalf of the Prince of Naples.[29]

The international cachet associated with the horse fair and the economic boost enjoyed by the city meant that some of the challenges accompanying the event were not tackled by the city's authorities. Nevertheless, some of these issues were regularly identified in local newspaper accounts during the nineteenth century. One of the major difficulties associated with the horse fair was the practice of horses being tested on Lincoln's streets before purchases were finalised. As a consequence, the city corporation appeared unable so readily to confine the horse fair, as it had the city's cattle sales, to the margins of the city. The spatial challenges associated with the event emerge clearly in the reports of the horse fair during the nineteenth century. The death of an elderly man as a result of a kick from the hind leg of an animal at the horse fair was reported in 1821.[30] The extent of the problem of accommodating horses for sale on the streets of the city can be gauged by the number of animals often involved. In 1869, some 5,000 horses were shown during the week, the majority of them displayed on the city's streets, most notably on the High Street and those adjoining it.[31]

By the 1890s, when the number of continental buyers was declining, more sustained criticism was made of the horse fair and its damaging effects upon passers-by. The cultural contrasts between townspeople and the temporary occupants of the city's streets during the horse fair were made particularly clear in a *Lincolnshire Chronicle* report of the horse fair in 1892. The newspaper noted that:

> The streets of the city have presented all those features of bustle and excitement so calculated to upset the nerves of the timid pedestrian who has proceeded along the thoroughfare with his 'weather' eye fixed with a doubting gaze upon the heels of every animal within range; the 'horsey' man, on the contrary, has been in his element ...[32]

By the beginning of the twentieth century, concerns about the horse fair and the way in which it took over the city were becoming even more conspicuous. The uneasy disjunction between the rustic, dangerous, masculine and relatively lawless world of the horse trader and the increasingly regulated, retail-orientated and feminised High Street became the subject of discussion. In 1903, for instance, the *Lincolnshire Chronicle* highlighted the effect the horse fair had upon the daily life of the city. The newspaper reported that there were enough horses at the fair 'to seriously interfere with vehicular traffic to stop the trams'.[33] The newspaper also noted the anxiety caused to 'nervous pedestrians who look askance at the business-like appearance of the hind-quarters of the hundreds of heavy animals backed up against the pavement'.[34]

In addition to the physical dangers presented to townspeople during the week of the horse fair, during the later nineteenth century especially, concerns were expressed about the alienation they experienced on the city's streets. Particular attention was paid to the unfamiliar, unrefined noises associated with the horse fair, many of which were reminiscent of an untamed rural world. The shouting of horse dealers on the city's streets and the sound of cracking whips came in for significant criticism.[35] In 1878, one report noted critically that during the horse fair, the Cornhill was 'crowded with rough specimens and equally rough "helpers" whose howling and yelling filled the air with discordant noises'.[36] According to the *Lincolnshire Echo* in 1894, the increasing sensibility of Lincoln's pedestrians prompted them to suffer 'bewilderment and alarm' as a consequence of 'a flood of the choicest of Queen's English' uttered by the horse dealers at the fair.[37] By 1897 these concerns resulted in actions being taken: horse dealers came before the city's magistrates and were fined for their 'obscene language on the Cornhill' during the horse fair.[38]

One group of rural visitors to the horse fair excited much comment within the pages of the local press: the significant number of Irish dealers came in for particular criticism for their behaviour. Reports of Irish drunkenness, violence and general bad behaviour during the horse fair occurred regularly during the nineteenth century. In 1859, for instance, the *Stamford Mercury* reported on how, during the week of the Lincoln horse fair, 'an Irishman was taken into custody on Tuesday night for being drunk, breaking windows and assaulting the police'.[39] In 1882 the *Lincolnshire Chronicle* focused upon the Irish visitors in its report of the

Figure 1.1 A general view from St Benedict's Square of Lincoln horse fair, looking north along the High Street towards the cathedral, c.1900. (Image courtesy of the Illustration Index, Lincolnshire County Council Cultural Collections, Ref. LCL2330)

horse fair. It noted how many Irish horses were chiefly located around the Cornhill and St Benedict's Square and 'as usual the men in charge [of the horses] have made these neighbourhoods particularly unpleasant to the occupants by reason of their unearthly yells and rough conduct'.[40] Eleven years later, the *Lincolnshire Echo*, with its offices in St Benedict's Square, reported on 'The Irish dealers at work', many of whom were based in the rural counties of Armagh and Down.[41] The newspaper noted that:

> the Irish Fair is as distinct from the English as if it were held at another season of the year … The visitors from the Green Isle are held but in poor account, though it has to be admitted that they bring into the city some of the finest horse flesh.'[42]

Recurring concerns with the horse fair related to the criminal activity associated with the event. A steady stream of stories is told of 'swindlers' separating owners from good quality horses, sometimes either without any form of payment or in exchange for sub-standard animals. In the *Stamford Mercury's* report of the horse fair in 1821, for instance, it notes many occasions where potential buyers have taken horses from potential sellers without payment.[43] Attempts were made by the town authorities to warn fair-goers of the presence of such criminals. The *Stamford Mercury* reported in 1832 that at the horse fair:

> The attendance of rogues and vagabonds is numerous … an extra body of police are stationed by the commissioners for the protection of the public during the fair and cautionary placards are freely posted on walls and carried about on boards.[44]

It was reported that many of these ne'er-do-wells passed themselves off as country horse traders, though as one newspaper report noted, many notorious characters were from Norwich, Lynn, Leeds etc.[45] In 1832, the *Stamford Mercury* drew a vivid picture of these villainous horse traders:

> many of them may be recognized during the course of the same day in several shapes: at one time in waggoners' frocks; and another buttoned up in farmers' great coats with whips in their hands, perhaps, and a half a dozen knots tied therein: all these minutiae of costume will go but little way, however, in

Figure 1.2 Lincoln horse fair on the High Street, looking north, *c.*1900. The disruption this event caused to retailers and shoppers in the city is evident. (Image courtesy of the Illustration Index, Lincolnshire County Council Cultural Collections, Ref. LCL214)

deceiving an experienced eye: the ruddy rural breadth of physiognomy is not to be counterfeited any more than the quiet and comfortable repose of countenance which has so little in common with the ruthless eye of the swindler and the pickpocket.[46]

By the middle of the nineteenth century a regular police presence was on hand in order to reduce the amount of criminal activity during April Fair week. Surviving police officer journals reveal much vigilance during fair weeks: in 1866, for instance, it was noted that 'it being Lincoln fair, a great number of suspicious characters was about'.[47] Newspaper reports at the end of the nineteenth century and in the early twentieth century regularly commended the Lincoln police for their handling of the horse fair and associated pleasure fair, when the town's population was swelled with the arrival of substantial numbers of visitors. The *Lincolnshire Chronicle's* report of 1882 is broadly typical:

> Several members of the force have done good service during the week ... as 'plain clothes' men and these, together with the placing of men in uniform ... have succeeded in maintaining order under, in many instances, trying and difficult circumstances.[48]

Notwithstanding the policing arrangements that appeared to be doing a reasonably effective job in curbing some of the lawlessness associated with the horse fair, many shopkeepers in particular were keen for the horse fair to be relocated, as the cattle market had been, away from the retailing heart of the city. During the 1860s, for instance, when there was much emphasis in newspaper reports on the uncomfortable interaction of the rural and urban occasioned by the horse fair, pressure was exerted to relocate the horse traders. As the *Lincolnshire Chronicle* reported during the horse fair in 1864: 'Business in the High Street except at the inns was almost entirely suspended and many tradesmen expressed a hope that ere long a more convenient place for holding the fair would be provided.'[49]

During the 1860s and 1870s several suggestions were made regarding the relocation of the horse fair. Improvements to the Cornhill, including the extension of pavements for pedestrians, rendered the area less suitable for the staging of the horse fair.[50] However, rather than removing the horse fair entirely from the city centre, it was agreed by the city council that the number of days allocated to the fair in the central parts of the city should be reduced and that, on the Thursday and Friday of fair week, horse sales should be confined to the southern end of the High Street 'below the Midland Railway Station'.[51] Some attempts had been made in 1878 to suggest relocating the horse fair to the junction of Broadgate and New Road, at the base of the hill upon which the city's cathedral was located. This prompted significant objection, particularly from one city councillor, a Mr Cannon. As the *Lincolnshire Chronicle* reported:

> He objected to horses being shown at the foot of New Road as by that road the elite of Minster Yard would descend ... and at the foot meet the

cosmopolitan elements from other parts of the city. They would have to pass through the hooting and miserable row [of the horse fair] ... to the utter annoyance of the citizens.[52]

This almost literal *de haut en bas* attitude prompted some derision among a number of councillors whose laughter was recorded in the newspaper report. The account, however, encapsulated the discomfort felt by some residents relating to the conspicuous threatening rural presence during the horse fair in the streets of the city. By the end of the nineteenth century, further discussions took place within the city council about the fuller regulation of the event. In 1898, for instance, it was suggested that tolls should be charged for horses attending the fair; that the horses should be enclosed in one space; and that the horse fair should be removed entirely from the High Street.[53] It was not until 1929, however, that a significantly diminished horse fair was removed from the city's streets and relocated to the city's West Common.[54]

While the city council appeared unwilling to remove the horse fair from the streets of Lincoln, others sought to dilute the presence of the April Fair by alternative means. Repeatedly, reports in the local press at the time of the fair make reference to cases of drunkenness, with associated violence occurring. To ameliorate the situation during fair week, gospel temperance meetings for the 'wandering people who annually visit our great April Fair', complete with a 'Fair Sunday free tea', were laid on by city philanthropists during the 1880s.[55] During 1886, when Lincoln's April Fair coincided with the week of Good Friday, the Bishop of Lincoln, Edward King, became involved directly in ministering to fairgoers by undertaking the 'Service of Three Hours'. According to the *Lincolnshire Chronicle*, 'Great pains have been taken to make this service widely known as the famous April horse fair was going on.' It reported that: 'about 1,500 people, many being frequenters of the fair, attended the cathedral, nearly 1,000 being present together at the end'.[56] The report concluded optimistically: 'The Bishop's simple, earnest and practical addresses were listened to with the deepest attention and evidently struck home.'[57] By 1893, the Rev. H. Joy, on behalf of the Committee of the Church of England Temperance Society, was arranging for the supply of non-intoxicating refreshments to the herdsmen and others who attended the fair in the cattle market.[58]

Such efforts by the temperance bodies during the April Fair week echo those undertaken during the statute hiring fairs which continued to take place in eastern England market towns during the period, Lincoln included. The work of Gary Moses has revealed the attempts made in East Yorkshire towns such as Driffield to curb the excesses of visiting rural workers to the town's annual statute fair which was marked by courting, drinking and fighting, as well as hiring. He highlights the attempts of a galvanised Anglican campaign in the third quarter of the nineteenth century that sought to suppress the high spiritedness of such occasions.[59] However, Moses explains that the fairs remained a vital and dynamic aspect of rural society in the East Riding and 'it was only when the institution of farm service went into fundamental decline in the twentieth century that the hiring fair experienced a dramatic transformation in its nature and form'.[60] A comparable situation appears to be evident in the case of Lincoln's horse fair, with its relocation from the city's streets only occurring following the terminal decline of the horse as a principal means of motive power within agriculture.

While within the city of Lincoln during the nineteenth century there appeared to be increasing unease at the presence on the city's streets of the horse fair and the movement of cattle, there was much less concern about the sheep fair. The largest sheep fair in Lincoln's calendar took place during April Fair week. In contrast to the horse fair, which saw the sale of many animals brought in to the county for the purpose of the fair and then sold to purchasers resident outside the county borders, the sheep fair was invariably much more orientated towards Lincolnshire itself. As the *Lincolnshire Echo* observed in 1893:

> the Sheep Fair exercises a much more direct influence upon the general trade of the district than does the horse fair. Of the many thousands of pounds which change hands in the stables quite half of the money is carried away to Ireland ... The pens on the other hand represent the indigenous substance of Lincolnshire. Of the 25,000 sheep which travelled hither by road and rail on Wednesday night not a tithe came from the other side of the county border.[61]

The Lincoln Longwool was a breed of significant standing during the nineteenth century. At a time when sheep were reared mainly for wool, the Lincoln breed was much valued. It had been subject to significant improvement by the middle years of the century, when a cross between a New Leicester ram and an Old Lincoln ewe developed 'Improved Lincolns'. By the 1840s the sheep of the county produced both better wool and mutton.[62] This was reflected in the prices these animals achieved at market. In the middle years of the nineteenth century, it was clear that the sheep fair was regarded as a prestigious element associated with Lincoln's April Fair. During the 1840s, the removal of the sheep fair to a new paddock on Monks Lane, to the east of the city, provided the animals and their handlers with significantly improved accommodation.

The enormity of the sheep fair is made clear in a number of the local newspaper accounts. In 1859, it was estimated that some 60,000 sheep were available for sale in pens in the Monks Lane market place.[63] To put this in context, by the 1870s there were estimated to be 1.5 million sheep in Lincolnshire, compared to a human population of 436,599.[64] The size of the sheep market is captured vividly in a description in the *Lincolnshire Chronicle* in 1864: 'More than two-thirds of the hill side to the right of the permanent market appeared covered with an immense fleece dotted here and there with forms of buyers, sellers and others.'[65] The picturesque nature of the sheep fair, the centrality of sheep to the local economy and the local pride often articulated in the Lincoln breed meant that for many of the middle years of the nineteenth century the sheep fair was spared the critical comments directed towards the horse fair by Lincoln's residents. Indeed, while the horse fair invading the streets of the city threatened the increasingly feminised retailing space at the heart of Lincoln, in some ways the sheep fair reclaimed the bucolic for women. During the 1850s and 1860s a number of local newspaper reports commented on the attractions presented to women by the spectacle of the sheep fair. In 1859, for instance, 'many ladies were on the ground of the sheep fair by 6am'; and in 1864 'the terrace running along the top of the field was lined with spectators, principally ladies who must have been highly gratified at the striking and busy scene which was presented'.[66]

By the final decades of the nineteenth century, however, the attractions of the sheep fair were considerably diminished as a spectacle, not least because of the much-reduced size of the event. As Catherine Wilson has noted, 'Between 1871–5 and 1891–5 the price of Lincoln wool fell by nearly 50% ... Wool which sold for 28.5 pence per pound in 1861 fetched 6.5 pence in 1902.'[67] This was in part a result of the reduced economic significance of the sheep. By the end of the nineteenth century, Lincoln's April sheep fair had been relocated from the city itself to the bordering West Common, reflecting its diminished status.

In conclusion, then, it seems that, through the nineteenth century, changes of attitude towards the incursion of rural visitors into the city were taking place in those in authority within Lincoln. As consideration of the April Fair through time reveals, some aspects of the event were successfully marginalised, thereby reducing the opportunity for interaction between the city's inhabitants and rural visitors. This was achieved earliest and with most success in the case of the cattle market, relocated from the central streets of the city to its eastern edge. The horse fair, perhaps the most prominent feature of the April Fair, proved more problematic to regulate. The city took pride in the event's international dimension, which was the subject of much reporting until the penultimate decade of the nineteenth century. However, the major inconvenience caused to the city's inhabitants by the horse trading on the central streets of the city was exacerbated in the final third of the nineteenth century, at a time when the city's retailing infrastructure had developed significantly to meet the needs of a rapidly growing urban and suburban population. The increasing alienation felt by the city's population towards the horse fair was reflected in the criticisms of the event in the pages of the local press. These not only highlighted the practical inconveniences caused by the horse fair but also emphasised the offence to sensibilities caused by the increasingly unfamiliar rural noises and bad language emanating from the city's rural visitors.

However, while an increasing detachment was discernible through the century between Lincoln's inhabitants and those involved with the trading of large animals within the city, one aspect of the April Fair, the sheep fair, did seem to retain a close link between the urban and the rural until its decline at the end of the nineteenth century. In part, no doubt, this was a consequence of the continuing close connections between the transactions at the fair and the fortunes of the local economy: while in the case of both cattle and horse sales at the April Fair the vendors and buyers did not necessarily have local connections, in the main the transactions at the sheep fair involved Lincolnshire agriculturalists and the sale of a local county product, the Lincoln Longwool sheep. As the *Lincolnshire Chronicle* stated in 1864 of the April sheep fair: 'Nearly all the agriculturalists in the neighbourhood were exhibitors.'[68] The impact upon the city tended to be less conspicuous than the horse fair: as a consequence of the local nature of the sales, those involved with the sheep fair did not tend to linger long in the city. The major business conducted at the sheep fair was often started very early and largely completed by mid-morning, which helped to soften the impact of the event upon the city's retailers, in contrast to the horse fair. Although the sensibilities of Lincoln's citizens appeared to be offended by the cattle and horses associated with the April Fair, as reported in the pages of the local press, a contrary view seemed to be held with regard to the sheep fair. Instead of repelling Lincoln's inhabitants, the sheep fair appeared to become some form of visitor attraction in itself, particularly for women visitors for whom the sight of 'an immense fleece' was regarded as particularly enticing.[69]

By the end of the nineteenth century, however, with the decline of the sheep fair, the principal components of the April Fair were not regarded positively by large numbers of Lincoln's inhabitants. Notwithstanding the city's links to the rural world through its manufacture of agricultural engineering equipment, interaction between the country and the city appeared to be increasingly troublesome. Within the pages of the local press, the rural worker's exposure to town life seemed increasingly to be the focus of patronising and disdainful comment. The *Lincolnshire Echo*, for instance, referred to the country labourer as 'dull and phlegmatic' in 1895.[70] It seems, therefore, that while in the larger urban centres and the metropolis aspects of rural life were being idealised and the consumption of bucolic imagery was avaricious, in urban centres more closely associated with countryside, by the end of the nineteenth century links to the rural were viewed by those in positions of cultural influence with some reservation.

Notes

1 J. Burchardt, *Paradise Lost: Rural Idyll and Social Change Since 1800* (London: I.B. Tauris, 2002).
2 M. Wiener, *English Culture and the Decline of the Industrial Spirit, 1850–1980* (Cambridge: Cambridge University Press, 1981).
3 Wiener, *English Culture and the Decline of the Industrial Spirit*, p. 14.
4 F. MacCarthy, *William Morris* (London: Faber & Faber, 1994), p. 412.
5 B. Reay, *Rural Englands: Labouring Lives in the Nineteenth Century* (Basingstoke: Palgrave Macmillan, 2004).
6 Reay, *Rural Englands*, p. 19.
7 T. Hardy, *The Mayor of Casterbridge* (1886), ed. M. Seymour-Smith (Harmondsworth: Penguin, 1978), p. 162.
8 B. Davey, *Lawless and Immoral: Policing a Country Town, 1838–1857* (Leicester: Leicester University Press, 1983), p. 2.
9 S. Royle, 'The Development of Small Towns in Britain', in P. Clark (ed.), *The Cambridge Urban History of Britain, Volume III, 1840–1950* (Cambridge: Cambridge University Press, 2000), pp.151–84.
10 N. Wright, *Lincolnshire Towns and Industry, 1700–1914* (Lincoln: History of Lincolnshire Committee, 1982), p. 224
11 D. Mills, 'Population, 1801–1901', in A. Walker, (ed.), *Monks Road: Lincoln's East End Through Time* (Lincoln: The Survey of Lincoln, 2006), pp. 16–17.
12 Mills, 'Population, 1801–1901', p. 17.
13 Wright, *Lincolnshire Towns and Industry, 1700–1914*, pp. 142–5.

14 H. Rider Haggard, *Rural England Being an Account of Agricultural and Social Researches Carried Out in the Years 1901 and 1902, vol. 2* (Cambridge: Cambridge University Press, 1902), p. 236.
15 *Lincolnshire Echo*, 16 May 1894.
16 M. Freeman, 'The Agricultural Labourer and the Hodge Stereotype, c. 1850–1914', *Agricultural History Review*, 49 (2001), pp. 172–86.
17 *Lincolnshire Chronicle*, 28 April 1899.
18 *Lincolnshire Chronicle*, 24 April 1885.
19 B. Bushaway, *By Rite: Custom, Ceremony and Community in England, 1700–1880* (London: Junction Books, 1982) and E. P. Thompson, *Customs in Common* (London: Merlin Press, 1991).
20 P. Joyce, *The Rule of Freedom: Liberalism and the Modern City* (London: Verso, 2003) and J. Schmiechen, 'The Nineteenth-Century Townscape and the Return of the Marketplace in Victorian History', in T. Larson and M. Shirley (eds), *Splendidly Victorian: Essays in Nineteenth- and Twentieth-Century British History in Honour of Walter L. Arnstein* (London: Ashgate, 2001), pp. 187–201.
21 P. Joyce, *The Rule of Freedom*, p. 81.
22 P. Dobraszczyk, 'Victorian market halls, ornamental iron and civic interest', *Architectural History*, 55 (2012), p. 174.
23 *Stamford Mercury*, 3 May 1844.
24 F. Hill, *Victorian Lincoln* (Cambridge: Cambridge University Press, 1974), p. 2.
25 L. Elvin, 'The May Hirings', *Fireside Magazine*, 4 (1967), p. 7.
26 *Stamford Mercury*, 26 April 1822.
27 *Lincolnshire Chronicle*, 29 April 1842.
28 *Lincolnshire Chronicle*, 28 April 1848.
29 *Stamford Mercury*, 23 April 1852.
30 *Stamford Mercury*, 27 April 1821.
31 *Lincolnshire Chronicle*, 30 April 1869.
32 *Lincolnshire Chronicle*, 29 April 1892.
33 *Lincolnshire Chronicle*, 24 April 1903.
34 *Lincolnshire Chronicle*, 24 April 1903.
35 *Lincolnshire Chronicle*, 29 April 1864.
36 *Lincolnshire Chronicle*, 26 April 1878.
37 *Lincolnshire Echo*, 21 April 1894.
38 *Lincolnshire Echo*, 21 April 1897.
39 *Stamford Mercury*, 29 April 1859.
40 *Lincolnshire Chronicle*, 28 April 1882.
41 *Lincolnshire Echo*, 20 April 1893.
42 *Lincolnshire Echo*, 20 April 1893.
43 *Stamford Mercury*, 27 April 1821.
44 *Stamford Mercury*, 27 April 1832.
45 *Stamford Mercury*, 24 April 1829.
46 *Stamford Mercury*, 27 April 1832.
47 Police Officers' Journals and Pocket Books: Lincolnshire Archives, CONSTAB 2/1/2/2/1, 23/4/66.
48 *Lincolnshire Chronicle*, 28 April 1882.
49 *Lincolnshire Chronicle*, 29 April 1864.
50 *Stamford Mercury*, 22 April 1864.
51 *Grantham Journal*, 13 April 1878.
52 *Lincolnshire Chronicle*, 8 March 1878.
53 *Lincolnshire Chronicle*, 6 May 1898.
54 L. Elvin, *Lincoln As It Was* (London: Hendon Publishing Company, 1974), p. 33.
55 *Lincolnshire Chronicle*, 27 April 1883.

56 *Lincolnshire Chronicle*, 30 April 1886.
57 *Lincolnshire Chronicle*, 30 April 1886.
58 Fairs and markets committee of Lincoln Corporation, minutes: Lincolnshire Archives, L1/1/20/1-3, 10/3/93 and 14/4/93.
59 G. Moses, 'Passive and Impoverished? A Discussion of Rural Popular Culture in the Mid-Victorian Years', *Rural History*, 22 (2011), pp. 197–9.
60 G. Moses, 'Rustic and Rude: Hiring Fairs and their Critics in East Yorkshire, c. 1850–1875', *Rural History*, 7 (1996), p. 169.
61 *Lincolnshire Echo*, 28 April 1893.
62 C. Wilson, *Lincolnshire's Farm Animals* (Lincoln: Society for Lincolnshire History and Archaeology, 2012), p. 20.
63 *Lincolnshire Chronicle*, 29 April 1859.
64 Wilson, *Lincolnshire's Farm Animals*, p. 21.
65 *Lincolnshire Chronicle*, 30 April 1864.
66 *Lincolnshire Chronicle*, 29 April 1859 and 30 April 1864.
67 Wilson, *Lincolnshire's Farm Animals*, p. 21.
68 *Lincolnshire Chronicle*, 30 April 1864.
69 *Lincolnshire Chronicle*, 30 April 1864.
70 *Lincolnshire Echo*, 16 May 1895.

2 Policing Brough Hill Fair, 1856–1910

Protecting Westmorland from urban criminals

Guy Woolnough

Brough Hill Fair in Westmorland, held annually on 30 September and 1 October, was medieval in origin but had its heyday after 1850.[1] Most Victorian annual fairs were held in a town centre or on its outskirts, whereas Brough Hill Fair was remote from even the nearest town. Fairs were a market for labour, livestock, food, drink and domestic goods, as well as offering amusements such as the boxing booth, shooting gallery, roundabouts and the Aunt Sally.[2] They attracted farmers, entrepreneurs and criminals; they were open to the honest and to the fraudulent, offering the fairgoer delights and excitement not routinely available elsewhere. Fairs were deemed to be on the edge of respectability and they attracted, interested or alarmed people from every stratum of society. A fair was a liminal event, a meeting place for town and country, to which crowds came with galvanised emotions and with hopes of exploiting the fair's opportunities. Andrew Walker's chapter, 'Lincoln's April Fair' in this volume, highlights this notion of the fair as a liminal or intermediary space. The liminality of Brough Hill Fair was delineated and regulated by the police, whose methods framed contemporary cultural attitudes. Ordinary policemen effectively defined, identified and dealt with the outsiders who were considered a threat to rural Cumbria.

Judd has said that fairs are as interesting as riots to the social historian.[3] This comment is very apt, for fairs, like riots, were closely implicated in contemporary discourses on social order, morality, economic change and progress. Whereas riots were relatively infrequent, fairs occurred several times a year in every county. Whereas riots were extremely difficult to control, fairs seemed susceptible to management by police. Powell-Frith's picture, 'Derby Day' (1858), gives an excellent insight into the mid-century idea of the fair, for it portrays the complexity of a fair as a social phenomenon by showing the meeting of all classes of Victorian society: sharpers, flashy young men and their female escorts, farm labourers, soldiers, Gypsies, entertainers and schoolboys are all rubbing shoulders.[4] The distinction between disreputable and respectable was not clear-cut. The dubious reputation of fairs is exemplified in a number of contemporary memoirs and works of fiction which contain graphic descriptions. Robert Loisan's memoir is typical in its fascination with his stories of 'gammy touts, broad fencers, ballad singers, patterers, prostitutes, thieves, tramps, snide pitchers, bad money passers and all the refuse of society [who] attend these [fairs]'.[5]

Much of the historiography of fairs has concerned urban fairs, exploring the way the event brought rustics and outsiders into town. But Brough Hill Fair was different: it was well away from any settlement and was readily represented in the press and in court proceedings as an incursion of urban Britain into rural Cumbria.[6] Some fairs were hiring fairs, like those featured in Hardy's novels, where labouring men and women could find farmers seeking workers; others (like Brough Hill) were stock fairs, but all types of fair were a magnet for sellers of goods and services, and for criminals.[7]

There are studies of fairs in the later nineteenth century which analyse their decline and show them to have been under attack from moral entrepreneurs.[8] Contemporary critics claimed they were losing their economic and commercial role, and were no longer proper for an urbanised, industrial age with expanding forms of 'rational recreation'.[9] In 1871, the Fairs Act created a means of closing down fairs which were 'unnecessary ... the cause of grievous immorality, and ... very injurious to the inhabitants of towns in which such fairs are held'.[10] These sorts of friction are made clear in Walker's chapter. None of these narratives was applied to Brough Hill Fair, which expanded and prospered in the Victorian age and faced no organised opposition, for the location of this fair was so remote that there were almost no 'inhabitants' who could be inconvenienced or shocked by the proceedings.[11] This was partly a regional difference: although fairs were being closed down or challenged in other parts of England, an extensive search of the local press has revealed no significant Cumbrian voice raised against fairs in general or Brough Hill Fair in particular. Only occasionally was a mildly pejorative remark offered, such as 'the usual array of potters' [vagrants] tents' and 'the many places of amusement which are provided by the itinerant charlatans'.[12] The vicar of Kirkby Stephen and local magistrate, James Simpson, heard some of the court cases arising from Brough Hill, but in his lengthy evidence to a Parliamentary Commission, Simpson emphasised the social benefits of fairs and made light of their moral dangers.[13]

Brough Hill Fair was thus very different from city fairs. It appears to have been a very traditional and unchanging rural fair in a remote location, but in fact it was closely implicated in the industrial changes in Britain, for the ponies sold there were vital in transport and in mining. Brough Hill at fair time was a place where industrial Britain came to thinly populated Westmorland to transact business. The role of the police was to manage the frictions generated by these interactions which, as this chapter will prove, were often represented as urban visitors preying on Cumbrian innocents.

The primary sources used in this research derive from the work of the police. Every case at Petty Sessions arising from the Fair has been compiled, from the inception of the Cumberland and Westmorland Constabulary in 1856, until 1910. The fair was policed, by turns, from two towns, Appleby and Kirkby Stephen. Different records have survived from each town and there are no complete runs of those records that have survived, but it has been possible to find press reports covering the few missing years, so that there is some evidence of police activity for every year.[14] The compiled data has been analysed by spreadsheet which allows a detailed, systematic and accurate description of what Brough Hill Fair was like: no contemporary published description gives such a clear idea of who attended, what was going on, or the types of sideshows and stalls.

This method has led to a micro-study which does not favour the narratives of the privileged or those in authority but gives a very clear idea of what the police were doing and thereby makes their priorities clear. The details examined in this chapter will show how the police progressed in their professional competence, from inadequacy in their handling of cases in the early years to efficiency by 1900 in pre-empting and convicting offenders.[15]

The police of Victorian Cumbria were literate and largely recruited from the labouring classes within the region.[16] In their work they were not only following orders from the chief constable, they were also informed or guided by local plebeian cultures.[17] The court records of Appleby and Kirkby Stephen do not accurately show the extent of criminality, offending and disorderly conduct at the fair, but the data demonstrates how the police identified or 'labelled' certain men as offenders.[18] There was significant under-reporting and under-recording of offences, and the police exercised deliberate discretion in failing to tackle some behaviour. In their handling of this fair, the police thus helped to sustain the idea of a discrete Cumbrian culture and to shape the region as an 'imagined community' within a broader British culture.[19]

Brough Hill Fair, a wild and unregulated gathering

Brough Hill, altitude 190 metres, is in the Pennines (a remote mountain range forming the 'backbone' of northern Britain).[20] It is in the parish of Warcop, which had a scattered and declining population of about 700 in the 1880s. The nearest town at five miles' distance to the south-east is Kirkby Stephen, which had a population of approximately 1,500 in the 1880s. Appleby, six miles west of the hill, had a similar population. The status of Brough Hill Fair was made clear in the *Cyclopedia of Agriculture* of 1855:

> one of the largest and most important in the United Kingdom ... the extensive common on which it is held is literally crowded with people, booths and stalls of woollen cloth and other merchandise, and immense numbers of horses, sheep, and cattle.[21]

It had long been an important rendezvous for shepherds and drovers, with more than 10,000 cattle reported in the late eighteenth century and 40,000 sheep in 1850, but by the 1860s the cattle trade was in decline.[22] Epidemics of foot and mouth disease (1865–80) and the growth of reputable auction markets ended droving, but accelerating demand for horses to work in mines, on trams and buses, for carriers etc. gave Brough Hill Fair new opportunities.[23] Tough working horses were bred on Cumbrian hill farms and in 1861 the railway arrived to within a mile of Brough Hill, which did not have the problems of space and location that hindered urban fairs as described by Walker in the previous chapter, so the fair expanded as a horse fair.[24] Every year it was reported in the press and was invariably described as the largest in the north, or even in the whole of the kingdom. For example:

Brough Hill Fair [is] in all probability the biggest horse fair in the United Kingdom … On that section of road were thousands of horses. It was lined with them, it was filled with a surging equine throng that passed and repassed from everlasting to everlasting. The sight inspired one with the thought that the horse dealers and breeders must be actuated with an earnest ambition to forward the time when every man, woman and child in the country shall have a horse of his or her own and another to lend out.[25]

Brough Hill itself was open, uninhabited and hosted a virtually unregulated fair with a wild reputation, similar in some ways to that of Appleby Horse Fair today. Although the landowner had the right to collect tolls, many fairgoers, with or without animals, simply entered from the open fell without paying.[26] The custom was for farm servants to be given a holiday to attend the fair, which was full of stalls offering refreshment, entertainment and goods for sale.[27] One Kendal newspaper expressed the contradictions of such a crowded, urban event occurring in one of the remotest places in England: 'Brough Hill, upon which at any other period of the year we scarcely ever see a human face, will now for two days and nights be populated almost as densely as any part of Manchester.'[28] A photograph of Brough Hill on fair day shows a number of Gipsy caravans in the middle ground, with tents, stalls and a large roundabout in the distance, but this picture will disappoint anyone looking for detail or excitement: all seems very quiet, despite the anticipated presence of swells, card-sharpers, pickpockets and prostitutes for which fairs were notorious.[29]

Nonetheless, Brough Hill Fair, just like its counterpart in Lincoln, was described in the local press as a magnet for the dishonest and disreputable. 'There were many depredations committed by the light fingered fraternity' is a typical comment on the fair.[30] Warnings of base coin and flash (phony) notes at the fair were regular.[31] Gangs or the 'flash mob' going to and from the fair were reported in the press: e.g. seven reprobates convicted at Penrith – 'The above parties were supposed to be on their way to Brough Hill', or the presence in Richmond market of 'several roughs and London pickpockets, who had experienced a very successful thieving career at Brough Hill Fair'.[32] Horse-dealing gave scope to dishonesty and there is plenty of anecdotal evidence of fraudulent dealing in animals; for example, the dialect poem, 'Jimmy Green at Brough Hill Fair':

It's an awful spot
For a roguish lot,
Is Brough Hill Fair –
An' ye'll ha'e to leeakoot,
An' be gaily cute,
If ye wish to manidge
an' keep a' square![33]

The hero of this verse negotiated the purchase of a fine yellow mare but it turned out to be a worthless dud, and the notes he had received as change for his £50 were fakes. Allowing for exaggeration, this verse agrees with contemporary descriptions of other fairs.[34] The repeated theme of these narratives was that townies came to the fair to cheat, rob or defraud naive Cumbrians like Jimmy. This idea, seen from a different perspective, is analysed by Christopher Ferguson later in this volume.

The work of the police

Before the foundation of the Cumberland and Westmorland Constabulary in late 1856, Brough Hill Fair was policed by special constables.[35] As the century advanced the Constabulary became more effective, successful and professional in their methods.[36]

Police professionalism generally can be seen as part of the advance of modernity and of organisational power with an expansion of accessible information;[37] the modernising state was both the product and the progenitor of policing policies and systems. The importance of the police force's role in modernisation has been emphasised in some histories and in the work of social scientists,[38] and, as will be clear from the Cohen case below, even the work of a humble Cumbrian police constable was necessarily implicated in this process.

The *Kendal Mercury* reported in 1861: 'Notwithstanding the great number of thieves and card sharpers who infested Brough Hill on the occasion of the fair this week, there was not a single case of robbery reported to the police.'[39] Newspapers and contemporary literature, which give a partial and subjective view, articulate contemporary opinion that Brough Hill Fair was a lawless occasion, whereas police records, expected to be comprehensive and objective, show surprisingly few prosecutions arising from Brough Hill Fair. Between 1857 and 1910, there were just 160 arrests and summonses, a rate of three per annum. Of these 160 cases, only one involved a female offender, whose case is detailed below. There were peaks: ten cases in 1883, nine on the occasion of a riot in 1894 and twelve in 1901, but in several years there were no prosecutions at all. Four factors tending to reduce the overall number of charges have been identified.

First, in the early years of the Constabulary (1856–1870) there were few charges brought against offenders at the fair because most cases of theft or fraud appearing before the magistrates were private prosecutions. Victims had to prosecute a case themselves and could be deterred by the cost or persuaded to withdraw. For example, in 1858 the *Westmorland Gazette* reported the case of Thomas Walker, a card sharper who had cheated a blacksmith at the fair. Walker was arrested with the assistance of a constable, but in court he offered the prosecutor (i.e. the blacksmith) six sovereigns to drop the charge, and this was accepted. The magistrate discharged Walker.[40] By the 1880s, however, most cases were prosecuted by police whose professional competence and willingness to meet the costs encouraged the public to entrust court cases to the local superintendent. Thieves and card sharpers could expect very little leniency once prosecutions were managed by police officers who, in theory, could not be swayed from their duty by bribes. This trend towards police rather than private prosecution has also been identified in Cumbria and in other constabularies in this period.[41]

The second factor was foot and mouth disease. In epidemic years (1865, 1866, 1869, 1870 and 1871) policemen were posted on roads leading to Brough Hill to check cattle coming to the fair and turn back, or even order the slaughter of, diseased animals.[42] These were years when the number of police prosecutions was very low because, according to the chief constable, his men who were posted outside the fair not only checked cattle but also turned back all vagrants heading to Brough Hill. In his opinion, vagrants committed most of the crimes at fairs.[43] Even though he repeated these claims several times, no one challenged the chief constable by asking the obvious question: did the number of charges brought by police fall in those years because they were busy outside the fair rather than being on the hill itself?

Discretionary policing is the third factor in keeping the number of cases low. For example, from 1856 to 1910 no prostitutes were charged with offences at the fair despite the opportunities presented by young men with money. Moreover, there were very few drink- related prosecutions arising from the fair. Of the seven drink cases, only one involved drunkenness on fair hill. One may infer that the police were prepared to tolerate prostitution and drunkenness at the fair, though the same constables when on the beat in towns and villages regularly charged drunks and prostitutes. Behaviour that was normally unacceptable was either tolerated at the fair, or was dealt with in extra-judicial ways that are described below.

The fourth factor is that the police used discretionary, ad hoc methods of detention which resulted in fewer offenders in the official records. A temporary lock-up on Brough Hill during the fair was mentioned occasionally in the records when describing the detention of an offender; other histories have described similar lock-ups in Wales and at the Derby.[44] Circumstantial evidence shows that offenders were detained in the lock-up on Brough Hill and released later without charge, for the *Westmorland Gazette* reported in 1878: 'During the day, the police made a raid on the light-fingered fraternity, and several were kept in durance, whilst others made their escape.'[45] However, the official records for 1878 show no fair-related prosecutions. The thieves were held in the lock-up for some hours without the police recording their detention in the Occurrence Book. Troublesome drunks and flagrant prostitutes may have been similarly detained when the police deemed it necessary. It is not possible to say who was held in the temporary lock-up, or how the police decided which offenders should be briefly locked up rather than charged, but one may assume that the people brought to court were those whom the police believed to merit prosecution, and so the official record gives a means of analysing police priorities and opinions, rather than of analysing offending.

The chief constable gave no orders relating to Brough Hill Fair, so operational decisions were made at the station level and the initiative to act against offenders at the fair rested with the policemen on duty.[46] The official records show the work of PCs and sergeants at the fair. The most frequent charges in the records were: gaming, 54 cases; theft and fraud, 44 cases; frequenting, 25 cases; cruelty to animals, 21 cases. Theft was the fairground crime that most exercised the anger of the Victorian public. Many thefts at Brough Hill Fair were of money or small items of property, whereas only 14 of the thefts and frauds related to animals.[47]

Often a horse thief or fraudster left the hill before his dishonesty was discovered, and the local police were unlikely to be involved. For example, in 1887 several farmers from Hawes had entrusted horses for sale to a local dealer, a young man named Brown, who had sold them as agreed at the fair. He then disappeared, rumoured to have left for New York with over £300 before any alarm was raised. No further news of Brown or the money appears in the press or elsewhere.[48] Only one significant fraud was dealt with by Cumbria police: in 1901 two men paid £225 for some horses with bad cheques. Two days later the fraud was discovered by telegraphing the bank named on the cheques, and Kirkby Stephen police arrested the men in the town.[49]

The police were unlikely to deal with serious animal theft, but they were very concerned with pickpocketing, which was the criminal menace that the newspapers highlighted. 'A strong force of police was on the ground, but there were few rows, and they were chiefly on the lookout for pickpockets and sharpers.'[50] There were considerable difficulties in catching pickpockets, who invariably operated in a gang; the person who lifted the property would immediately pass it on to an accomplice, so that bringing a successful prosecution was difficult.[51] The first Brough Hill Fair policed by the Constabulary (1857) showed the difficulty. John Metcalfe, a farmer on his way from the fair after dark, was approached by Harriet Metcalfe, 'a very fast young lady'. Harriet charmed the farmer, but when a close embrace occurred her accomplices appeared, presenting themselves as two passers-by, and she rushed off with feigned embarrassment and the farmer's wallet containing more than £85. The police identified and apprehended the offenders, and on the following day Harriet and two men were arrested. The money was not recovered and the evidence was not strong enough for the magistrates, who released the accused.[52] The Kirkby Stephen Occurrence Books, wherein all reported thefts should have been recorded, illustrate the difficulty of catching and convicting pickpockets. Seventeen thefts by pickpockets were reported, in only five of which cases there was an arrest, and only two of these ended with a conviction.

However, the police used the Vagrancy Act to prosecute men for 'frequenting', or loitering with intent to commit a felony: that is, they were planning to steal.[53] In the second half of the nineteenth century, police forces developed techniques to deal with pickpocketing, particularly through their increasing skill in detaining 'frequenters'.[54] Most of those charged with frequenting pleaded guilty, but the few cases where the accused pleaded not guilty provide an insight, through the detailed evidence given in court, into how the police operated. For example, in 1900 Sergeant Illingworth and Constable Sheffield waited at Penrith station for four men whom they followed onto the train to Warcop (20 miles) and then onto the hill where, having made detailed notes of their behaviour, they made the arrests.[55] They had secured a gang which included George Cohen, who had several previous convictions (using different names) as a pickpocket since 1889.[56] One cannot doubt that this was a carefully planned operation, for when Cohen appeared with his accomplices at the Quarter Sessions their case was undermined by detectives from London and Manchester who identified them.[57] The police proved that the men were loitering without any genuine business at the fair, that they were behaving suspiciously in how they moved through the crowd and that they had previous convictions under the Vagrancy Act. With this evidence, their conviction was inevitable.

A Manchester news report of 1896 provides an example of how Cumbria police were able to get intelligence about the plans of an itinerant criminal gang:

> YESTERDAY'S POLICE INTELLIGENCE … Frederick Scarborough … was charged with loitering about the Market-place with intent to commit a felony … [he was] captured by [Detective Sergeant] Wilson, to whom he proffered information respecting the proposed visit of two notorious thieves to Brough Hill Horse Fair [if] he was allowed to go.[58]

There were networks of intelligence between police forces in different parts of Britain and, although these communications have left few records, one can see them operating in the cases of Scarborough and Cohen; Cumbrian police cooperated regularly with other forces to share intelligence.[59]

During the fair, plain-clothes police were on duty at the railway stations through which the townies attending the fair travelled. Frequenters were followed onto the hill in order to gain evidence. Police were also looking out for card-sharpers, who, operating in twos or threes, conned their victims with the 'three card trick'.[60] The police saw pickpockets and card-sharpers as the same category of offender: they arrived in the same way and they were caught in much the same way. As with frequenters, the evidence against sharpers was their suspicious behaviour. Some frequenters and some sharpers had upon their person flash notes, which were not forgeries within the meaning of the law, for although they seemed to be Bank of England notes, the wording was 'Bank of Engraving' or 'Elegant'.[61] These notes helped the sharpers for if a 'successful' punter was tricked into accepting flash notes it was no crime. Phrases such as 'They were endeavouring to induce some youths to gamble with them' and 'betting money with country people and cheating them out of it', used by the police to describe these offences, reveal their priority of protecting naive Cumbrians.[62] A pickpocket who had flash notes or a roulette table (see the Metcalfe case above) was readily identified as a sharper.[63]

When a riot occurred at the fair in 1894, the *Westmorland Gazette* commented:

> Brough Hill Fair has been a happy hunting ground for sharpers and rowdies for many generations; but if they begin to organise parties for plunder and riot like that of Monday night the resources of civilisation will have to be more carefully organised too.[64]

Pickpockets, thieves, card-sharpers and 'other rowdies' were readily lumped together by police and press, so that they saw the arrest of a card-sharper as equal to the arrest of a pickpocket as a means of reducing property crime. However, the prosecution of a card-sharper was easier because the evidence was more objective: it was straightforward to see and describe what the offender was up to, and to produce the tools of his trade in court.

For the police and the press, the important targets for interdiction were male thieves, pickpockets and card-sharpers, who constituted 123 of the 160 prosecutions arising from Brough Hill Fair (see Figure 2.1). The largest remaining category of offence, cruelty to animals, was not seen as a priority by many Cumbrians and was rarely prosecuted by the police. Police constables, although experienced in dealing with farm animals, were reluctant to take on such cases.[65] All but two of the 21 cruelty cases at the fair were prosecuted by RSPCA inspectors, who were peripatetic, middle-class 'off-comers'.[66]

Animal cruelty was the charge most likely to be faced by Cumbrians and locals. The strong local bias in cruelty charges is simply explained by the problems faced by the RSPCA inspectors. All cruelty cases proceeded upon summons, but an 'off-comer' could more easily get away with giving the inspector a false name and address than could a local. Policemen were required by their handbook to cooperate with RSPCA officers, so an inspector who demanded the name of an offender was

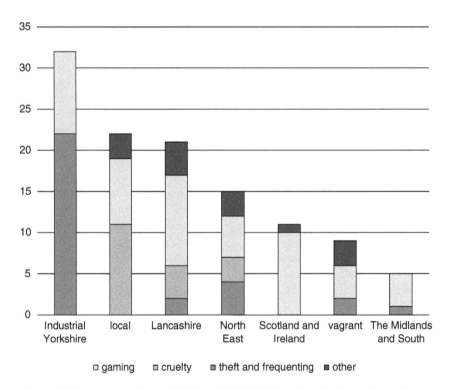

Figure 2.1 Prosecutions: Brough Hill Fair 1857–1910. Figure showing the numbers of persons from each region, organised by category of offence. Compiled using the stated places of residence given by those charged with offences at Brough Hill, extracted from police records, court records and news reports. Note: 'Local' has been taken as Cumbria and places within twenty-five miles of the hill, reaching into Pennine Durham and Yorkshire. All Yorkshiremen charged came from industrial towns: Leeds, Bradford, Wakefield, Skipton etc. Vagrants were listed as 'no fixed address'.

more likely to receive a correct answer if the person was a local whom the police recognised. Figure 2.1 represents the idea that the policing problem at Brough Hill Fair was urban criminals. A contemporary Cumbrian examining the proceedings of the courts or the local press would readily conclude that the greater part of the disorderly and law-breaking element at the fairs involved men from the industrial cities of the north. Many of those arrested arrived by train from industrial towns, gave addresses in urban areas and their previous convictions were often from the cities. Although this interpretation is supported by the table, it is not an accurate representation of the actions of criminals at the fair but the outcome of the working methods of the police who set out to deal with what they saw as a 'flash mob' comprised of thieves, pickpockets and card-sharps. They developed working practices to enable them to spot, arrest and successfully prosecute these men. They were not looking out for female offenders, but they did find and arrest the type of men they wanted. The police used intelligence, they operated at the railway stations where they believed they had a good chance of spotting their quarry; they knew what evidence was needed and how to collect it. The police were the important agents in determining the persons and the behaviour that needed to be controlled or stopped.

Conclusion

Brough Hill Fair was atypical in many ways. It prospered when other fairs were in decline, it was unchallenged when many fairs were being closed and it was largely unregulated at a time when (as Walton, Walvin and Crone have explained) other fairs were being 'civilised'.[67] These differences derived from its remote location, and its success grew from the importance of its primary commodity to industrial Britain: horses. Brough Hill Fair brought people from the industrial cities to rural Westmorland. Police policy, to protect Cumbria, determined their tactics in dealing with foot and mouth disease and with thieves. Police strategy favoured locals but was rooted in the implicit idea of the fair as a liminal event, a front line between honest, decent Cumbrians and disreputable outsiders from the industrial cities, who were seen as an external threat. The police exercised their discretion in identifying and dealing with certain types of male offenders, prioritising offences such as pickpocketing and card-sharping, and tolerating, for example, drink- and prostitution-related offences. Police tactics and consequent successes were reported very favourably in the Cumbrian press. They arrested those whom they targeted, and thereby defined the sort of persons generally believed to be a problem and a threat to Cumbria, and they clearly satisfied public opinion as expressed in the local newspapers. In constructing this group of outsiders the police delineated the liminality of Brough Hill Fair and reinforced the 'imagined community' of Cumbria.

Notes

1   The old county of Westmorland has been part of Cumbria since 1973. W. Addison, *English Fairs and Markets* (London: Batsford, 1953), p. 120; R.R. Sowerby, *Kirkby Stephen and District* (Kendal: Wilson, 1948).

2 Good descriptions are to be found in D.K. Cameron, *The English Fair* (Stroud: Sutton Publishing, 1998), I. Starsmore, *English Fairs* (London: Thames and Hudson, 1975) and S. Alexander, *St. Giles's Fair, 1830–1914 Popular Culture and the Industrial Revolution in 19th Century Oxford* (Oxford: Ruskin College, History Workshop, 1970).

3 M. Judd, '"The Oddest Combination of Town and Country": Popular Culture and the London Fairs', in J.K. Walton and J. Walvin (eds), *Leisure in Britain, 1780–1939* (Manchester: Manchester University Press, 1983), pp. 11–30, p. 12.

4 Powell-Frith, W., 'Derby Day', Manchester City Art Galleries, 1893/4; first exhibited 1858.

5 R. Loisan, *Confessions of Robert Loisan, alias Rambling Rob* (No publisher identified, c. 1870), at East Riding Archives and Local Studies Service, Beverley, Yorkshire; W. Green, *The Life and Adventures of a Cheap Jack: by one of the fraternity* (London: no publisher identitifed, 1876); G. Sanger, *Seventy Years a Showman* (New York: E. P. Dutton, 1927); C.G. Leland, *The Gypsies* (Boston, MA: Houghton, Mifflin and Co., 1886).

6 Alexander, *St. Giles's Fair*; H. Cunningham, 'The Metropolitan Fairs' in A.P. Donajgrodzki (ed), *Social Control in Nineteenth-Century Britain* (London: Croom Helm, 1977), pp. 163–184; Judd, "The Oddest Combination"; J. Catt, *Northern Hiring Fairs* (Chorley: Countryside Publications, 1986); S. Caunce,'The Hiring Fairs of Northern England, 1890–1930: A Regional Analysis of Commercial and Social Networking in Agriculture', *Past and Present*, 217.1 (2012), pp. 213–46.; G. Moses, '"Rustic and Rude": Hiring Fairs and their Critics in East Yorkshire c.1850–1875', *Rural History*, 7.2 (1996), pp. 151–75; G. Moses, 'Reshaping Rural Culture? The Church of England and Hiring Fairs in the East Riding of Yorkshire c.1850–1880', *Rural History*, 13.1 (2002), pp. 61–84.

7 R. Perren, 'The Marketing of Agricultural Products from Farm Gates to Retail Store', in E. J. T. Collins (ed), *The Agrarian History of England and Wales, vol.VII, part 2.* (Cambridge: Cambridge University Press, 2000), pp. 953–998; p. 980. Caunce, 'The Hiring Fairs of Northern England'.

8 Judd, '"The Oddest Combination", pp. 12–28; J. Fiske, *Understanding Popular Culture.* (Boston: Unwin Hyman, 1989), pp. 74–7; R.W. Malcolmson, *Popular Recreations in English society, 1700–1850* (Cambridge: Cambridge University Press, 1973), pp. 30–4; R. Crone, *Violent Victorians: Popular Entertainment in Nineteenth-Century London* (Manchester: Manchester University Press, 2012), pp. 43–7.

9 J. Page, *The story of the Manchester Fairs* (Manchester: Heywood, 1887); R. Nash-Stephenson, 'On Statute Fairs: their Evils and their Remedy', in *Transactions of the National Association for the Promotion of Social Science* (1858); *Royal Commission on Market Rights and Tolls. Minutes of evidence, Vol. VII. With appendices.* Parliamentary Papers, C.6268-I: p. 288.

10 The Fairs Act, 34 & 35 Vict., c.12.

11 The author has found no organised opposition to Brough Hill Fair in the national or local press.

12 *The Westmorland Gazette* (hereafter *WMG),* 8 Oct 1870; 6 Oct 1878, p. 7. Other newspapers explored are: *Carlisle Journal, Carlisle Patriot, Kendal Mercury (KM), Lancaster Gazette (LG), Whitehaven News.*

13 H.S. Tremenheere, *Commission on the Employment of Children, Young Persons, and Women in Agriculture (1867). Second Report of the Commissioners, with appendix part I* (London, H. M. Stationery Office, 1868), pp. 548–50.

14 *Kirkby Stephen Police Occurrence Books,* Cumbria Archive Service, Kendal Archive Centre (hereafter KAC), WS/Cons 4/1 1857–1880; WS/Cons 4/2, 1883–1894; WS/Cons 4/3, 1894–1902; *KS Police Charge Books,* KAC, WS/Cons 4/10 1874–1888; WS/Cons 4/11, 1888–1915; *KS Petty Sessions Court Registers,* KAC WTPS/KS no.1, 1880–1894; *Appleby Petty Sessions, court minute books,* KAC, WTPS/A, 1851–1903; *Appleby Petty Sessions, Court Registers,* KAC, WTPS/AA/AB 1880–1886.

15 Emsley has written of the increasing professionalism of police in *The Great British Bobby* (London: Quercus, 2009), pp. 169–76. Others have described the growth of professionalism in Victorian England in sport, the army and public health, e.g. P. Bailey, *Leisure and Class in Victorian England* (London: Methuen, 1978), pp. 139–52; G. Harries-Jenkins, 'The Development of Professionalism in the Victorian Army', *Armed Forces & Society*, 1:4 (1975), pp. 472–89; S. Novak, 'Professionalism and Bureaucracy: English Doctors and the Victorian Public Health Administration', *Journal of Social History*, 6:4 (1973), pp. 440–62.

16 *Returns of the distribution and constitution of staff, Cumberland Police* (includes Westmorland), Cumbria Archive Service, Carlisle Archive Centre (hereafter CAC), SCons 2/19, 1866–1873; 2/20, 1874–1890; 2/21, 1891–1901; *Descriptions of persons appointed, Cumberland Police*, SCons 2/7, 1865–1884; *Kendal Police, record book of policemen*, KAC, WS/Cons 10/1, 1860–1947.

17 G. Woolnough, *Policing Petty Crime in Victorian Cumbria* (PhD dissertation, Keele University: 2013), pp. 195–248.

18 H.S. Becker, *Outsiders: Studies in the Sociology of Deviance* (New York: The Free Press, 1963).

19 A.P. Cohen, *Belonging: Identity and Social Organisation in British Rural Cultures* (Manchester: Manchester University Press, 1982), pp. 1–18. See also B.R.O. Anderson, *Imagined Communities: Reflections on the Origin and Spread of Nationalism* (London: Verso, 2006).

20 Grid ref: SD 765156.

21 J.C. Morton, *A Cyclopedia of Agriculture, Practical and Scientific, by Upwards of Fifty of the Most Eminent Practical and Scientific Men of the Day*, vol. 2 (London, 1855), p. 366; *Nottinghamshire Guardian*, 10 October 1850, p. 5; *Northern Echo*, hereafter *NE*, 1 October 1870, p. 5; 2 October 1893, p. 6.

22 J.V. Beckett, *Coal and Tobacco: the Lowthers and the Economic Development of West Cumberland, 1660–1760* (Cambridge: Cambridge University Press, 1981), p. 5; *Nottinghamshire Guardian*, 10 October 1850, p. 7.

23 F.W. Garnett, *Westmorland agriculture 1800–1900*, (Kendal: Titus Wilson, 1912), p. 132.

24 M.E. Shepherd, *From Hellgill to Bridge End: Aspects of Economic and Social Change in the Upper Eden Valley 1840–95* (Hatfield: University of Hertfordshire Press, 2003), p. 211; T.F. Bulmer, *History, Topography and Directory of Westmorland* (Manchester: Bulmer, 1885), p. 278.

25 Taken from a cutting from *Yorkshire Weekly Post* of 10 October 1908, held at KAC, WDFC M 2/27/4.

26 Westmorland Federation of Women's Institutes, *Some Westmorland Villages* (Kendal: Westmorland Federation of Women's Institutes, 1957), pp. 192–3. In 1867 a toll-collector was seriously assaulted and knocked unconscious when he attempted to levy a toll on some men on horseback on the road. *WMG*, 3 November 1867, p. 4.

27 *NE*, 1 October 1870, p. 4.

28 *KM*, 1 Oct 1859, p. 5.

29 The few pictures of Brough Hill Fair discovered by the author may be seen at *http://www.guywoolnough.com/brough-hill-fair-images-of-the-fair/* (posted 10 June 2015, accessed 19 June 2015).

30 *LG*, 17 Oct 1863, p. 5.

31 For example, see: *Newcastle Courant*, 22 October 1852, p. 4; *NE*, 16 October 1885, p. 7.

32 *KM*, 24 October 1852, p. 8; *Yorkshire Post and Leeds Intelligencer*, 5 November 1884, p. 8.

33 The last four lines of this extract may be read as: 'You will have to look out and be very cunning if you wish to manage to keep all square.' Rev. T. Clarke, W. Bowness and R. Southey, *Specimens of the Westmorland Dialect, Reprinted from the Westmorland Gazette* (Kendal: Atkinson & Pollitt, 1870), p. 40.

34 E.g. Loisan, *Confessions*; Leland, *The Gypsies*.

35 Parliamentary Papers, 1846. *Report from the Select Committee of the House of Lords on the Burdens Affecting Real Property,* House of Commons Papers (411, 411-II) VI Pt. I.1, VI Pt. II.1., pp. 517 and 1288.

36 Woolnough, *Policing Petty Crime,* pp. 192–3; M.J. Wiener, *Reconstructing the Criminal: Culture, Law, and Policy in England, 1830–1914* (Cambridge University Press, 1990).

37 A. Giddens, *Modernity and Self-identity* (Cambridge: Polity Press, 1991), pp. 14–20; A. Giddens, *A Contemporary Critique of Historical Materialism, vol.2: Nation and Violence* (Cambridge: Polity Press, 1985), pp. 12–14.

38 T.A. Critchley, *A History of Police in England and Wales* (Montclair, NJ: Patterson Smith, 1972); D. Taylor, *The New Police in Nineteenth-Century England: Crime, Conflict and Control* (Manchester: Manchester University Press, 1997); L. Radzinowicz, 'Towards a National Standard of Police', in M. Fitzgerald, G. McLennan and J. Pawson (eds), *Crime and Society Readings in History and Theory* (London: Routledge & K.P. with Open University Press, 1981), pp. 60–85; C. Emsley, *The English Police: a Political and Social History* (London: Longman, 1996); M. Neocleous, *The Fabrication of Social Order: a Critical Theory of Police Power* (London: Pluto Press, 2000).

39 *KM* 5 October 1861, p. 5.

40 *WMG* 9 Oct 1858, p. 4. This discharge did not precisely accord with the chief constable's orders, first stated in 1857, repeated 1878, when he instructed his men to examine carefully and arrest all 'suspected parties' and vagrants. General Orders no. 14 and no. 384, *Chief Constable's General Orders,* CAC SCons 1/4, 7 May 1857 and 26 Oct 1878.

41 This was a national trend. See C. Emsley, *Crime and Society in England, 1750–1900* (London: Pearson Longman, 2005), pp. 191–3.

42 Report of the Chief Constable, *Westmorland Quarter Sessions Minute Book 1859–1875,* KAC WQ/M/32, 1859–1875, 5 January 1866; 15 October 1873.

43 *Report of the Chief Constable,* KAC WQ/M/32, 1859–1875. 7 April 1866; *WMG,* 7 October 1871 p. 5; Dunne, J., [Chief Constable] *Correspondence between the Home Office and Chief Constable of Cumberland and Westmorland on Suppression of Vagrancy* (Parliamentary Papers, House of Commons Papers, 158 liii.157, 1869), pp. 1–5.

44 *KS Occurrence Book, KAC,* WS/Cons 4/1 1857–1880, 7 Oct 1874. Williams, K., *The English newspaper* (London: Springwood Books, 1977); Jones, D.J.V., *Crime in Nineteenth-Century Wales* (Cardiff: University of Wales Press, 1992), pp. 125–6.

45 *WMG,* 5 Oct 1878, p. 5.

46 The Chief Constable did issue orders relating to foot and mouth at the fair, as noted above. *General Orders from the Chief Constable: 1857–1897* (CAC SCons 1/14); *1888–1897* (CAC SCons 1/114).

47 Many were dealt with as civil cases, e.g. *Lancaster Gazette,* 16 April 1861; *York Herald,* 28 Oct 1882 & 6 January 1883; *North Eastern Daily Gazette,* 12 October 1888.

48 *NE,* 27 Oct 1887, p. 3. Reports of lesser frauds were frequent in the press: e.g., a youth conned into swapping a £50 horse for one valued at 30 shillings. *NE,* 7 October 1886, p. 5.

49 *Lancashire Evening Post,* 2 October 1901, p. 4.

50 *WMG,* 8 Oct 1870, p. 5.

51 The *modus operandi* is explained by D. Philips, *Crime and Authority in Victorian England: the Black Country, 1835–1860* (London: Croom Helm, 1977), pp. 207–13.

52 *Morning Post,* 12 Oct 1857, p. 8. The report says nothing about Harriet sharing the same surname as her victim.

53 B.M. Gregg, *A Police Constable's Guide to his Daily Work* (London: Effingham Wilson, 1919), pp. 243–4.

54 Jones, *Crime in Nineteenth-century Wales,* p. 211; V.A.C. Gatrell, B. Lenman and G. Parker, *Crime and the law: the social history of crime in Western Europe since 1500* (London: Europa, 1980), pp. 275–8.

55 *Appleby, Court Minute Books, KAC,* WTPS/A, 1851–1903: 2 Oct 1900

56 Cohen and his gang gave addresses in Glasgow and Birkenhead. *Prisoners tried at Quarter Sessions and Assizes, Cumberland and Westmorland. Record of persons brought before Quarter Sessions and Assizes.* Metropolitan Police, The National Archive, PCOM 2/451, 14 October 1907.
57 *Manchester Courier and Advertiser*, hereafter *MCA*, 20 Oct 1900, p. 3.
58 *MCA*, 29 September 1896, p. 3.
59 This is supported by the wealth of trivial paperwork that survives at *Maryport Police Station, Correspondence*, CAC SCons 4/75, 23 October 1877.
60 *KS Occurrence Book*, KAC, WS/Cons 4/1 1857–1880, 30 September 1865; *North-Eastern Daily Gazette*, 3 October 1884, p. 5; *MCA*, 29 September 1896, p. 3.
61 *WMG*: 9 October 1858, p. 4; 7 October 1876, p. 5; *Appleby, Court Minute Books*, KAC, WTPS/A, 1851–1903, 1 Oct 1901.
62 *KS Occurrence Book*, KAC, WS/Cons 4/1 1857–1880, 2 Oct 1876; WMG, 24 Nov 1894, p. 5.
63 In 1875 one man arrested for frequenting had a flash note; another was listed as a 'billiard marker', which identified him as a gambler. *Kirkby Stephen Police Charge Book*, KAC, WS/Cons 4/10 1874–1888, 30 September 1875.
64 *WMG* 5 October 1894, p. 5.
65 A case in Kirkby Lonsdale confirms their disdain for cruelty prosecutions: a constable found two men man-handling a pony and was telling them to stop when a Lancashire barrister ordered him to prosecute the men for cruelty. The police constable involved referred the case to a veterinarian and his superintendent who both agreed with the constable that the men's treatment of the horse was not cruel. *Kirkby Lonsdale Police Occurrence Book*, KAC WS/Cons 2/8, 5 Oct 1898.
66 Christopher Nicholls and Edwin Chivers prosecuted cruelty cases at Brough Hill Fair, Islington, Stoke on Trent, Dundee, Alnwick, Runcorn, York, Manchester, Portsmouth and the Isle of Wight. *KS Charge Book*, KAC, WS/Cons 4/10 1874–1888, 30 September 1879, 30 September 1897; *Western Daily Press*, 14 December 1877, p. 7; *Staffordshire Sentinel*, 25 March 1879, p. 4; *Dundee Courier*, 29 September 1880, p. 2; *Alnwick Mercury* 10 September 1881, p. 4; *Cheshire Observer*, 12 November 1887 p. 6; *York Herald*, 1 September 1900, p. 10; *Portsmouth Evening News*, 28 June 1895, p. 3; *MCA*, 28 April 1900, p. 4. See also: M.J.D. Roberts, *Making English Morals: Voluntary Association and Moral Reform in England, 1787–1888* (Cambridge: Cambridge University Press, 2004); B. Harrison, 'Religion and Recreation in Nineteenth Century England', *Past and Present*, 38 (1967), pp. 98–125.
67 Walton and Walvin, *Leisure in Britain;* Crone, *Violent Victorians.*

3   Urban Unitarians vs. rural Trinitarians

Town liberals in a planter culture

John A. Macaulay

While the planter elite of the Old South dominated the region well past the Civil War, the growth of cities attracted a growing professional class whose presence and size threatened that dominance. By 1850 the South had 770 lawyers, 8559 teachers and twice as many doctors, most living in either Charleston, Savannah, New Orleans, Richmond, Augusta or other urban areas peppered across the region. With different outlooks, occupations and locations these urban professionals made for 'uneasy neighbours' to the landed gentry – the custodians of political, economic, cultural and social power in the Old South. In addition to arguing that the reshaping of such relationships was not solely dependent on local circumstances but also on the tensions within the Unitarian church on a national scale, this chapter demonstrates how religious differences played a key role in urban–rural configurations in other contexts.

Jonathan Daniel Wells recently chronicled the emergence of this 'Southern Middle', placing its origins decades before the Civil War, and argued that as a class they favoured 'progress', economic diversification and self-improvement. He contends that early on, emboldened by their numbers and fed in part by evangelicalism, the middle class sharpened its commentary on the planter class, and, by doing so, fostered class tensions that increased anxiety within the region. Using the Whig Party as its political vehicle, the middle class criticised elements of the planter culture, such as elite luxuries, the honour code, duelling and the lack of economic diversification, while at the same time promoting education, intellectual improvements, temperance and other reforms. These efforts not only separated them from the planter class but also from labourers, yeomen and even their northern middle-class counterparts, as the latter grew fearful of competition from southern industries and southern labour. But by 1850, as sectional tensions increased and the Whig Party disappeared, Wells contends that the Southern middle class largely abandoned partisan politics, instead deferring dominance to the planter class.[1]

In my 2001 publication, *Unitarianism in the Antebellum South: The Other Invisible Institution*, I chronicled this faith and its adherents below the Mason-Dixon line and demonstrated how the movement stood out against the norms of that time and place. Like Wells's portrait of the professional classes, Southern Unitarianism was liberal, 'middle' (economically, politically, and culturally), and urban in an otherwise conservative, elite, and rural world. But while Wells's

Southern middle class was inspired religiously by an evangelical and implicitly Trinitarian fervour, sharing at least the latter with the planter elites, yeoman and labouring classes, Southern Unitarians remained untouched by both religious elements and this made them even more of a real and imagined threat to the planter class than their urban professional peers. The 'uneasy' relationship between themselves and others therefore often morphed into suspicion, and worse, active opposition. While their churches were most successful in urban areas, their Unitarian faith stood out against the Trinitarian norm of both the planter class and religious orthodoxy. And their Northern coreligionists only made this delicate situation worse. While some Northern Unitarian ministers looked on 'country' life with disdain, others took the faith in radical new directions, and still others blurred the line between church and state through political activism, especially political abolitionism. Faced with a Southern orthodoxy that erroneously labelled them 'Deists' and associated them with the growing antislavery cause of their Northern counterparts, Southern Unitarians held on as long as they could. Most lost their churches, organisational strength, and visibility.[2]

And yet, they survived, and most even thrived, casting a shadow of influence on the South much greater than their size. Even as their church doors closed, Southern Unitarians still remained 'disconcertingly respectable' to Trinitarian orthodoxy and planter elites as they came to dominate the intellectual, professional and literary circles of the South's urban landscape. But how did they overcome these odds, move from foe to friend and shift from rival to neighbour? How could a Unitarian mayor be voted into office for six terms in Savannah, Georgia? How could Unitarian ministers in Charleston and New Orleans come to be revered and respected by Presbyterian divines?

Theirs was less a concerted strategy than a mode of survival that became more a way of life. That life included keeping a low profile with unobtrusive posturing, making religious and cultural appropriations, intentionally separating from their Northern counterparts and purposefully aligning with the planter class. That alignment with the planter class came to signify much more about the 'uneasy' relationship between these two groups and how they came to reconcile some of their differences. As Northern Unitarians increasingly aligned themselves with the growing industrialisation of that region, Southern Unitarians became stronger advocates for the supremacy of the agrarian economy, a hierarchical social order and the genteel culture it inspired. And while attacks by Trinitarians forced many Unitarians below the Mason-Dixon Line to close their doors, Southern Unitarianism didn't die out. It simply found other ways to survive outside of institutional religion. Sometimes that meant forging a place for itself in new and different ways just below the surface of the religious landscape, and other times, well above it. Perhaps most curious about their religious experience was that in spite of the apparent damage done by local Trinitarians, Southern Unitarians didn't see them as their biggest threat. Instead, they reserved that designation for their Northern counterparts, who they believed had fallen victim to the poisons of evangelical emotionalism, the political fanaticism of abolitionism and the dangers of the new industrial order.

Unitarians versus Trinitarians and the aftermath of theological uneasiness

In 1821, Dr. Samuel Miller, professor of ecclesiastical history and church government at Princeton University, drew the line for orthodoxy and summarily declared war on Unitarians. To the members of the First Presbyterian Church of Baltimore he declared that the 'system of the Unitarians is nothing less than a total denial and subversion of the Christian religion'.[3] This was not an isolated charge. Accusations against Unitarians mounted in the early years of the antebellum period as churches sprang up in urban areas across the South. Following Dr Miller's earlier declaration, David Henkel published a pamphlet in 1830 in Virginia entitled *Against the Unitarians*, attacking Unitarians for claiming Christian status.[4] Seven years later in Charleston, the editor of the Baptist journal, *The Southern Watchman*, printed a scathing article on the 'religious delinquencies of Unitarianism and the threat that it posed to the Christian world. Unitarians', the editor declared, 'in the esteem of all but themselves, have descended ... in the scale of error [and] have plunged many fathoms in the gulf of impiety.'[5]

Toward the end of his ministry, Dr Samuel Gilman, minister of the First Unitarian Church of Charleston, recalled the heated climate both he and members of his congregation had faced earlier: 'The very name Unitarian bore with it an offensive odor ... Bitter speeches ... were daily circulated against us with the activity of current coin... Most persons ... seemed to shrink from the employment of the epithet Unitarian.'[6] For Gilman, the differences that existed between Southern Unitarians and orthodoxy were more questions of 'arithmetic' than 'true theology'. Southern Unitarians emphasised a divine 'union' between Father and Son, while the latter stressed a divine 'unity'. Gilman declared: 'The differences between the two parties, for which Unitarians are so bitterly and unsparingly denounced and excommunicated, is simply this: Unitarians believe in the closer union between Father and Son; Trinitarians, as far as we can comprehend them, contend for a unity, or identity.'[7]

Epistemologically, an ontological 'unity' was incomprehensible to liberal Christians, who, nurtured in the philosophical framework of Scottish Common Sense Realism, sought an 'understanding' of God's revelation through their innate 'consciences'. 'I think it to be impossible that any thinking being could suppose,' Gilman declared, 'that Jehovah himself resigned his existence for our sins.' He explained Christ's divine nature and existence on Earth as 'immeasurable degrees of power and wisdom ... poured out upon and closely connected with his human nature, by the Spirit of God'. For him, the idea of divinity being 'poured out' was inherent in John's invocation of the Word being 'spoken' or begotten by God, in the first line of his Gospel ('In the Beginning was the Word, and the Word was with God and the Word was God.') Moreover, Southern Unitarians confirmed the Virgin Birth, the divinity of Christ, believed he was the Son of God and the Messiah, insisted that he be called 'Saviour', and believed that their faith, like that of other Christians, required equally compelling responses from its adherents. Gilman concluded, 'In whatever degree we honour the Father, to that same degree it is clear that we honour the Son and Messenger whom he has sent.' Indeed, there is much credence in (at least the Southern version) of the Unitarian claim that they were 'misunderstood' by orthodoxy and were maligned by those ignorant of their faith and Christian principles.[8]

Historians have seen these attacks as the end of Unitarianism in the South. The few discourses that deal with the topic usually pause here and emphasise the decline of the faith in the would-be Confederate States.[9] But this decline has been exaggerated and misunderstood. Historians have failed to explain not only what happened to Southern Unitarians after they lost their churches, but also how Southern Unitarians were able to sustain their position of prominence among the South's urban professional, intellectual, civic and commercial elite.

It is true that for many Southern Unitarian congregations, attacks by Trinitarians, tension within their own denomination and the erroneous association of Southern Unitarians with all things Northern proved too difficult. Out of seven Unitarian churches in the would-be Confederate states, all in urban areas, only two, in Charleston and New Orleans, managed to remain organisationally active on the eve of the Civil War. But this did not mean that Unitarians ceased to exist or stopped holding their beliefs altogether. Southern Unitarians who found themselves without a church building for worship often decided that the most practical option was to duck into the more orthodox churches to better ride out the evangelical storm. They may not have had a church building with a Unitarian title to call home, but they were able to practise 'their old and primitive faith' in local Southern churches that were more tolerant of their theology and with whom they had more in common than with their Northern coreligionists.[10]

Cities and Unitarians

As was the case with the cities in which they lived, the influence of Unitarians on the religious landscape of the antebellum South remained greater than their numbers. Although cities contained only a small part of the South's population during the antebellum period and Unitarians appeared to comprise only a small fraction of the South's religious groups, both cities and Unitarians more than made up for their size. Unitarianism attracted some of the urban South's most influential literary, professional, commercial and mercantile classes. Prominent doctors, lawyers, writers, editors, mayors, corporate officers and merchants espoused Unitarian beliefs and were drawn to Southern cities not only for their own vocations but also for the intellectual stimulation, opportunities for benevolence and greater sense of freedom these urban areas engendered in allowing them to practise their religion.

Unitarian contributions to all of the professional vocations remained disproportionately strong throughout the antebellum period as Unitarians ascended through the South's professional classes and formed close associations with other Southerners, often assuming prominent national and local roles. In addition to serving as president of the Bank of South Carolina, for example, Unitarian the Honorable Thomas Lee of Charleston was also United States District Court judge for South Carolina. And the same Charleston Unitarian congregation boasted at least ten doctors, one of whom, James Moultrie, Jr, served both as vice-president and president of the American Medical Association. In Savannah, Richard Arnold served as the first secretary of the American Medical Association, was mayor of the city for six terms, founder of the Savannah Medical College and head of the Board of Education. In New Orleans, the Reverend Theodore Clapp not only served as minister of the Unitarian church but was also designated 'chair of the Adjunct Professor of Anatomy' at the medical school of the University of New Orleans (which later became Tulane University). During summers when epidemics ravaged the city, Clapp devoted countless hours to attending to the sick and bereaved. In Clapp's congregation, Christian Roselius served as attorney general of the state of Louisiana, while Joseph Oglesby and Samuel H. Kennedy controlled much of the Western trade from their seats in New Orleans and were influential in the development of railroads into and outside of Louisiana, Texas and Mexico.

Some of the South's most distinguished editors of newspapers and journals were also Unitarians. Daniel Whitaker edited the *Southern Literary Journal and Magazine of Arts* and the *Southern Quarterly Review* and made frequent contributions to the *National Intelligencer*, the *Christian Register*, the *Charleston Courier*, and the *New Orleans Times*. After selling the *National Intelligencer*, Joseph Gales edited the *Raleigh Register* and served as mayor of Raleigh for nineteen years. His son, Joseph Gales, Jr, along with William Seaton, Joseph Gales's son-in-law, later regained and co-owned the *National Intelligencer*. John Moncure Daniel was a prominent and controversial editor of the *Richmond Examiner*, L.W. Spratt edited the *Charleston Standard*, and A. M. Holbrook edited the *New Orleans Picayune*. In addition to his work in medicine and mayoral responsibilities, Dr Richard Arnold published *The Georgian*.[11]

As part of the new professional class in the urban South, Unitarian ministers enjoyed the most intimate association with these powerful and influential Southerners, and the fact that they were privileged to minister to such an array of prominent laymen brightened the ways in which they were perceived by the outside community and the ways in which they perceived themselves. Unitarian ministers met regularly with other ministers for theological and academic discussions. Gilman and Jasper Adams, Episcopal president of Charleston College, met regularly to read German Biblical criticism together. Moreover, Gilman was a frequent and regular speaker at various clubs and organisations in Charleston. By 1850, he could declare that 'with the clergymen of this city … it has ever been my good fortune to hold the most-friendly relations'.[12]

Unobtrusive posturing: the word

But relations were not always friendly. Indeed, it is hard to fathom how these statements of 'friendly relations' in the 1850s can be reconciled with the theological attacks Unitarians faced in the 1820s. But the relationship between Unitarians and Trinitarians differed in the North and South, as did their origins, their faith and the political economies in which each group found itself. As I have argued elsewhere, the very origins of Unitarianism in the North (not the South) began as some established ministers attacked the emotional influence and transient nature of the First Great Awakening, an evangelical movement that swept Protestant Europe and British America in the early mid-eighteenth century. In New England especially the movement challenged established church authority and incited division between traditionalists, who insisted on the continuing importance of ritual and doctrine, and revivalists, who encouraged emotional involvement. In the 1740s, Boston minister Charles Chauncy took special aim at evangelists like George Whitfield, William Tennent and James Davenport, and was as troubled by the itinerant usurpation of their clerical pulpits as he was by the arousal of the 'horrendous passions' of the audience. As religious liberals faced the Second Great Awakening's backlash against the rational extremes of the eighteenth century's Enlightenment, they developed 'a firm opposition to revivalism and the whole pietistic emphasis on a religion of the heart'. Accordingly, Unitarians, North and South, mobilised and started utilising tracts and pamphlets instead of revivals to cater to the head over the heart. By 1860, Unitarian tracts had become, in the words of Sydney Alhstrom, 'the most distinguished collections of denominational literature that *any* [emphasis added] American church had produced'. Not surprisingly, Unitarians took great pride in their literary achievements and placed the 'written word' many times over that of the 'spoken word' from the pulpit. In the 1820s, in one area in which Unitarians, North and South, agreed, both groups took to the pen and the press to counter Trinitarian attacks.[13]

Established churches founded the American Tract Society in 1825 in large measure as an evangelistic and missionary extension of the Second Great Awakening. Over the course of the nineteenth century the society published millions of copies of religious devotionals, moral tracts, hymnals, and periodicals. But the founding of the American Tract Society came only *after* Unitarians in the North and South had already organised similar societies. In 1821, Jared Sparks started the *Unitarian Miscellany* in Baltimore and soon had agents scattered throughout the South. In the early 1820s Joseph Gales published thousands of Unitarian pamphlets, blanketing Raleigh and the surrounding area. He did this so that 'these [and other Unitarian] extracts may find their way into newspapers and other periodical works ... without [many] suspecting they contain the favorite sentiments of the Sect which is everywhere spoken against ... and Prejudice may in this way be undermined!' Within a few years, he declared, 'I believe we have put a stop to the preaching of our Clergy on the subject, for, as we could not give them Sermon for Sermon we published a Pamphlet for every Sermon they preached.' In Augusta, Georgia, the Reverend Stephen Bulfinch began a literary periodical called the *Unitarian Christian* to assert what he described as 'their Christianity and their right to fellowship among Christians and to serve as an outlet for more general literary material'.[14]

In Charleston, Gilman declared, 'We know of no better mode by which Unitarians can counteract its annoyances ... than by giving our publications as wide a circulation as may be consistent with fair and proper measures.' In 1821, four years before the founding of either the American Unitarian Association in Boston or the American Tract Society, he and members of the First Unitarian

Church of Charleston formed the Charleston Unitarian Book and Tract Society, the first organisation in the United States for the circulation of Unitarian literature. The society met with unforeseen success. In 1831, on the tenth anniversary of its founding, Gilman declared that the society had not only retained its ground, but increased in 'favor and usefulness, far beyond the expectations of its original projections'. 'It began with about 30 subscribers,' he recalled, 'but during the last six years, its average number of members has never been lower than seventy. About 200 different works have been distributed.'[15]

In countering attacks by evangelicals Unitarians realised the great importance of the written over the spoken word. The written word kept the sanctity of individual conscience intact and aided in maintaining 'reasonableness' over the emotional zeal of evangelical preaching and revivalism. Unitarians believed that the written word allowed an individual to be more reflective, sound and reasonable in matters of faith, provided a quiet forum for argument, catered to the head over the heart and assumed a much lower profile than the visible signs of a church steeple or the audible strains of Sunday sermons. In short, the written word provided Southern Unitarians with the perfect tool for unobtrusive posturing, and allowed them to establish a liberal faith just below the surface of the South's religious landscape.

Religious and cultural appropriation

Throughout the urban South there existed a core of rational Christianity that was shared by Unitarians and Protestants alike. This core allowed for a certain fluidity and similarity of thought between these seemingly antagonistic groups that can today be seen as orthodox, despite the then frequent cries between them of 'Deist' and 'Sceptic'. Southern Unitarians believed that outside attacks and labels grossly misrepresented their faith and their theological positions. Paul K. Conkin has argued that 'what these labels too easily conceal and what critics like to downplay is that all the early Unitarian ministers were avowed, serious, conscientious Christians who simply wanted to reform and purify the church'. They believed that the Bible was the Word of God and while they rejected the triune God, they 'continued to baptize in the name of the Father, the Son, and the Holy Spirit'.[16]

While the polemics between Southern Unitarians and the 'orthodox' community raged early on, these labels could not stick for long, particularly in places like Charleston and New Orleans, as the educated classes saw more similarities than differences in their theological, political and cultural outlooks and their epistemological assumptions. This was true of the Episcopal Church in the South especially during the entire antebellum period. Not only did Unitarian congregations in the South frequently look to Episcopal (not to mention Anglican) seminaries and churches for clergy for their pulpits, they also frequently found sympathisers and future members among their ranks. The Episcopal and the Unitarian churches were perhaps the least touched theologically, socially and politically by evangelical influences and many Episcopalians rented pews in the Unitarian churches to attend when convenient and when they so desired.

Many of the South's educated elite often flirted with the Southern version of Unitarianism and in the process helped to blur the lines between what constituted orthodoxy and what did not. While John C. Calhoun and William H. Crawford, Democratic-Republican Presidential nominee from Georgia, espoused Unitarian views, they did not necessarily flaunt them. Nevertheless, their theological positions did help to assuage the initial hostilities and elevate the liberal faith out of the trenches. Gilman, Clapp and other Southern Unitarians took over from there. According to Presbyterian minister Dr Benjamin Morgan Palmer: 'The social and amiable qualities of Mr. Clapp endeared him greatly as a man ... the large majority of his hearers could not appreciate this clamor about doctrine and many of the truly pious ... were disposed to sympathise with him as one unkindly persecuted.' Presbyterian minister James Henley Thornwell described Gilman as having 'a genial sympathy with his kind, a spirit full of love to all that God has made beautiful ... pure, gentle, confiding, shrinking from the very thought of inflicting gratuitous pain, these qualities are everywhere so conspicuous, that one must not be told, why the circles of Dr. Gilman's intimacy are so devoted to their pastor and friend'. When Gilman died, the Charleston *Courier* described the funeral as 'the most solemn occasion since Calhoun's death'.[17]

Southern liberals like Gilman and Clapp and Southern conservatives like Thornwell and Palmer were indebted to a philosophical way of thinking that offered them a broad foundation on which to reconcile some of their differences, and in essence share a common Southern Christian rationalism. Scottish Common Sense Realism was largely instrumental in precipitating a correspondence between Gilman and Thornwell in the late 1850s that demonstrated both mutual respect between them and shared theological assumptions and positions. As newly appointed editor of the *Southern Quarterly Review*, Thornwell solicited articles from Gilman on Thomas Brown, perhaps the most Idealist of the Common Sense Philosophers at Edinburgh.

Scottish Common Sense Philosophy was as ubiquitous as it was flexible. It was not so much a set of conclusions as a way of thinking that could commend itself to a variety of thinkers. It was characterised by a commitment to the ultimate meaningfulness of what human beings know, feel, desire and decide. It rested on three epistemological assumptions: (1) observation is the basis of knowledge; (2) consciousness is the medium of observation and (3) consciousness contains principles that are independent of experience and impose order on the data of experience. Thus, consciousness was anterior to experience and regulated what the mind and body saw, felt, heard, etc. These constituents of consciousness comprised what was known as 'common sense'. Unlike the Scepticism of David Hume and John Locke that doubted certain concepts, such as causality, that tie experiences together to establish order, Common Sense Realists believed that consciousness strove for both order and understanding, revealing that a 'natural and original judgement' accompanied one's perceptions of the world. By embracing Realism, Southern Unitarians distanced themselves from the more radical elements of both Deism and Scepticism, and tied themselves to the philosophical assumptions of other Southern Christians. For them, Common

Sense Realism provided not only the tools needed for a 'rational orthodoxy', but also a means by which to legitimise their 'Christian' status to Southerners and to push for ecumenical reform among the various denominations.

Along with an enlightened and Realist sense of 'order' and 'understanding', Southern Unitarians steadfastly maintained as paramount the sanctity of individual conscience in matters of religion and politics. 'Liberal Christianity,' Gilman declared, 'aims to secure more and more the respect and tenderness of the church toward individual conscience, instead of crushing and absorbing the conscience of the individual in the will and the despotism of the church.'[18] It is for this reason that Southern Unitarians seldom if ever initiated theological attacks upon orthodox circles but waited until false allegations demanded a response, which by then was defensive rather than offensive in nature. These defensive responses reflected the genteel culture of the Southern mind. The right and sanctity of individual conscience did not exist in a vacuum and Southern Unitarians were mindful of its place within the context of time and place. David Molke-Hansen argues that intellectual cultivation in Charleston was by its very nature a social occasion in which everybody knew everybody and the personalities, friendships and dynamics these relationships engendered dictated the terms of discourse. For the Charleston intelligentsia, 'to criticize or disagree was permissible; to attack directly or disparage (though done often enough) was not'.[19] This helps to explain why theological attacks could not last long in the South. Southern Unitarians believed that not only were they unwarranted, they also ran counter to the Southern norm.

Separating from the North

As the years progressed, Southern Unitarians became increasingly troubled that Unitarians in the North were making abolitionism the ultimate expression of national reform, were using the pulpit (the 'spoken word') to make it a political issue and were holding revival meetings to gather emotional zeal and ferment for the cause.Through their written expositions of liberal faith Southern Unitarians believed that they had maintained the purity and rationality of the Unitarian faith, kept it on a 'broad and liberal' foundation that minimised doctrinal and denominational differences and with their emphasis on individual conscience, 'render[ed] unto Caesar' by keeping politics out of the pulpit.[20]

On December 22, 1850, A.M. Holbrook, editor of the New Orleans *Daily Picayune* and himself a Unitarian, openly rebuked the 'pulpit treason' of Unitarian minister Theodore Parker, who, he declared, had violated the clerical 'duty of non-interference'. He then recommended the 'Thanksgiving Sermon' of local Unitarian minister Theodore Clapp, which the *Picayune* carried and printed on the front page. Throughout the sermon, Clapp cited the name of the most influential Unitarian in the United States, William Ellery Channing, and was as bothered by his interference in Southern affairs as he was by the recent change in his position on slavery.[21] Years earlier, Channing declared that if nothing but political action could remove slavery, 'then slavery must continue'. But with the publication of

Slavery in 1835, Channing changed his position and called on his parishioners and readers to openly renounce the institution, as he himself pushed for its abolition.[22] Like many Southerners, Clapp believed that industrial capitalism in the North provided more than sufficient material for ardent reform and that Channing and Northern Unitarians were turning a blind eye to their own problems in order to claim moral authority. 'Let them direct their united and vigorous efforts towards meliorating the condition of the suffering, impoverished and immoral thousands at home,' he declared, 'instead of wasting their declamation and resources upon visionary projects that relate to remote parts, over which it is not possible for them to exert the slightest salutary influence.'[23]

In *Patterns of Antislavery among American Unitarians*, Douglas C. Stange has taken Channing's comments into account and assesses the change within and the nature of Unitarian political activism, accounting for the early divisions, and delineating the forces that ultimately triumphed in propelling the Northern ranks of the denomination to articulate and incorporate an antislavery political position within its national convention platform in 1860. Stange chronicles the activity and careers of ministers in the North who often found it their duty to wear political hats along with their clerical robes. Throughout New England, one could find a Unitarian minister who was also an attorney, a governor, a state legislator, a political party activist, a congressman or a United States senator.[24]

Dr Richard D. Arnold, mayor of Savannah, repeated Theodore Clapp's concerns with Channing. He scribbled the following line in his scrapbook: 'We are now in the midst of a war waged against us by our quondam Brethren of the North in order to subjugate us to make us bow supplicating for mercy at their feet.' To support this claim, Arnold glued to the pages of his scrapbook a newspaper article of 3 February 1856 entitled 'The Reaction Against the Abolitionists-American Civilization Versus Puritan Fanaticism'. Arnold believed that Unitarian ministers in the North formed the vanguard of the abolitionists, and that through their lapse into religious emotionalism and heightened political agitations they had revealed their true blood, 'Puritan fanaticism'.

> The fertile source of the ever-recurring mischief is the Puritan idea of the superiority of their sect over other men, and a mysterious divine right which they claim to possess of dictating to all mankind – a right which they held to be higher than the authority of the Bible and the constitution, and which ought to be maintained at all hazards, even with Sharp's, rifles, bayonets and cannon balls.[25]

Joseph Lewis in Kabletown, Virginia, lamented the 'destruction' of Northern Unitarianism by the encroachment of the secular on the sacred and the increasing willingness of its ministers to taint the pulpit with political agendas. Admonishing Unitarians in the North, Lewis declared:

> The number of ministers that fall – your vitiated literature which is thrown broadcast over the country – misrepresentations, exaggerations, the ignoble

appeals of certain politicians to the masses to excite their passions & their prejudices for the sole object of gaining political power. Such is the aspect of northern society as it presents itself to me, & what is to save it from destruction, but the ministers of the Gospel returning to the faithful and earnest discharge of their duties by preaching the Kingdom of heaven & leave the affairs of Caesar to statesmen. Who ever heard of a minister of the Gospel being a statesman? ... A true statesman understands the proverb uttered by our Savior, 'cast not your pearls before swine' – but it appears a large portion of the North has not the slightest conception of the truth conveyed by it.[26]

In New Orleans, former New Englander, Thomas Adams argued that the American Unitarian Association might have sustained a greater missionary presence in the West and the South, if not for the political deviations of its ministers. 'Had the clergy of that denomination confined their preaching to the truths of Christianity and to the abolition of sins prevailing among their own people,' Adams declared, 'quite an important sum of money might annually flow into your treasury.'[27] M.J. Rice, secretary of the board of trustees of the New Orleans church, expressed the board's desire to secure a minister with 'good judgment' who could preach the Gospel without introducing any personal or political 'crusade' into the congregation or the community.[28]

Not surprisingly, Southern Unitarians edited and sent back those religious publications from the North that they believed generated theological discord, and that delved into political areas that many thought were beyond the realm of the pulpit, and that tended to compound the problems they already faced. In Charleston, the congregation declared:

> The course pursued by a large majority of our Unitarian brethren at the North … has been such, that, to protect ourselves in the quiet enjoyment of our domestic rights, we find it expedient to forego the use of most of their religious publications, and the irksomeness of this course (an alternative which, in common with most all other denominations of Southern Christians, we have been compelled to adopt) is much enhanced because of our very isolated position. We say this rather in sorrow than in anger, but neither the fanaticism of the North, nor the averted looks of those around us, shall deter us from maintaining our old and primitive faith … the liberal spirit that has distinguished our members, and has never failed to meet every demand heretofore made upon it …we surely will not withhold a few dollars, when needed to maintain our independence as a Southern congregation of 'liberal Christians.'[29]

But this statement in 1857 did more than accompany the return of unwanted literature. It formally split the American Unitarian Association, one of the last remnants of denominational unity in the South, into separate sectional entities. In so doing, Southern Unitarians purposefully aligned themselves to the planter culture and to the ideals of an agrarian economy, the social order it established, the genteel customs it inspired, and appropriated their faith to that of Southern orthodoxy.

Purposeful alignment with planter class

Throughout the antebellum period the Southern economy remained dependent upon seaport and river towns to export cotton and other hinterland and lowland staples to Europe, the North, and the outside world. Because of the nature of the agrarian economy, Southern urban culture ebbed and flowed as town populations fluctuated with the waves of the seasons and on the hands of an agricultural clock. Southern towns like Charleston, New Orleans, Augusta, Savannah and Mobile typically slept from late spring to early fall, awoke with the arrival of the first cotton or tobacco shipments, and arranged their social and cultural calendars around the staple markets. When harvests peaked in October, farmers and country shoppers flocked to town to restock. Commerce bustled until Christmas, enjoyed a small pause, and then from January through April, boats jammed the harbours, hoping to make the mid-January rush to European destinations in order to be back by mid-April for their second cargoes. By June, business slowed down and many Southern urban dwellers retreated to the country, the hinterlands, their plantations, the North, or to European destinations.

Historians William and Jane Pease have argued that many urban tradesmen used their profits not for furthering their businesses or increasing their incomes, as Northern industrialists and capitalists would do, but instead to buy land, plantations, and slaves. Rather than seeking individual materialistic gain, the Peases argue, many Southern merchants bartered their urban wares for such intangible country values as social prestige, gentility, and political power. In Mobile, in addition to his work in agricultural commodities exchange, Unitarian merchant Herbert C. Peabody owned vast tracts of land and numerous slaves, as did George E. Gibbon in Charleston and John Leeds in New Orleans, just to name a few.

But merchants were not the only ones who sought elements of agrarian distinction and social prestige. The South's growing number of urban professionals aspired to various levels and elements of planter status. In the late 1820s, Augusta Unitarian minister Daniel Whitaker gave up the pulpit and became a planter in the South Carolina low country, devoting himself to the production of the Southern staples of cotton and rice. Other town ministers like Gilman and Clapp, though not investing in large tracts of country land, purchased or rented slaves for domestic betterment and social prestige. In Unitarian congregations throughout the South, both ministers and laity owned slaves and land. In Savannah, Unitarian minister Dexter Clapp wrote that there were slave owners in every Southern Unitarian congregation and that in nearly all of these churches, 'almost every member owned slaves'.[30]

Throughout the urban South, the possession of slaves served both symbolic and functional purposes for Unitarians. Slave ownership served as a symbol of prestige and gentility, and when coupled with their own professional careers, helped to determine the social relationships, associations and organisations in which Southern Unitarians would lead and join. These relationships and associations tied Unitarians closer to other Southerners, to a growing sense of sectional consciousness and Southern identity, and helped them, when under attack, to shape an underground network of liberal faith hiding just below the surface of institutional religion.

Slave ownership, land, power, and prestige also strengthened the distinctions of class and fuelled the established intricacies of a hierarchical society. Hierarchy in Charleston, New Orleans, and other port cities in the South defined what Moltke-Hansen calls the 'channels of intercourse, the conventions of discourse, and to a great degree, cultural expectations and values'. The community and literary culture of Charleston was 'dominated by Episcopalians and Presbyterians of British and Huguenot extraction, plantation heritage, [and] cosmopolitan education and prejudice,' Moltke-Hansen explains.[31] As Episcopalians and Presbyterians controlled first- and second-place positions in towns across the South, Unitarians came in a very close third.

Because they chose to emphasise theological agreement rather than discord, Southern Unitarians were able to rise above the theological attacks of earlier years, tying themselves closer to other rational Southern Christians, and in the process instil in Southern urban religion an ecumenicism that was not always apparent on the surface. As one Northern Unitarian described Clapp's church: '[T]here is less Sectarianism in this place than in any I was ever in. The prevailing spirit is liberal. Unitarians, Calvinists, Episcopalians, Catholics, and Nothingarians, contributed towards building the Methodist Church.' In Savannah, J. Allen Penniman declared, '[Our society] is made up of Unitarians, Presbyterians, Baptists, & Methodists, and has been from the beginning of my labors here.' Moreover, in 1855, Clapp and members of his congregation chose to drastically alter the sign out front of their church after The First Congregational Unitarian Church of New Orleans burned. When the new church was completed, these Southern liberals, in order to discard the trappings of sectarianism, appropriate their faith to Southern orthodoxy, and erase the Unitarian name from its synonymy with Northern Unitarian abolitionism, changed their name to The Church of the Messiah.[32]

By tying themselves to Southern Trinitarians instead of their Northern coreligionists, Southern Unitarians became stronger advocates for the supremacy of the agrarian economy, a hierarchical social order, and the genteel culture it inspired. In doing so, these Southern urban liberals made themselves 'easy' neighbours to the rural planter class.

Notes

1 J. Wells, *The Origins of the Southern Middle Class, 1800–1861* (Chapel Hill: University of North Carolina Press, 2004), pp. 209, 224.

2 J. A. Macaulay, *Unitarianism in the Antebellum South: The Other Invisible Institution* (Tuscaloosa: University of Alabama Press, 2001).

3 S. Miller, D.D. *Letters on Unitarianism Addressed to the Members of the First Presbyterian Church of Baltimore* (Trenton, N.J.: George Sherman, 1821), p. 9.

4 D. Henkel, *Against the Unitarians: A Treatise on the Person and Incarnation of Jesus Christ, In Which Some of the Principal Arguments of the Unitarians are Examined* (New Market, Va., 1830).

5 J. B. Whitridge, *Calling Things by Their Right Names: A Brief Reply To An Article Under That Title, In the Southern Watchman of May 19, 1837. By a Layman* (Charleston: Walker and James, 1937), p. 4.

6 S. Gilman, *The Old and the New: Discourses and Proceedings at the Dedication of the Re-Modeled Unitarian Church* (Charleston: Samuel G. Courtenay, 1854), p. 20.

7 S. Gilman, *A Sermon on the Introduction to the Gospel of St. John* (Charleston: Unitarian Book and Tract Society, 1825), p. 5.

8 Gilman, *St. John*, p. 12–13.

9 R. Adams, *The Charleston Unitarianism Gilman Began With*, Kenneth B. Murdock (ed.) (Cambridge: Harvard University Library, 1952). S. E. Alhstrom, *A Religious History of the American People* (New Haven: Yale University Press, 1972). A. A. Brooks, *A History of Unitarianism in the Southern Churches: Charleston, New Orleans, Louisville, Richmond* (Boston: American Unitarian Association, [n.d.]. C. Eaton, *Freedom of Thought Struggle in the Old South* (New York: Harper and Row, 1964). E. Morse Wilbur, *A History of Unitarianism in Transylvania, England and America* (Boston: Harvard University Press, 1952). C. Wright, *The Beginnings of Unitarianism in America* (Boston: Starr King Press, 1955). C. Wright, *The Liberal Christians: Essays on American Unitarian History* (Boston: Beacon Press, 1970). G. H. Gibson, 'Unitarian Congregations in Ante-Bellum Georgia' in *Georgia Historical Quarterly* 54 (1970). G. H. Gibson, 'Unitarian Congregations in the Antebellum South' in *Proceedings of the Unitarian Historical Society* 12, pt.2 (1959). C. Gohdes, 'Some Notes on the Unitarian Church in the Ante-Bellum South: A Contribution to the History of Southern Liberalism' in *American Studies in Honor of William Kenneth Boyd by Members of The Americana Club of Duke University*, David Kelly Jackson (ed.) (Durham: Duke University Press, 1968). D. W. Howe, 'A Massachusetts Yankee in Senator Calhoun's Court: Samuel Gilman in South Carolina' in *New England Quarterly* 44 (1971).

10 G. W. Logan, et al. *Annual Reports Rendered by the Managers of the Charleston Unitarian Book and Tract Society On the Occasion of Its Thirty-Sixth Anniversary, Sunday, August 9, 1857* (Charleston: Walker, Evans & Co., 1857), 9–10.

11 For a detailed account of Unitarian laity see Macaulay, *Unitarianism in the Antebellum South*, pp. 57–78.

12 Gilman, *Old and New*, p. 20.

13 Alhstrom, *A Religious History of the American People*, pp. 673, 303, 391, 398.

14 Joseph Gales to Jared Sparks, 2 August 1822, Joseph Gales to C. H. Appleton, 20 June 1821, Gales collection. Joseph Gales Papers, Southern Historical Collection, University of North Carolina, Chapel Hill.

15 Gilman, *Old and New*, p. 21.

16 P. K. Conkin, *American Originals: Homemade Varieties of Christianity* (Chapel Hill: University of North Carolina Press, 1997), p. 68.

17 See J. Duffy (ed.) *Parson Clapp of the Strangers' Church of New Orleans* (Baton Rouge: Louisiana State University Press, 1957), 36. *Southern Quarterly Review*, n.s. (3d), I (1856): 430. [Charleston] *Courier*, 18, 11 February, 1858.

18 Gilman, *Old and New*, p. 66.

19 D. Moltke-Hansen, 'The Expansion of Intellectual Life: A Prospectus,' in *Intellectual Life in Antebellum Charleston*, Michael O'Brien and David Moltke-Hansen (eds) (Knoxville: University of Tennessee Press, 1986), p. 20.

20 Editorial by A. M. Holbrook, [New Orleans] *Daily Picayune*, 22 December 1850; Theodore Clapp, 'A Thanksgiving Sermon, Delivered in the First Congregational Church, New Orleans, December 19, 1850,' *Daily Picayune*, 22 December 1850. Hereafter cited as 'Thanksgiving Sermon.'

21 Thanksgiving Sermon.

22 W. E. Channing, *The Works of William E. Channing, D.D.* (Boston: American Unitarian Association, 1882), pp. 844–46. W. E. Channing, *Slavery* (Boston: James Munroe and

Co, 1835), p. 7. For a detailed account of Channing's change in position, see 'The Conversion of William Ellery Channing,' in E. Rugemer, *The Problem of Emancipation: The Caribbean Roots of the American Civil War* (Baton Rouge: Louisiana State University, 2009).

23 Thanksgiving Sermon.

24 D. C. Stange, *Patterns of Antislavery among American Unitarians, 1831–1860* (Rutherford: Fairleigh Dickinson University Press, 1977), pp. 100–120.

25 Richard D. Arnold Scrapbook [paper and date unknown], Richard D. Arnold Papers, Southern Historical Collection, Wilson Library, University of North Carolina, Chapel Hill, pp. 140–41.

26 Joseph B. Lewis to the AUA, 28 January 1858, AUA Letters.

27 Thomas Adams to the American Unitarian Association, 31 December 1858, AUA Letters.

28 M. J. Rice to the AUA, 17 May 1856, AUA Letters.

29 G. W. Logan, et al. *Annual Reports Rendered by the Managers of the Charleston Unitarian Book and Tract Society On the Occasion of Its Thirty-Sixth Anniversary, Sunday, August 9, 1857* (Charleston: Walker, Evans & Co., 1857), pp. 9–10.

30 W. H. Pease and J. H. Pease, *The Web of Progress: Private Values and Public Styles in Boston and Charleston, 1828–1843* (Athens and London: The University of Georgia Press, 1991), 40–53. Dexter Clapp, 'Letter on the Religious Conditions of Slaves,' *Monthly Religious Magazine* 3 (May 1846), p. 207.

31 M. O'Brien and D. Moltke-Hansen (eds) *Intellectual Life in Antebellum Charleston* (Knoxville: University of Tennessee Press, 1986). p. 20.

32 *Christian Register* 10 April 1841. J. Allen Penniman to the Secretary of the A.U.A, 13 August 1849. A.U.A. Letters.

Part II
The changing world of work

4   Country butchers and the city in the Exe Valley, 1840–1900

Julia Neville

Introduction

In 1863 John Pearcy, a butcher living in a village a few miles from Exeter in the English south-western county of Devon, placed an advertisement in *Trewman's Exeter Flying Post*, to announce that he:

> begs to inform his patrons that, for their greater accommodation and convenience, he has taken the shop 214 High Street (*four doors below Queen Street*) where he will in future attend, instead of in the Higher Market as heretofore…[1]

Pearcy was a 'country butcher', a butcher with a farm in the countryside where he reared and fattened animals, slaughtered them and then brought in the meat ready dressed to sell in a nearby town. His advertisement showed that, in the twenty years since he was first mentioned as a butcher, he had progressed to the most classy form of retailing, the High Street shop rather than the covered market. He had also extended the acreage of his farm. Seven years later, however, he was declared bankrupt. He had to give up the shop and the farm and move away from the village. His story was not unique. Although the country butcher was a well-established figure in stock-farming regions of England in the first half of the nineteenth century, and demand for meat increased throughout the century, by 1900 butchers of that kind had virtually disappeared from small villages close to town markets. The functions of the producer-retailer had been split between specialist farmers and specialist retailers.

In this chapter it is argued that, though some of the factors that contributed to the disappearance of country butchers were features of agricultural life, others were generated within the urban environment where they sought to sell their produce. The argument is grounded in a case study of the butcher families in seven villages in the lower Exe valley, all within six miles of Exeter, the major market for their meat. It draws in detail on census and parish records, together with information from Exeter's three local newspapers, to reconstruct what happened to nine families between 1840 and 1900. Then, by intercalating these narratives with material about the city of Exeter, including the city archives, government papers and local newspapers, it demonstrates how the management of the market halls, the changing pattern of retail and the increased regulation of issues relating to public health created an environment in which the country butcher found it difficult to operate on traditional lines.

The context for the case study

The geographical area of the study covers seven villages, bordering or close to the lower Exe around the point where the River Culm flows into it: Nether Exe (650 acres); Huxham (830 acres); Brampford Speke (1150 acres); Stoke Canon (1217 acres); Rewe (1346 acres); Poltimore (1430 acres); and Upton Pyne (2200 acres).[2] None of the villages was very large and, as the nineteenth century progressed, the overall population gradually declined as shown in Table 4.1.[3] The main activity in the villages was farming, although the paper mills at Stoke Canon and Huxham employed a more industrial workforce.

Exeter, the county town, was the natural market for the produce from these villages. By the early nineteenth century the city had lost the cloth trade that had brought it prosperity in medieval times and its rate of growth had slowed. The population in 1831 was 28,000; by 1901 it had risen only to 47,000. The city remained an administrative and ecclesiastical centre, and became a railway centre, but there was little new industry. Nonetheless the area within and just outside the old walls was overcrowded and new suburbs began to stretch out along the main roads. Congestion on the city's streets, the highways from London and Bath to Plymouth and Cornwall, was exacerbated by the fact that there was no separate market place. Sellers set up their stalls and buyers made their purchases along the street frontages. There was a Butcher Row, and a shambles, but many butchers sold from stalls along or just off the High Street. The corporation, successor under the 1835 Municipal Corporation Act to the 'chamber' of aldermen and councillors that had governed Exeter for centuries, took forward their predecessors' plans for modernising the markets and moving them away from the street frontages into covered market halls, providing greater order to public life and greater cleanliness. In fact, unable to decide between rival factions in different quarters of the city, the corporation built two separate market halls, no more than three hundred yards from each other. It was a ludicrous decision, and saddled the city with a debt it

Table 4.1 Population changes in the lower Exe valley, 1841–1901

	1841	1851	1861	1871	1881	1891	1901
Brampford Speke	393	432	466	436	425	308	316
Huxham	150	156	133	124	132	111	138
Poltimore	263	282	339	309	309	363	301
Rewe & Nether Exe	301	248	260	286	284	246	297
Stoke Canon	490	454	452	447	425	364	373
Upton Pyne	514	481	458	427	406	471	384
Total	2142	2053	2108	2029	1981	1863	1909

Data taken from Census Enumeration Books, 1841–1901.

could never pay off. Maintaining two substantial market halls meant that, unlike other cities, Exeter was never able to make profits from its general markets for reinvestment, as cities as far apart as Carlisle, Huddersfield and Reading did.[4] This was particularly unfortunate since, as Newton has identified, the dominant characteristic of the corporation throughout the nineteenth century was 'fiscal prudence'.[5] Rather than use revenue from other sources to improve the markets, the council allowed them to deteriorate.

The history of the decline and disappearance of the country butchers can be discussed as part of the history of rural social change, or as urban history, demonstrating attempts by municipal authorities to impose order and cleanliness within the crowded city. For the purpose of this chapter, however, the argument has been set in the context of the evolution of food distribution and food retailing, although studies of this for the early part of the nineteenth century are limited. Schmiechen and Carls attribute the lack of detailed studies of local authority responses to the growing demand for food in the nineteenth century, generated by the rising population and greater affluence, to the 'lack of consolidated data', and the absence of central systems of accounting and regulation.[6] This is indeed problematic: direct comparison between this study and one of the few other detailed local studies, Scola's on the markets and shops of Manchester and Salford, has proved impossible because, for example, the rate-books he used have no parallel in the Exeter archives.[7] A broad framework for understanding the development of food retailing does, however, exist. Jeffreys first classified the methods of distribution in 1954, identifying itinerant hawkers, periodic markets and fairs, producer-retailers and fixed retail units.[8] It is clear that the country butchers were producer-retailers as Jeffreys describes them, 'craftsmen … experienced and knowledgeable as to the quality and value of the goods they offered for sale', trained by apprenticeship in the skills of animal management, slaughtering and cutting and dressing meat for sale.[9] There is less agreement, however, about how and when these different retailing systems evolved or gained supremacy, and most effort has so far been directed at explaining the evolution of the retail shop into chain stores, supermarkets and malls. The late eighteenth and early nineteenth centuries are less well charted, and have even been described as a 'primordial retail swamp'.[10] Jeffreys' early view that the pace of urban and industrial development in the nineteenth century 'swept away' the market trader and the hawker has been overturned in favour of a recognition, articulated by Shaw, for example, that the old systems co-existed with the new throughout the century.[11] In particular the retail shop and the covered market continued to co-exist. Phillips's analysis of local Market Acts in England shows that the peak period for passing acts authorising the construction of new urban markets was the 1850s and 1860s, although Market Acts in Devon and Cornwall peaked at a slightly earlier date.[12]

Within this shift from selling in the market hall to selling from fixed retail units lies the history of the disappearance of producer-retailers such as the country butchers. One of the few studies to discuss this is that of Scola, who found in Manchester that by the mid-nineteenth century 'most traders in markets were no longer producer-retailers, but retailers' and dates this change to possibly as early as 1815.[13] This is quite different from the experience in Exeter's markets where references to the country butchers in the markets continue beyond the middle of the nineteenth century.

The case study

The Butchers

The study has investigated the fortunes of nine families. Those studied consist of all heads of household described as 'butcher' on either the 1841 or 1851 census returns from the study area, their butcher sons and grandsons (Beedell, Chamberlain, Chambers, Symes from 1841; Greenslade, Nethercott and Pearcy from 1851). Two other families whose heads of household were referred to in the 1840s as having butchers' stalls on the Exeter market were included, although their 1851 occupations are listed on census returns respectively as 'farmer' and 'dairyman' (Hunt and Smith).[14] Changes to the butchers' businesses run by these nine families are discussed in three phases, 1841–1860; 1861–1875; 1876–1901.

The earliest period, 1841–1860, appears to have been a time of great prosperity for many of the families. Thomas Beedell of Upton Pyne and North Street, Exeter, and Thomas Chamberlain of Stoke Canon and High Street, Exeter, were among the country butcher elite with a farm in the village and a city-centre shop. During these two decades they settled the next generation in the same business: Thomas Beedell junior and his brother Henry appear as 'butcher' and 'farmer' respectively in the household return for 1851. Beedell also probably assisted his son-in-law, William Symes, to set up as a country butcher in Brampford Speke. Symes is listed as a butcher in Exeter in White's 1850 *Directory*, but in Brampford Speke in 1861. Chamberlain's elder sons, John and Thomas, were settled in butchers' businesses outside the study area while younger sons Frank and Abraham continued the family business. When Thomas senior died in 1849 his widow, Sarah, took on the business with her younger sons.[15]

Becoming a country butcher was a career to aspire to in the 1840s. John Pearcy, son of a Plymtree farmer, took on a farm in Poltimore, married the daughter of Poltimore butcher William Chambers, and is first recorded as a butcher at the Exeter market in 1845.[16] By 1851 he appears on the census as a butcher and farmer, employing two apprentice butchers. Philip Greenslade, son of a well-known Stoke Canon cattle dealer, is first mentioned with a stall on the Higher Market in 1850,[17] and is described as a butcher on the 1851 Stoke Canon census. One of John Pearcy's two apprentices in 1851 was Charles Smith, son of Charles Smith of Huxham, described as 'dairyman' on the same census. Charles senior is unaccountably missing from the 1841 census although parish register information shows his sons were baptised there in the late 1830s[18]. As mentioned above, he ran a butcher's stall on Exeter market. He was described as a 'pork butcher' in White's 1850 *Directory*. 'Pork butchers' were specialists, but this end of the business required less capital than selling the full range of beef, mutton and pork. It seems that Charles had ambitions for his son to extend the range of the business and was prepared to pay to apprentice him to another butcher. John Smith of Stoke Canon, either another son of Charles or his nephew, also appeared selling pork at Exeter market in 1845.[19] Richard Hunt, Pearcy's second apprentice, was also the son of a man who had a pork butcher's stall on Exeter market and wanted his son to learn the full range of the trade. The final 'new' butcher identified on the 1851 census was Daniel Nethercott of Rewe, described as 'dairyman and butcher'. Dairying was often associated with pig rearing, as the pigs could be fattened on surplus milk. Nethercott had been a dairy hand in a village a few miles from Rewe in 1841.

To counterbalance the additions to the group, two of the 1841 butchers left the lower Exe valley during the 1840s, both from Poltimore. George Symes moved to Aylesbeare, a larger village further east. By 1861 he had evidently decided that the future lay in retail butchery in a more populous place, and moved to Heavitree, a village adjacent to Exeter and rapidly developing as one of its larger suburbs. William Chambers moved into Exeter itself, where he is found as a butcher in both 1851 and 1861.

By comparison with this stable and prosperous period, that from 1861 to 1875 was one of uncertainty, turbulence and failure. Richard Hunt, Pearcy's former apprentice, described himself as 'butcher' in 1861 but was living on a smallholding in Stoke Canon with his brother Abraham, and it is unclear where, if at all, he was employed as a butcher. By 1871 he had disappeared from the records. Daniel Nethercott of Rewe was listed only as a dairyman in 1861 and by 1871 had descended still further down the occupational scale to become an 'agricultural labourer'. Charles Smith senior was still a dairyman in 1861, while Charles junior was employed as a butcher in a large village down on the Exe estuary. Charles junior appears to have returned to help his ageing father during the 1860s as he is evidently the C. Smith referred to in a case of embezzlement, related to a youth employed at the Smiths' market stall, heard at the Exeter Quarter Sessions in January 1865.[20] In 1871, however, a year after his father's death,[21] although recorded on the census return as a butcher in Huxham, Charles was no longer living on the property tenanted by his father, which was inhabited by another dairyman.[22] The business appears to have been split. Meanwhile his cousin (or brother) John Smith, in Stoke Canon, had diversified into a baker's business. He is listed as a baker on the census returns for 1861 and 1871, but his Christmas show of pork on the market is referred to in 1870 and a newspaper reference in 1874 described him as a butcher.[23] A further son of Charles Smith, Samuel, also appeared on the 1861 census for Poltimore, listed as a butcher and resident with his mother-in-law. It is probable though not proven that he worked at that point for John Pearcy, who was still at that time expanding his business but is listed with only one resident apprentice, his wife's nephew, Thomas Chambers. By 1871 Samuel and his family had moved into Exeter, where he was working as a pub landlord.

At the other end of the scale, Thomas Beedell senior moved further up the Exe to take on a farm without a butcher's business, where his son Henry became farm manager. Thomas junior took on the business in Upton Pyne and Exeter. After Thomas senior's death, however, the two sons sold up and by 1871 both were running pubs in fast-developing areas of London. Only Thomas's son-in-law, William Symes, remained in business as a farmer-butcher, though apparently without a market stall.

John Pearcy's rise to the acquisition of a High Street shop and his subsequent spectacular fall into bankruptcy were noted earlier.[24] (Thomas Chambers, his 1861 apprentice, moved to Christchurch, Dorset, where he was a retail butcher in 1871.) Bankruptcy was also the fate of the youngest of the Chamberlain brothers, Abraham. Sarah Chamberlain and her son Frank both died in 1856, and Abraham continued to run the family business on the High Street and in Stoke Canon. In 1862 he was declared bankrupt, and gave up the shop. He started again with a market stall, but in 1864 announced that he was going to give up and go to London.[25] By 1871, however, he had returned to the Exeter area and was working as a butcher in the large village where his eldest brother, John, owned a farmer-butcher business.[26]

By 1875, therefore, the number of butchers in the study area had dwindled and this process continued. By the time of the 1881 census, Charles Smith was working as a gardener in London. John Smith went bankrupt in 1882, still described as 'butcher and baker'.[27] William Symes moved on during the 1880s from the country butcher business in Brampford Speke and is found in 1891 elsewhere, described merely as 'farmer'.

The only remaining country butchers in the villages by the mid-1880s were the Greenslades. Both Philip junior and William followed their father as butchers, with Philip taking on the Stoke Canon business and William taking a farm with a slaughter house in Poltimore where he is described as a butcher in 1881. Philip senior had expanded the Stoke Canon business at some point after the Chamberlains had left in 1864, taking on their 'desirable … butcher's shop, dwelling house, slaughter house, yard, orchard, arable and pasture fields'. This had to be let 'with immediate possession' in 1876, possibly as a result of Philip senior's death, suggesting that the scale of their joint business may have reduced at that stage.[28] In 1882 Philip junior was declared bankrupt and the sale of his goods included his beam, scales and weights as well as his meat block, indicating that he no longer intended to practise as a butcher.[29] He continued to work as a farmer and cattle dealer, but not as a butcher.

His brother William continued to describe himself as 'butcher' and remained in business in Poltimore until after 1921. It does not appear, however, that he ever took a stall or a shop in Exeter, and he presumably sold direct to the town's retail butchers. His eldest sons, though trained as butchers, left the family business.[30] By the end of the century William Greenslade was the sole representative of the original nine families to remain in the area, and he no longer retailed meat in Exeter. There were new butchers in Stoke Canon and in Brampford Speke, but they did not take market stalls or shops in the city. The traditional country butcher as producer-retailer selling in the city had disappeared from the lower Exe valley.

The City

The city authorities had been warned by a vestry meeting shortly before the implementation of the new Exeter Markets Act in 1840 that it was important to ensure that provision was made for the country butchers in the new covered markets, and that they should not be charged too much.[31] The corporation, nonetheless, keen to recoup their costs, raised charges for stalls to 2s 6d on market days and 1s 6d on other days, considerably more than had been charged before the new markets were built.[32] Collection of these rents and of the tolls on transactions was outsourced to the highest bidder at auction, the 'lessee of the market tolls', who was required to pay the corporation the sum he had bid but was free to keep any profit he made by his diligence in letting space and collecting payments.[33] The lessee's wish to maximise his profits and the corporation's wish to ensure order within the new markets resulted in the publication of a new set of bye-laws to regulate buying and selling in the city.[34] The early 1840s featured several prosecutions for breach of the bye-laws, brought by the lessee or the Town Clerk before a bench of magistrates almost all of whom were themselves serving councillors or aldermen. The outcomes of some cases, such as that in 1843 of a butcher who was fined for refusing to move to another stall when directed to do so by the superintendent of the markets, had general applicability and were designed, as the Town Clerk said, 'to teach butchers … that they would not be allowed to interfere with the arrangement of officers'.[35] Of particular concern to country butchers, however, were those regulations that sought to confine buying and selling on market days to the market halls alone. This meant that opportunistic sales to retail butchers or to private individuals were liable to a market toll.[36] Even more irksome to the country butcher was the levying of transaction tolls on those who were not city residents for selling from shops on the streets. Since a number of country butchers had apparently taken shops while the new markets were being constructed, this aroused widespread concern, as exemption was only granted to the permanently resident rather than to those who paid rates or could prove they were on the list of Parliamentary voters.[37] The Town Clerk argued that:

> The Market Act was framed for the purpose of protecting the rights and privileges of the inhabitants against the practices of strangers who were in the habit of coming in to the city, selling marketable commodities in what manner and place they thought proper to the injury of the inhabitant traders.[38]

The only lower Exe valley butcher prosecuted during this campaign was Beedell of Upton Pyne, who escaped a fine by being able to prove that members of his family were permanent residents on the premises, but country butchers from other areas were fined for their actions.[39] The Town Clerk's reference to 'strangers' suggests that the ideals of 'Free Trade' had no influence on the corporation's protectionist approach towards its resident traders.

By 1850 there were 50 retail butchers in the city of Exeter and the area immediately east of its old walls. This volume of shops, to serve a population still not much in excess of 32,000, may be the reason why the Town Clerk felt no need to make concessions to the country butchers. The use of the covered markets by country butchers appears to have been declining as early as 1855, when the lessee of the market tolls applied to the Markets Committee to remove six butchers' stalls from the Lower Market and reuse the space for vegetable and fruit sellers.[40] After that there were reports of falling tolls, and when the market charges and tolls were let at auction in 1857 it was at a reduced rate, again suggesting a loss of business.[41] The Markets Committee tried to fill some of the space in the halls by permitting the building of fixed retail shops around the perimeter.[42] The lessee apparently sought to boost his income from other sources: a letter to the *Western Times* in 1863 accused him of allowing his cronies to unlock the market gates after the city police officer had closed them, and then to operate coffee stalls that attracted 'bad characters', especially girls.[43] The amount of repair and renovation required in the markets was regularly reported by the surveyor to the Markets Committee, but many of the items he noted were deferred or never tackled.[44]

In the 1850s, too, the corporation's intermittent initiatives to tackle the sale of unwholesome meat were given a greater focus by national concerns for public health, particularly reflected in the 1855 Nuisances Removal and Diseases Prevention Act. The corporation appointed a sanitary committee, a medical adviser and a sanitary inspector and initiated prosecutions of butchers for being in possession of meat unfit for human food. In 1856 there were seven successful prosecutions before the Exeter magistrates. John Pearcy was one of those prosecuted for possession of unfit meat in 1858, although the magistrates only levied a small fine as the meat had not actually been for sale when seized.[45]

In the last quarter of the nineteenth century the viability of the markets was further threatened by the growing practice of door-to-door selling, or, in the case of butchers, calling for orders. In 1877 the corporation had tried to reassert its authority by successfully appealing the decision of magistrates, on a 'trivial technicality', not to fine a country carrier for selling meat without paying the toll. In spite of this, selling outside the market became regularised on payment of a licence fee.[46] The Town Clerk was certainly aware, as he indicated during his evidence to the Royal Commission on Markets and Tolls in 1888, that the benefit of holding a market was not merely its revenue-raising capability but the opportunity it afforded for customers to compare prices, and thus to prevent the scandal of the 'butchers' rings' that operated to fix prices in 'Lincolnshire, Yorkshire, Kent and other agricultural counties', uncovered in 1886.[47] Rather than take action to rejuvenate the markets, however, the corporation preferred to maintain a rigorous regime of compelling door-to-door salesmen to pay for licences.

In 1888 an inspector for the Royal Commission on Markets and Tolls, which had been set up in order to identify whether existing market arrangements could be considered to restrict trade, visited Exeter's Higher Market on a Friday (market day). He spoke to two country butchers, neither from the lower Exe valley. Both of them said: 'The market is going down.' One added that on Tuesdays there were only two butchers in the market. He attributed the falling off in the market to the 'many shops in town', and implied that he only continued to attend on Tuesdays so as not to disappoint his regular customers.[48] The conclusions of the inspector were that: 'The cattle market here is very prosperous; the general market cannot be kept up even by the system of hawkers' tolls, which here is elaborately enforced', and he highlighted the 'absurdity' of building two markets in the first place.[49] The markets lingered on into the twentieth century but were never again to be more than traditional Devon 'pannier markets', to which country producers brought their wares in baskets.

The disappearance of the country butcher

The narrative that emerges from the case study is of the disappearance by the 1880s from small villages close to the city of the traditional country butcher, a producer-retailer slaughtering and preparing livestock on his farm to sell in the nearby town. In the 1840s and 1850s this had been perceived as a good career for a young man to be apprenticed to, but by the 1880s young men were actively turning away from it, and those that remained as butchers on country farms seem to have sold their produce to the retail butchers in town rather than direct to customers for home consumption. The principal period of change appears to have been the 1860s and 1870s, and it occurred not only among the butcher elite with a shop as well as a market stall but further down the scale as far as the 'pork butchers' who coupled dairying and rearing pigs. Some butchers went into urban retail shops; others became farmers. A high proportion of them went bankrupt; some went into other trades; and some of those who had trained as butchers never made a living from it. Nationally butcher numbers expanded between 1841 and 1901 at a rate greater than the population as a whole did; more meat than ever before was eaten;[50] yet butcher numbers in the city of Exeter remained relatively stable and, as the study has demonstrated, country butchers from the small villages nearby declined to the point of extinction.[51]

By examining the role played by the city, the focus of changes has been the use of the city-owned market halls and the relationship of country butchers to the more general retail environment. The market halls had been intended to provide a modern, clean, safe shopping environment, particularly for those who came in from the villages around to sell to the population of Exeter. The case study shows some of the unwelcoming attitudes, overhead costs of rentals and tolls, restrictive practices and new public health requirements for which country butchers had to allow. There were other costs and demands too. The country butcher who 'put up' at an inn was charged for the stabling of his horse and parking of his wagon, and possibly for the use of a shed to store his meat and a porter or butcher's boy to carry it.[52] To maximise the opportunities to sell meat, those that did not have access to permanent retail facilities probably not only had a stall in the market on Tuesdays and Fridays but attended the Saturday evening meat market, where the poor bought the cheapest meat for their Sunday meal. The city authorities were never willing to let the butchers close this before 11 p.m. so that, as evidence of cases at the toll gates shows, the butcher or his wife might have difficulty in packing up, driving off and reaching the toll gate before midnight when their day ticket would expire.[53]

It is therefore not surprising that some country butchers chose to become farmers, avoiding the additional overheads and labour required in the dressing and retailing of the meat. Exeter's cattle market, as the Royal Commission's inspector quoted above remarked, thrived while its general markets did not. Changes in transport, particularly the development of railways along the Exe valley between 1844 and 1885, enabled farmers to sell to dealers from London and Bristol and retail butchers in Exeter to arrange for meat they had seen on the farm to be sent in from the railway station.

Another factor determining the country butcher's solvency was the change in consumer culture during the period, both in relation to the means of distribution and to food itself. The location of the transaction of food purchases shifted as more retailers began to offer the greater convenience to the purchaser of house-to-house calls. The covered markets had been designed to encourage Exeter's expanding middle class to test the prices by comparing different stalls. By the time of the Royal Commission visit in 1888, this had changed. The Town Clerk's assistant explained that:

> Formerly you went to the market and bought your meat, but now the butcher comes for orders … The very poor go to market to try what they can pick up cheap … tradespeople call at the houses of the middle and higher classes for orders.[54]

Such a service was more readily organised from a fixed retail shop than from a small village away from the mass of the population. It fitted into a pattern evolved by other food retailers: the milk deliverer, the greengrocer, the baker and even the fish merchant.

According to Collins, meat consumption rose between the mid-1840s and 'around 1873', and prices for meat and dairy products held up well into the 1880s, rather than falling in the 'Great Depression' of the 1870s.[55] Changes arising from the introduction of imported meat are unlikely to have affected country butchers until the 1880s. Imported processed or canned meat was available earlier, but not in widespread use. It was not until frozen meat became available that imported meat began to form a significant proportion of meat consumed.[56] Collins, who noted that the way in which farmers responded to changes in demand still requires investigation, has suggested that consumer preferences influenced the meat trade towards the production of 'smaller leaner joints from earlier maturing animals'.[57] This change is attested in local newspaper accounts of butchers' Christmas displays: a farmer was praised in 1835 for a heifer whose 'fat was many inches thick on the ribs', but by 1852 butchers were praised for having 'learned the folly of piling up the grease too high upon their beasts'.[58]

Such a change was part of the other environment in which the country butcher operated: the country rather than the city. Farming practices altered during the nineteenth century, although livestock farming was less dramatically affected than arable farming. The nature of practice changed at a quicker pace from the 1830s, influenced by the development of science, particularly chemistry, to raise productivity. Animal feeding began to include a higher proportion of root vegetables and products such as cattle cake, and feed preparation was eased by new machinery such as root slicers.[59] These developments, which enabled the production of market-ready animals at a younger age, made it more likely that those who could farm on a larger scale and invest in more expensive feed and machinery would be successful. Interest in breeding better stock also intensified, led by the gentry and large-scale farmers, and again requiring access to capital to secure pedigree animals. The operation of a small-scale country butcher, commonly farming less than fifty acres, became less economically viable. Lack of capital to cover risks was also a problem, particularly when everyday diseases such as foot-rot and pleuro-pneumonia were virtually untreatable. There were also periodic outbreaks of foot-and-mouth disease and other epidemics, most notably the *Rinderpest* or cattle plague, which arrived in England in 1865 and took more than two years to eradicate. For the first time an outbreak of animal disease engaged national and local government agents in measures to prevent its spread. The Exeter cattle market was closed for more than two years, and two at least of the lower Exe valley butchers fell foul of the regulations restricting animal movements and were fined.[60]

The businesses of the country butchers were not all on the same scale, and they were affected differently by different factors in their operating environment. However, the complexity of the producer-retailer business was a challenge to business management skills, and several butchers made the decision either to farm or to run a purely retail business. Changes in agricultural practice and to the style of meat preferred gave larger businesses an advantage. Changes in transportation gave new opportunities for sale of stock and transport of fresh milk, thus uncoupling the dairying business from the pig farming that had utilised former waste products. Above all, the environment of the city that provided their retail opportunities changed. The covered markets had been intended as the acme of retailing for producer-retailers, but the corporation, instead of promoting their use, allowed them to decay and fall into disuse. Pearcy, who thought he could afford it, moved out of the markets in 1863 into a shop; Chamberlain, starting again with a market stall in 1862, was unable to make a go of it; Charles Smith, once he had relinquished the dairy side of the business in 1870, was unable to make a living from his market stall. Although city officials recognised the potential value of the market in ensuring fair prices, they responded to consumer wishes for tradesmen to call at the house for orders, and taxed the transactions rather than take measures to improve the popularity of the markets. Without such support the traditional practice of the country butcher in a small village near to and dependent on the city markets was doomed to extinction.

Conclusion

This case study has examined a small number of country butchers in a specific location, and demonstrated how many of their businesses vanished during the 1860s and 1870s, and identified major factors in this decline as the change in the retail environment in the city where most of their customers lived and a lack of support from the city council for their trade. The cordial and mutually supportive relationships between the council and local farmers in South Yorkshire described by Sarah Holland in this volume certainly had their parallel in Devon. The city was prepared to play host to the Devon Agricultural Society's County Show, to make common cause over the outbreak of cattle plague and to institute a Christmas fat stock show. The farmers who became involved in these events, however, were those with substantial land holdings rather than the country butchers with limited acreage and little wealth who were rarely perceived to merit special consideration.[61]

The change in Exeter seems to have occurred considerably later than Scola's findings for Manchester, where he considered the country butcher was already in decline by 1830, possibly even by 1820. The contrast between what happened in fast-growing industrialised modern Manchester and in the slow-growing old-fashioned county town of Exeter would benefit from exploration in other cities and their rural hinterlands to identify the variables that affected the different pace of change in different towns. What seems certain is that the history of the Victorian country butcher cannot be understood purely as part of the rural history of the farms where they raised their stock, but requires an understanding of the complexities of the changing retail environment of the towns they served.

Notes

1 *Trewman's Exeter Flying Post (FP)*, 16 December, 1863.
2 Figures for total acreage taken from W. White, *History, Gazetteer and Directory of Devonshire* (London: White's,1850) (henceforth White's 1850 Directory), pp. 196, 293, 183, 201, 204, 293.
3 Information from the 1841–1901 censuses is taken from the data supplied by the Ancestry family history service, http://home.ancestry.co.uk/. Data for Huxham, Nether Exe, Poltimore, Rewe and Stoke Canon was accessed in July 2013. Data for Brampford Speke and Upton Pyne was accessed in May 2014. It should be noted that a portion of Brampford Speke civil parish was transferred to Upton Pyne in 1889, affecting the 1891 and 1901 censuses for those parishes. The enumerator for Huxham and Poltimore in 1891 was confused about the parish boundary between the two and mis-assigned some properties from Huxham to Poltimore, creating anomalies in the totals.
4 J. Schmiechen, J. and K. Carls, *The British Market Hall: A Social and Architectural History* (New Haven: Yale University Press, 1999), p. 44.
5 R. Newton, *Victorian Exeter* (Leicester: Leicester University Press, 1968), pp. xvi–xvii.
6 Schmiechen and Carls, *British Market Hall*, pp. ix, 144.
7 R. Scola (1975) 'Food Markets and Shops in Manchester, 1770–1870', *Journal of Historical Geography*, 1:2, p. 163.
8 J.B. Jeffreys, *Retail Trading in Britain, 1850–1950* (Cambridge: Cambridge University Press, 1954), pp. 1–2.
9 Jeffreys, *Retail Trading*, pp. 2, 182.
10 N. Alexander and G. Akehurst, G. (1998), 'The Emergence of Modern Retailing, 1750–1950', *Business History*, 40:4, p. 15.
11 G. Shaw, 'The Study of Retail Development', in J. Benson and G.Shaw (eds), *The Evolution of Retail Systems, c.1880–1914* (Leicester: Leicester University Press, 1992) pp. 4–6.
12 M. Phillips, 'The Evolution of Markets and Shops in Britain', in J. Benson and G. Shaw (eds), *Evolution of Retail Systems c.1880–1914* (Leicester: Leicester University Press, 1992), pp. 58–62, particularly Tables 4.1 and 4.2.
13 Scola, 'Food Markets and Shops', pp. 154, 163.

14 *Exeter and Plymouth Gazette* (EPG), 24 December 1847; *Western Times* (WT) 20 December 1845.

15 *FP*, 12 July 1849.

16 *FP*, 25 December 1845.

17 *EPG*, 5 January 1850.

18 Devon Heritage Centre (DHC) 2811A, *Huxham Register of Baptisms*, 1838.

19 *FP*, 25 December 1845.

20 *WT*, 6 January 1865.

21 DHC2811A *Huxham Register of Burials*, 1870.

22 Although the new dairyman is also called Smith, it does not appear that there was any family connection.

23 *FP*, 28 December 1870; 2 December 1874.

24 References for Pearcy giving up the shop and his bankruptcy are *FP*, 14 December 1870; *London Gazette*, 16 June 1871; *FP* 5 July 1871.

25 *WT*, 13 and 20 December, 1862; *FP* 23 December 1863; 22 June 1864.

26 Abraham's five year old son is listed on the 1871 census for the village in Broadclyst, a few miles east of Exeter, as born in Broadclyst; if Abraham did go to London it can only have been for a short period.

27 *WT*, 25 September 1883.

28 *FP*, 11 October 1876.

29 *EPG*, 23 September 1882; 4 October 1882.

30 Frederick is mentioned as a butcher in *WT*, 12 July 1893, though listed as a farmer on the 1901 census and as a roads contractor on the 1911 census (Poltimore). Samuel was listed as a butcher on the 1901 census (Poltimore).

31 St John's Vestry, *WT*, 18 April 1840.

32 Lists of charges do not appear in the Exeter City Archive, but a newspaper report in 1834 stated that the minimum charge for a market stall was £8 per annum (EPG, 15 March 1834). At 2s 6d for one stall on a single market day the minimum annual charge under the new regime would have been £13.

33 *EPG*, 22 March 1841.

34 DHC, Exeter City Archive (ECA) *General Purpose and Markets Committee Minutes*, 2/12, 22 August 1840; 4 October 1841.

35 *EPG*, 11 February 1843.

36 For example, those described in *EPG*, 3 April and 22 May 1841.

37 *FP*, 13 June 1844.

38 *WT*, 6 November 1841.

39 *EPG*, 6 November 1841.

40 DHC ECA, *Markets Committee*, 2/13, 1 October 1855.

41 *EPG*, 15 September 1855; 12 September 1857.

42 DHC, ECA, *Markets Committee*, 2/13, 1860s, various.

43 *WT*, 16 January 1863.

44 *WT*, 11 January 1862.

45 *FP*, 14 February 1858.

46 *FP*, 19 December 1877.

47 *Devon and Exeter Gazette* (DEG), 9 January 1886.

48 Royal Commission on Markets and Tolls, 1889, Vol. III, *Minutes and Evidence*, p. 276. House of Commons Parliamentary Papers on line. Accessed 11 September 2013.

49 Royal Commission on Markets Vol. III (1889), p. 281.

50 R. Perren, *The Meat Trade in Britain, 1840–1914* (London: Routledge & Keegan Paul, 1978), p. 3, Table 1.1.

51 Entries in city directories, though the information from them was not necessarily compiled on an identical basis, show 50 butchers in 1850; 45 in 1870; 40 in 1889 and 41 in 1902.

52 *WT*, 11 October 1862.

53 *WT*, 12 February 1867.

54 Royal Commission on Markets and Tolls, (1889) Vol III, p. 276.

55 E.J. Collins, 'Rural and Agricultural Change', in E.J. Collins (ed.), *Agrarian History of England and Wales,* Vol. VII, 1850–1914 (Cambridge: Cambridge University Press, 2000), p. 150.

56 Burnett, J. *Plenty and Want: England* (London: Nelson, 1966)*,* pp. 100–1.

57 Collins, 'Rural and Agricultural Change', p. 200.

58 *EPG*, 26 December 1835; *WT*, 25 December 1852.

59 Collins, 'Rural and Agricultural Change', p. 107.

60 Greenslade, *WT* 16 February 1866; Smith, *EPG*, 22 June 1866.

61 *EPG*, 15 Jan, 19 Feb 1864; *WT* 15 Aug 1865; *DEG* 8 Nov 1884.

5   Doncaster and its environs

Town and countryside – a reciprocal relationship?

Sarah Holland

Town and country are often perceived as distinct entities, frequently in conflict with one another during the mid-nineteenth century, because of rapid urbanisation and industrialisation.[1] Studies specifically of the country town have tended only to look briefly at the relationship with agriculture and the countryside, within a much broader analysis of the urban.[2] Country towns have often been interpreted as autonomous spheres upon which rural hinterlands were dependent.[3] The relationship between town and countryside is therefore frequently depicted in terms of the impact of the urban on the rural and of change in the countryside. Examples cited include the loss of land to urban building, urban employment opportunities leading to rural depopulation, agriculture being forced to adapt to urban demands and a range of profound social, economic and landscape changes.[4]

This traditional perspective underestimates the complex interrelationships between urban centres and their rural hinterlands. Neither town nor country operated in a vacuum. The extent to which the economic activities of town and country influenced and affected one another was particularly prevalent in the north of England during the mid-nineteenth century. This was a period of prosperity for agriculture, and a prosperous countryside provided the basis for industrialisation, both by supplying food or raw materials and providing a market for industrial products.[5] G. E. Cherry and J. Sheail explore the paradox of industrialisation and urbanisation, contending that the potentially destructive urban and industrial processes also stimulated interest in, and concern for, the countryside and rural life.[6] Jonathan Brown argues that 'the relationship between the town and its countryside was much more intimate' than merely trade encounters on market day, with a market town's fortunes closely intertwined with those of agriculture.[7] While there has been an acknowledgement of these interrelationships, the emphasis has still largely been on urban demands and transformation. The role of the rural and agriculture in this relationship is minimised. Yet just as urban demand impinged on agricultural production, agriculture demanded better marketing facilities and access to knowledge and skills. Thus, the urban–rural relationship can be characterised as one of mutual dependency. This chapter uses a case study of one northern English town and the surrounding agricultural district to analyse that reciprocal relationship in more depth, and to evaluate the usefulness of such an approach.

A reciprocal relationship suggests a cooperative interchange of ideas and actions. In the context of the urban–rural relationship, this will include ideas and actions that were favoured by, and/or perceived to be of benefit to, members of both communities. Effective reciprocal relationships are constructed upon a foundation of defined rights and responsibilities, and are sustained by ensuring the balance between them is maintained. Social hierarchies, including landownership in the countryside and municipality in towns, often provided the stability that ensured decisions and actions were enacted. Success was dependent upon consultative processes and mutual respect, and was often indicative of social and economic conditions in the specific locale.

The extent of these reciprocal relationships can be measured through the detailed examination of the motivations for, and outcomes of, decisions and actions affecting both town and country. As Brown argues, the connection between town and country was not a constant but differed according to time and place.[8] A comprehensive analysis of council minutes and local newspapers, in conjunction with other relevant sources, provides evidence of both the official and more popular perceptions of decisions, ideas and actions. The process of negotiation and mediation between the key stakeholders in town and country thus comes under scrutiny. The way in which language was employed and motivations, decisions and actions were depicted reveals the extent of positivism and mutual co-dependency, and indeed the presence of tension and disagreement.

Doncaster offers a particularly interesting example of a reciprocal relationship between town and country. In the mid-nineteenth century, Doncaster was a country market town on the cusp of change. The arrival of the Great Northern Railway in 1848 and the establishment of the Great Northern Railway Works in 1853 stimulated this process. Subsequent industrial activity in the town was nucleated initially on the north side of the town in close proximity to the railways, which were used to transport raw materials and distribute finished products. This applied to Fawcett's steam corn mill and Marshall's agricultural machinery workshop, both of which were established in West Laith Gate in 1868, and the Victoria Mustard Mill and Elwes' steam-powered saw mill located in Marshgate in the second half of the nineteenth century.[9] The population of Doncaster and its suburbs increased from 12,967 in 1851 to 39,404 in 1901, and the agricultural villages of Hexthorpe and Balby, on the periphery of the town centre, were transformed into railway suburbs.[10] Doncaster thus underwent significant growth, both physically and in terms of its population, in this period.

Nevertheless, the surrounding countryside was not heavily industrialised until the development of the collieries in the late nineteenth and early twentieth centuries. Until then, agriculture continued to employ a large proportion of the population. Demand for agricultural produce increased in response to the growth and commercialisation of Doncaster, and new market buildings were constructed in the town to cater for the expanding supply and demand networks. In this transitional period of industrialisation and urbanisation the balance between urban industrial and rural agricultural interests was crucial. This chapter explores two key ways in which a reciprocal relationship between town and country was both promoted and constituted by development of the market infrastructure and knowledge networks in operation throughout the Doncaster district, and considers whether this relationship was typical or atypical in this period.

Market towns served a rural hinterland, providing a variety of services for farming communities, of which the market itself was of particular importance.[11] The market place was also a spatial metaphor for the relationship between town and country, a potential site for conflict and compromise, and in Doncaster it came to symbolise the evolving relationship between the town and its environs. This was particularly reflected in the market infrastructure, which was altered and enlarged during this period. As Mark Girouard argues, 'most market places were given convenience and character by a series of buildings ... ranging from purely utilitarian structures to buildings of some elaboration and importance'.[12] The ability to provide suitable facilities in an age of expansion determined the relative success of markets, and their architectural design represented the balance between the needs of agriculturalists and the civic ambition of the town. Some of the smaller markets in the Doncaster district were already in decline by the early nineteenth century. Tickhill market, for example, was 'almost disused' in 1822, and by 1837 was described as being 'of small importance'.[13] Concurrently, the markets of neighbouring towns such as Sheffield, Leeds and Wakefield were expanding as large-scale investment transformed the available facilities. It was therefore imperative for Doncaster to improve its market infrastructure too.

Between the 1840s and 1870s, the markets underwent a series of infrastructural changes, initiated and paid for by Doncaster Corporation. As municipal bodies, corporations often represented town power and dominance. Neville's chapter on country butchers in the Exe Valley shows how, in that region, municipal power equated to unwelcoming attitudes, prohibitive rentals and tolls, and restrictive practices targeted at non-townspeople (see Chapter 4). In contrast, Doncaster Corporation's proactive role in market improvements is indicative of a much more positive relationship between town and country in the district, and specifically of the high esteem in which agriculture was held there. In March 1840 the Corporation resolved that is was expedient that 'some alteration tending to the improvement of the Market Place generally be effected'.[14] Among the arguments presented in favour of investing in new market buildings was the need to keep pace with competitors 'in an age when change and improvements are rapidly extending throughout the greater part of the country'.[15] Yet the Corporation's argument went beyond mere emulation of its competitors. From the outset, the projected benefits for both town and country were at the fore of decisions made by Doncaster Corporation; for example, the dialogue in the relationship between town and country was evidenced in the minutes of the market committee meetings. Council representatives argued that extensive improvements to the market place in Doncaster would 'not only add greatly to the appearance but afford considerable advantages to the Town and Neighbourhood' in terms of the local economy.[16]

One of the first improvements to be made was the erection of a covered corn market.[17] Many towns found that existing market facilities were not sufficient to deal with growth in the corn trade in this period.[18] The prominence of the corn market in Doncaster's improvements reflected the importance of the grain trade in the district: wheat was the principal crop grown in the majority of villages around Doncaster.[19] Previously trading had taken place in the open, making the covered corn market 'desirable' and from the Council's perspective 'in compliance with the repeated expressed wishes of the Farmers and others attending the market'.[20] The advantage of protection in all seasons for those attending the corn market was again emphasised in the plans laid before the Council by Mr Butterfield (bailiff to the Corporation).[21] On completion, newspaper reports confirmed that the requirements of agriculturalists and merchants had been addressed. The *Doncaster Gazette* wrote: 'Of particular importance to both buyers and sellers of corn were the three key design elements of space, light and shelter, which were incorporated into the new corn market.'[22] Both official and popular accounts interpreted the new corn market in terms of the benefits being bestowed on town and country alike, which is indicative of the reciprocal relationship between them.

The location of the new market buildings demonstrates the extent to which the relationship between town and country was physically as well as metaphorically important. The ability of market towns to take advantage of transport networks was often vital to their success.[23] Doncaster had a long legacy as a key transport hub, being situated on the River Don and the Great North Road, the main trade route between London and Scotland. In 1840, when the location of the new corn market was being discussed, the chief mode of transit from seller to consumer was via the River Don. It was therefore crucial to maintain the strategic position of the market in relation to the river and the wharves.[24] Moreover, the links between the prosperity of town and country and improvements to the navigation by the River Dun [*sic*] Company were acknowledged in a speech by the mayor at an event to celebrate the opening of the new corn market. He emphasised the economic value of such improvements both to inhabitants of the town of Doncaster, 'our agricultural friends' and to the merchants who 'buy their produce for those mighty consumers, the manufacturing districts'.[25]

This municipal sensitivity to both parties did not go unnoticed. Agriculturalists from the Doncaster district subscribed to a dinner held in honour of the mayor and the Corporation on account of the improvements being made. The event was a mutual show of appreciation with various toasts proposed demonstrating the importance of balance between town and country, and the relative roles and responsibilities of the Corporation and local agriculturalists. A representative for the agriculturalists hoped that further improvements would follow, as 'he was convinced, that every improvement which the Mayor and Corporation made for the benefit of the agriculturalists would cement still stronger the bond of friendship and good will which existed between them and the town of Doncaster'.[26]

The new corn market was erected amid the controversy and upheaval of the campaign to repeal the Corn Laws. The Corn Laws, arguably the most influential and controversial agricultural policy of the period, imposed taxation on imported corn and inhibited free trade, and thus were integrally linked to both agriculture and industry.[27] Representatives of both the Anti-Corn Law League and the Pro-Corn Law movement (1839–1846) promoted the importance of forging positive relationships between town and country, citing agriculture and industry as both being intrinsically linked to the success of the nation.[28] The mayor, Joseph Birley, emphasised his commitment to pursuing additional improvements to the market facilities, and also his affirmation of the importance of agriculturalists in the district. He promised that 'whatever change might happen in the laws or legislature of the country', the agriculturalists 'would never be debarred of that fair and legitimate remuneration which their hardy industry and honest capital so freely entitled them to'.[29] The mayor's comments, in alluding to the Corn Laws, suggest an acute awareness of the wider impact of change and of the Corporation's responsibility to protect agriculture in this climate. It reaffirmed their recognition that the prosperity of Doncaster and its environs was to be built upon a foundation of strong industry and agriculture, and the unity of town and country.

Likewise, Edmund Denison MP toasted the complementary efforts of the mayor and Corporation and the agriculturalists in the project, and 'hoped and trusted it might cement between the respective parties, that bond of union which would make them brothers, and promote their interests'.[30] Not only were these remarks well received but they also represented his wider political view that the prosperity of manufacturing and commerce depended on the prosperity of the agricultural interest. This was reflected in his political campaigning and particularly in his pro-Corn Law stance.

Denison had previously argued that the Repeal of the Corn Laws would place farmers and labourers in a worse position than ever in what he described as 'the most dangerous experiment the country had ever made'.[31] Concurrently, representatives of the Anti-Corn Law League had argued that the Corn Laws inhibited both agriculture and industry, and that the prosperity of agriculture depended upon commerce and manufacturing being permitted to flourish, which in turn necessitated free trade.[32] Undoubtedly both factions used a similar argument as a mode of propaganda to further their cause, but in doing so they highlighted their mutual recognition of the importance of the reciprocal relationship between town and country in the Doncaster area at the time.

Further toasts echoed this sentiment that town and country were inextricably linked. T. Walker, Esq. argued that: 'On the prosperity of agriculture depended not only this town and neighbourhood, not only this kingdom, but the whole world.'[33] Mr F. Carr added that 'commercial prosperity could not be good unless the agricultural prosperity was good likewise' because 'these two great interests must go along hand in hand together'. He not only hoped that the Corporation would continue to assist the agriculturalists but also considered it to be their duty to do so in order to 'promote the interests of the town at large'.[34]

The Corporation soon made further improvements to the market infrastructure in Doncaster. In February 1845, the market committee recommended the removal of the old Shambles and some houses in order to create the necessary space for a new general market hall, which was subsequently erected.[35] Increasingly the civic ambitions of the Corporation came to the fore. The market committee was particularly anxious that the new market hall would correspond aesthetically with the townscape and be a credit to the Corporation. In accordance with this, several recently erected market buildings were inspected in order to ascertain the best plans.[36] A report in the *Doncaster Gazette* also argued that continued improvements to the markets would, when completed, be 'an honour to the town, not only by their appearance, but by their immense usefulness and accommodation'.[37] Reports of the opening of the new general market hall in 1849 commented on the facilities provided for both the buyer and seller, including the new weighing machine and provision for meat and butter.[38] Thus, in spite of civic motivations, the new market hall still responded to the needs of agriculturalists by providing better marketing facilities.

Other improvements were responsive to the composition of agriculture in the Doncaster district. The importance of sheep and cattle, reflected in livestock returns, motivated the Corporation to construct new wool and cattle markets in 1863.[39] Livestock markets were subject to great scrutiny during the mid-nineteenth century as they were linked to issues of public health and urban improvement, with improvement acts empowering towns and cities to remove them from the streets.[40] Wakefield, Leeds and Manchester had already addressed these problems through investment programmes. In comparison to these, and Doncaster's earlier improvements, the new cattle and wool markets were much more modest undertakings but responded directly to the needs of local agriculturalists.[41] The Mayor once again delivered a speech on the completion of the new market facilities, emphasising the role of the Corporation and his belief that 'the agriculturalists were great friends of the people of Doncaster'.[42] It is worth noting that although the focus was on the relationship between Doncaster and its rural hinterland, increasing quantities of wool were brought to the market by railway from other counties.[43]

The continuing need to improve market facilities in the town was the focus of a report published by the *Doncaster Chronicle* in February 1867. As early as 1861, the Corporation had intimated the need to enlarge the covered corn market, and yet nothing had happened.[44] By the time of the report, Wakefield had enlarged its corn exchange in 1862 and a new corn exchange had opened in Leeds in 1864. The *Chronicle* argued that it was short sighted not to borrow money and invest in continually upgrading their market facilities. The report emphasised the growth in Doncaster, of the town, its population, its markets and its prosperity, but stressed that: 'This cannot last, however, if we stand still while other towns around us are ever "up and doing".'[45] It argued 'the markets are the very main spring of our action – the whole and sole bulwarks of our existence as a community'.[46] The report provided a public focus for discussions about improving the corn market, which was subsequently rebuilt rather than enlarged.

The erection of the new Corn Exchange in 1873, which replaced the earlier covered corn market, was a physical embodiment of the even greater civic aspirations of the Corporation, both in terms of its architecture and of its purpose.[47] Architecture was a recognised method of conveying civic pride during the Victorian period, providing visual statements of confidence.[48] The new Corn Exchange adopted a classical style of architecture, incorporating both Tuscan and Doric columns and featuring a sculptured frieze of the Roman god Genius blessing both agriculture and the civic buildings of Doncaster.[49] It was also designed to be more than just a place to sell and buy corn, as it also contained a space designated for concerts and performances.[50] The opening ceremony included an orchestral concert hosted by Messrs Meacock and Son, which demonstrated the multifaceted uses of the new building.[51] The Mayor, William Clark, delivered a speech in which he expressed his pride in the beauty of the new Corn Exchange he was officially opening.[52] He described it as one of the 'grandest and most comfortable corn exchanges' in the country.[53]

Nevertheless, the new Corn Exchange embodied the importance of agriculture through architectural imagery. Classical figures and symbols representing agriculture adorned the front of the building, and foliage was incorporated into the interior ironwork. The practicalities of trade were also integral to the design of the Corn Exchange, and the agriculturalists of the Doncaster district once again held a dinner in honour of the Corporation.[54] The Exchange, although still at the heart of the market place, was not rebuilt on the same location as the existing covered corn market, as the strategic importance of the wharves was no longer as great. The development of the railway network significantly altered the transportation of agricultural goods to and from market, and became crucially important.[55] In 1873, the mayor was reported as arguing that although 'Doncaster was not a manufacturing place, it ... was the centre of a large railway district, and it was to this fact that he attributed the success of their markets'.[56] The *Doncaster Chronicle*, reflecting on the immensity of the changes taking place, argued that the quick response of the agriculturalists in arranging a dinner in honour of the mayor and Corporation was testimony to the fact that it had met their needs.[57] The mayor emphasised that the dinner was indeed proof of the success of the markets and of the agriculturalists' approval of the improvements.[58] The event was orchestrated to promote the Corporation's progressiveness. The dinner was advertised in local papers, requesting the attendance of gentlemen interested in the town and trade of Doncaster and the agriculture of the district.[59]

Notably, however, at a meeting held to discuss the public dinner, opposition was voiced based on cost and the greater need for other improvements. It was argued that the new Corn Exchange was an improvement that the farmers did not want, which would destroy 'the ready money principle of the pitch market'.[60] Many favoured pitched markets, where farmers brought all the grain they had to sell, as being more honest. Sample markets on the other hand relied on the sample grain brought to market being representative of the rest to be sold. Yet sample markets were better suited to the new Corn Exchanges being constructed.[61] The transition from pitch to sample market was often controversial, and the criticism may have been an attempt to preserve tradition or aimed at the increasing civic ambition present in the town. It did not, however, impede plans, and as the *Doncaster Chronicle* reported, 'it was unanimously decided to entertain the Corporation to a dinner in commemoration of the opening of the Exchange'.[62] Civic pride was a prominent theme at that dinner. It was argued that Doncaster had 'many advantages which even a city might envy' and was in a position to supersede the neighbouring corn market at Wakefield in both quality and price.[63] Even though civic ambitions increasingly motivated the Corporation to build grander and more elaborate buildings, they continued to stimulate the positive relationship.

Reciprocal relationships between town and country were further fostered through knowledge networks.[64] The mid-nineteenth century witnessed a growth in agricultural societies in response to the demand for agricultural knowledge, innovation and experimentation in order to inform more efficient agricultural practices.[65] This was of mutual benefit to both town and country, and the mechanisms by which these knowledge and skill networks operated and were successful relied on effective urban–rural relationships. Few villages had their own agricultural society, whereas market towns were home to district-wide societies and had the opportunity to stage larger agricultural shows. As Nicholas Goddard argues, agricultural societies based in large towns facilitated the interrelationship of opinion 'for landowner, occupier and labourer alike'.[66] Doncaster had both an agricultural society and farmers' club, and hosted the agricultural shows of the Royal Agricultural Society and the Yorkshire Agricultural Society. These meetings and shows had broader spatial and social implications, interconnecting the town with the surrounding villages. Consequently, Doncaster became a hub of knowledge production and dissemination at the centre of an agricultural district.

Successful agricultural societies and shows bestowed prestige on the town and introduced new agricultural ideas and innovative practices to the countryside. Both local agriculturalists and Doncaster Corporation encouraged and supported the formation of an agricultural society in the town. While the establishment of agricultural societies was characteristic of the era, the complex dynamics between town and country are less well understood and Doncaster provides an instructive example. The dialogue between the key stakeholders from town and country once again reveals the extent to which ideas and actions were reciprocated. At the celebratory dinner for the completion of the first Corn Hall in 1844, the issue of a town-based agricultural society was raised. Thomas Dyson of Braithwell, an owner-occupier farmer, argued that it was the responsibility of all agriculturalists to establish such a society, and of the Corporation to support them in doing so. Dyson reasoned that a town where so many local farmers frequented the markets, many of whom had been awarded prizes at the Yorkshire and Royal Agricultural Society shows, should have its own agricultural society. He was reported as contending that: 'There were so many conveniences for an Agricultural show in Doncaster, and such a body of men to support it, that he must say it would be a disgrace to them if they did not come forward and establish one.'[67]

The mayor and Corporation of Doncaster also supported the formation of a local agricultural society and show, and assumed shared responsibility for doing so. The mayor said he had great confidence that 'whenever the subject should be properly brought before the Corporation, they would lend every facility in their power, to render the Doncaster Agricultural Show beneficial and important'. Edmund Denison, MP, not only agreed that such a society would be advantageous but declared that 'he would take the liberty of starting a project for a Doncaster Agricultural Association for the exhibition and improvement of stock, and cattle, and implements'.[68] Once again, civic ambitions and support for agricultural interests were united in a project. As Louise Miskell has argued, large towns were increasingly competitive in agricultural matters and agricultural societies and shows were a way in which this manifested itself.[69] According to Miskell, agricultural shows consequently tended to escalate far beyond their original remit. This particularly applied to the large annual shows of the Royal Agricultural Society of England that towns competed to stage. In 1860, Doncaster Corporation resolved that 'a strenuous effort should be made to obtain the holding of the meeting of the Royal Agricultural Society of England in 1861 at Doncaster'.[70] It would be a further thirty years before Doncaster fulfilled this ambition, but the desire to do so underpinned their efforts to ensure the success of their own agricultural society and shows.

The success of the Doncaster Agricultural Society (DAS) and its shows relied upon the relative roles and responsibilities of town and country being complementary. The aim of the DAS was to further the cause of agriculture, specifically 'the advancement of pursuits connected with the farm and all its varied departments'.[71] It therefore required the input of agriculturalists from the surrounding countryside, in addition to the support of the Corporation. At the celebratory dinner in 1844, an agriculturalist spoke of his experiences of participating in such agricultural societies and associations, describing them as apprenticeships. Such was their importance that he offered his assistance and experience in the formation of an agricultural society in Doncaster. Local farmers went on not only to consume the knowledge formulated in the town but also to actively contribute to its creation. Many local farmers belonged to the DAS, whose inclusive membership policies made it possible for even small farmers to participate. The emphasis was on active participation, with the *Doncaster Chronicle* advocating the importance of the DAS and the necessity of farmers exhibiting at the shows.[72] The *Chronicle* reports argued that prize-winning produce stimulated competitiveness and productiveness as well as loyalty, and that active participation in agricultural societies and shows was an integral part of agricultural improvement.[73]

The Doncaster Agricultural Society also conducted research into new practices and products, and published their findings. The primary objective of this research was the advancement of local agricultural production, with the underlying motive of promoting economic prosperity. The DAS argued that geology influenced agriculture, and that accordingly new ideas and innovative practices had varying impacts. Their evaluation of the use of new ideas and techniques therefore made specific reference to geological variations.[74] For example, a report on the use of bones as manure concluded that they were particularly beneficial on the limestone and lighter soils around Doncaster, but not on the heavy clay soils.[75]

In addition, the DAS conducted research that was beneficial on a much wider scale. Crop disease had potentially devastating economic implications, and turnip fly was a recurring problem that threatened to destroy turnip crops across England. Turnips were another of the principal crops grown in the Doncaster district, primarily for animal fodder. A poor harvest of turnips had a direct impact on the livestock, as it could no longer be successfully overwintered. This occurred in 1858 when the November Fair in Doncaster was inundated with livestock, many of which were inferior and had to be sold cheaply if at all.[76] The DAS consequently researched, wrote and published a widely distributed and frequently cited report on the problems of turnip fly and how to prevent it. The report was based on the returns of over one hundred farmers in England and Wales, and was advertised as being of 'immense importance to farmers in general'. It featured in prominent farming journals such as *The Farmers' Magazine* in England and the *New York Farmer* and *American Gardener's Magazine* in America, but it also had immediate resonance in the Doncaster district.[77]

This chapter has shown that strong reciprocal relationships characterised the interactions between Doncaster and its environs. Through the active participation of local agriculturalists and Doncaster Corporation, the market infrastructure and knowledge networks fostered and represented positive urban–rural relationships. Three key determinants were crucial to this process: economy, human agency and geography. The economy of the Doncaster district remained predominantly agricultural during the nineteenth century. Agricultural prosperity and suitable marketing facilities underpinned the achievements of both town and country, and required cooperation and participation from both the urban and rural populations. Human agency promoted this reciprocal relationship, uniting town and countryside in decisions, actions and responses. Within this reciprocal relationship, either Doncaster Corporation or local landowners and large farmers occupied hierarchical positions of power. Nevertheless, perspectives of, responses to and participation in these processes were more inclusive than in some other regions and constituted both active and positive interaction, resulting in effective reciprocal relationships. Geography, or spatial dynamics, also contributed to the strength of this reciprocal relationship. Doncaster market occupied a strategic position in the country that was enhanced by the river and railway connections. Moreover, the physical intimacy of Doncaster and the surrounding villages promoted mutual cooperation, which was stimulated by the decisions and actions of those in both town and country.

This does not negate the fact that tensions between town and country did surface, but the ability for balance and unity to be retained was testimony to the strength of the reciprocal relationship between Doncaster and its rural environs. Political arguments of the mid-nineteenth century often asserted that economic prosperity was dependent on the union of agriculture and industry, which would suggest the foundations for reciprocal relationships between town and country were established. Yet, as shown in the wider literature and elsewhere in this book, tension and disagreement frequently occurred when the two converged. The extent to which the positive urban–rural relationship in the Doncaster district was perhaps atypical ultimately requires further research, though it does have an interesting counterpart in the Unitarians' alliance with the rural planter class in the American South, as explored by John Macaulay in Chapter 3.

In evaluating a reciprocal relationship model as a mode of enquiry, it is important to acknowledge that while reciprocal relationships were not present everywhere, the underlying dynamics that made this possible in Doncaster can be explored elsewhere. The majority of towns and cities in England had new market buildings and agricultural societies in the mid-nineteenth century, but this did not necessarily equate to a reciprocal relationship. The way in which the relationship between town and country was managed, and how it was articulated, determined its nature. The language used by representatives of town and country, and that of newspaper reports describing urban–rural relationships, was crucial. The concept of a reciprocal relationship provides a lens through which to view urban–rural relations, and the three key determinants outlined (economy, human agency and geography) can be applied as interpretive filters. This approach offers a new perspective through which to re-evaluate relations between town and country, and has the potential to explore reciprocal relationships on a much larger scale.

Notes

1 J.D. Marshall, 'The Rise and Transformation of the Cumbrian Market Town, 1600–1900', *Northern History*, Vol. 19 (1983), pp. 129–130; G.E. Cherry and J. Sheail, 'Town and Country: An Overview' in E.J.T. Collins (ed.), *The Agrarian History of England and Wales, Vol. VII, 1850–1914*, Part II (Cambridge: Cambridge University Press, 2000), p. 1540.

2 C.W. Chalklin, 'Country Towns' in G.E. Mingay (ed.), *The Victorian Countryside* (London: Routledge and Kegan Paul, 1981); M. Girouard, *The English Town: A History of Urban Life* (Yale University Press, 1990); C. Chalklin, *The Rise of the English Country Town, 1650–1850* (Cambridge: Cambridge University Press, 2001).

3 Chalklin, 'Country Towns', pp. 276, 286; D. Brown, 'The Rise of Industrial Society and the End of the Self-Contained Village, 1760–1900?' in C. Dyer (ed.), *The Self-Contained Village?: The Social History of Rural Communities 1250–1900* (Hatfield: University of Hertfordshire, 2007), pp. 114–137.

4 G.E. Mingay 'Introduction: Rural England in the Industrial Age' in G.E. Mingay (ed.), *The Victorian Countryside*, pp. 3–4.

5 I. Berend, *Economic History of Nineteenth Century Europe* (Cambridge: Cambridge University Press, 2013), pp. 128–9; Cherry and Sheail, 'Town and Country', p. 1542.

6 G.E. Cherry and J. Sheail 'The Urban Impact on the Countryside: Introduction' in E.J.T. Collins (ed.), *Agrarian* History, pp. 1515–16.

7 J. Brown, *The English Market Town: A Social and Economic History 1750–1914* (Marlborough: The Crowood Press, 1986), pp. 7–8.

8 Brown, *The English Market Town*, p. 15 .

9 D. and E.M. Holland, *A Yorkshire Town: The Making of Doncaster* (iBook edition, 2012), p. 53.

10 Holland, *A Yorkshire Town*, p. 27.

11 Chalklin, 'Country Towns', p. 276; Chalklin, *Rise of the English Town*, p. 2.

12 Girouard, *The English Town*, p. 17.

13 E. Baines, *Directory of Yorkshire*, 1822, Vol. 1 (Leeds, 1822), p. 418; W. White, *History, Gazetteer and Directory of the West Riding*, 1837 (Sheffield, 1837), p. 297.

14 Doncaster Archives, AB2/2/3, *Council Minutes*, 11 March 1840.

15 Doncaster Archives, AB2/2/3, *Council Minutes*, 11 March 1840.

16 Doncaster Archives, AB2/2/3, *Council Minutes*, 11 March 1840.

17 S. Holland, 'The Evolution of a Northern Corn Market: Doncaster 1843–1873', *Northern History*, 51:2 (September 2015), pp. 233–49.

18 P. Smart, 'Corn for Sale! The Markets and Corn Exchanges in Reading and Wokingham', *Berkshire Old and New*, 30 (2013), p. 21.

19 S. Holland, 'Contrasting Rural Communities: The Experience of South Yorkshire in the Mid-Nineteenth Century' (Unpublished PhD Thesis, Sheffield Hallam University, 2013), pp. 94–5.

20 Doncaster Archives, AB2/2/3, *Council Minutes*, 9 May 1843.

21 Doncaster Archives, AB2/2/3, *Council Minutes*, 9 May 1843.

22 *Doncaster Gazette*, 5 May 1844, p. 5; *Doncaster Gazette*, 17 May 1844, p. 5.

23 A. Howkins, 'Types of Rural Communities' in E.J.T. Collins (ed.), *Agrarian History*, p. 1339.

24 Doncaster Archives, AB2/2/3, *Council Minutes*, February 1841.

25 Doncaster Archives, AB2/2/3, *Council Minutes*, February 1841.

26 *Doncaster Chronicle*, 18 October 1844, p. 5.

27 A. Howe, *Free Trade and Liberal England 1846–1946* (Oxford: Clarendon Press, 1997), p. 1; C. Schonhardt-Bailey, *From the Corn Laws to Free Trade: Interests, Ideas and Institutions in Historical Perspective* (Massachusetts Institute of Technology, MA, 2006), pp. 107–108.

28 Howe, *Free Trade and Liberal England*, p. 1; Schonhardt-Bailey, *From the Corn Laws to Free Trade*, pp. 107–108.

29 *Doncaster Chronicle*, 18 October 1844, p. 5.

30 *Doncaster Chronicle*, 18 October 1844, p. 5.

31 *Doncaster Gazette*, 28 February 1840, pp. 6–7.

32 *Doncaster Gazette*, 3 May 1839, p. 5; Doncaster Archives, DD/WA/P/19, *Speeches delivered in Leeds*, 1841; Doncaster Archives, DD/WA/P/25-26, *Speeches delivered by Aldam*, 1843.

33 *Doncaster Chronicle*, 18 October 1844, p. 5.

34 *Doncaster Chronicle*, 18 October 1844, p. 5.

35 *Doncaster Gazette*, 28 February 1845, p. 5; Doncaster Archives, AB/2/2/19/4, *Council and Committee Records of Doncaster Corporation, Finance Committee including Markets, 1843–1847*, 17 February 1845, 4 December 1845, 16 January 1846, 10 July 1846, 23 July 1846; Doncaster Archives, DZMD/569, *Order of Procession for the laying of the First Stone*, 24 May 1847.

36 Doncaster Archives, AB/2/2/19/4, *Council and Committee Records of Doncaster Corporation, Finance Committee including Markets, 1843–1847*, 23 June 1845, 28 January 1846.

37 *Doncaster Gazette*, 2 February 1849, p. 5.

38 *Doncaster Gazette*, 18 May 1849, p. 5; *Doncaster Gazette*, 25 May 1849, p. 5; *Doncaster Gazette*, 1 June 1849, p. 5; *Doncaster Gazette*, 8 June 1849, p. 5.

39 *Doncaster Chronicle*, 30 January 1863, p. 5.

40 Grady, 'The Cattle and Meat Trades in Leeds', pp. 139–140.

41 *Doncaster Chronicle*, 30 January 1863, p. 5; *Doncaster Chronicle*, 29 May 1863, p. 4.

42 *Doncaster Gazette*, 12 June 1863, p. 5.

43 *Doncaster Gazette*, 12 June 1863, p. 5.

44 Doncaster Archives, AB2/2/5, *Council Minutes*, 25 October 1861.

45 *Doncaster Chronicle*, 15 February 1867, p. 5.

46 *Doncaster Chronicle*, 15 February 1867, p. 5.

47 *Doncaster Gazette*, 11 April 1873, p. 5; *Doncaster Chronicle*, 18 April 1873, p. 8; Holland, 'Evolution of a Northern Corn Market'.

48 A. Briggs, *Victorian Cities* (London: Odhams, 1965), pp. 42–3; P. Jones, *The Sociology of Architecture: Constructing Identities* (Liverpool: Liverpool University Press, 2011), p. 53.

49 *Doncaster Chronicle*, 18 April 1873, p. 5.

50 *Doncaster Gazette*, 11 April 1873, p. 5; *Doncaster Gazette*, 9 May 1873, p. 6; *Doncaster Chronicle*, 9 May 1873, p. 6.

51 *Doncaster Chronicle*, 4 April 1873, p. 5; *Doncaster Chronicle*, 18 April 1873, p. 5.

52 *Doncaster Gazette*, 9 May 1873, p. 6.

53 *Doncaster Gazette*, 9 May 1873, p. 6.

54 *Doncaster Gazette*, 11 April 1873, p. 5; *Doncaster Chronicle*, 18 April 1873, p. 5.

55 R. Perren, 'The Marketing of Agricultural Products: Farm Gate to Retail Store' in Collins (ed), *Agrarian History*, p. 968.

56 *Doncaster Chronicle*, 18 April 1873, supplement.

57 *Doncaster Chronicle*, 18 April 1873, supplement.
58 *Doncaster Chronicle*, 18 April 1873, supplement.
59 *Doncaster Chronicle*, 11 April 1873, p. 1.
60 *Doncaster Chronicle*, 7 March 1873, p. 5.
61 Brown, *The English Market Town*, pp. 18–9.
62 *Doncaster Chronicle*, 18 April 1873, supplement.
63 *Doncaster Chronicle*, 18 April 1873, supplement.
64 S. Holland, 'Knowledge Networks in Mid Nineteenth Century England: A Case Study of Agricultural Societies in the Doncaster District', *Knowledge Networks in Rural Europe since 1700 Conference*, 27–29 August 2014, University of Leuven, Belgium; Holland, 'Contrasting Rural Communities', pp. 130–5.
65 N. Goddard, 'Agricultural Institutions: Societies, Associations and the Press' in E.J.T. Collins (ed.), *Agrarian History*, p. 655.
66 Goddard, 'Agricultural Institutions', p. 686.
67 *Doncaster Chronicle*, 18 October 1844, p. 5.
68 *Doncaster Chronicle*, 18 October 1844, p. 5.
69 L. Miskell, 'Puttting on a Show: the Royal Agricultural Society of England and the Market Town, c. 1840–1876', *Agricultural History Review*, 60:1 (2012), pp. 37–59.
70 Doncaster Archives, AB2/2/5, 9 May 1860
71 Doncaster Archives, DD/BW/E11/126, *Battie-Wrightson Miscellaneous Papers*, Doncaster Agricultural Society Leaflets.
72 *Doncaster Chronicle*, 1 October 1847, p. 8.
73 *Doncaster Chronicle*, 31 March 1871, p. 5.
74 Holland, 'Contrasting Rural Communities', p. 133.
75 *Journal of the Royal Agricultural Society of England*, Vol. 2, 1841, p. 320; *The Farmer's Magazine*, Vol. 5, July to December 1836, p. 419; *New York Farmer and American Gardener's Magazine*, Vol. 10, 1837, p. 278
76 *Doncaster Gazette*, 19 November 1858, p. 5.
77 *The Farmer's Magazine*, Vol. 1, May to December 1834, pp. 336–7; *New York Farmer and American Gardener's Magazine*, Vol. 9, 1836, p. 333; *Journal of the Royal Agricultural Society of England*, Vol. 2, 1841, p. 207; H. Stephens, *The Farmer's Guide to Scientific and Practical Agriculture*, Vol. 2 (1862), p. 74.

6   'Following the tools'

Migration networks among the stone workers of Purbeck in the nineteenth century

Andrew Hinde and Michael Edgar

Introduction

This chapter is concerned with migration patterns and networks in the nineteenth century among a specific occupational group: the stone workers of the Isle of Purbeck, in the southern English county of Dorset. By focusing on a specific group, we hope to set the migrants' experience more fully in its social, economic and historical context than has been possible in many previous studies of population mobility in nineteenth-century England.[1] Although we do not have access to residential histories of the kind analysed by Colin Pooley and Jean Turnbull in perhaps the best-known recent study of nineteenth-century British migration, we are able to look at the destinations of out-migrants from Purbeck using a transcription of the whole of the 1881 census of England and Wales.[2]

The chapter begins by describing various aspects of the economy of nineteenth-century Dorset and the Isle of Purbeck in particular. The main characteristic of the latter was its dual dependence on agriculture and the quarrying of building stone. This section also introduces the peculiar history of the stone trade and the recruitment of stone workers. The two following sections present, respectively, analyses of in-migration to and out-migration from the Isle of Purbeck, focusing on the period between 1841 and 1881, by applying well-established methods to data from the census enumerators' books (CEBs) and parish registers. We then use the 1881 CEB transcriptions to look at the destinations of out-migrants involved in the stone trade, which leads into a discussion of our conclusions in the light of other contributions to this volume.

The stone trade of the Isle of Purbeck in the nineteenth century

During the nineteenth century the county of Dorset was largely agricultural. Fishing and other maritime activities were carried out along the coast, and there was a small industrial sector in the few towns, such as Dorchester and Poole, but the vast majority of the population was based on the land. Rapid population growth in the late eighteenth and early nineteenth centuries created a surplus population in the countryside, but the relative remoteness of Dorset meant that out-migration – at least to other parts of England and Wales – during the early decades of the nineteenth century was not intense. The result was an impoverished, underemployed rural labour force receiving some of the lowest wages in England.[3]

There were, however, two areas within Dorset where men might find employment outside agriculture: the Isle of Portland, to the south of Weymouth, and the so-called Isle of Purbeck in the south-east of the county (Figure 6.1). Here the quarrying of fine building stone had been carried out for centuries, and it provided an alternative means of getting a living. In this chapter the second of these areas – the Isle of Purbeck – will concern us and, within that area, the stone workers. In order to interpret migration patterns among the stone workers of Purbeck, some background information is necessary.[4]

The Isle of Purbeck is in fact a peninsula. Its 'island' designation stems from the landward (western) end being largely delimited by watercourses. To its north is Poole harbour, and to the south and east the open sea. Despite its proximity to the town of Poole, it has long been an isolated area, and even now may only be entered easily by a single main road from Wareham or via a ferry across the entrance to Poole harbour.[5]

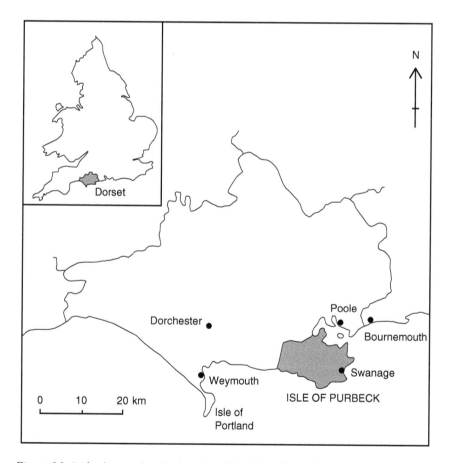

Figure 6.1 Author's map showing location of the Isle of Purbeck in the county of Dorset.

Stone has been quarried in Purbeck since Roman times. During the Middle Ages Purbeck marble (actually a polished limestone) was used in ecclesiastical buildings throughout England. By the seventeenth century, Purbeck quarries were producing stone for general building purposes, and especially for paving. A great deal of Purbeck stone was used in the rebuilding of London after the fire of 1666, and there were also contracts to supply stone for sea defences and fortifications along the south coast.[6] Tens of thousands of tons of Purbeck stone were used in the construction of Ramsgate harbour between 1750 and 1771.[7] Population growth and urbanisation ensured that the demand for Purbeck stone for paving, especially in London, continued into the nineteenth century. The stone was transported from Purbeck to London and elsewhere by sea.

The quarries were small; almost all were family concerns, each employing six to twelve men.[8] Many were worked by a sole proprietor who would, in the first instance, employ his sons. Any additional labour needed would be hired. Sometimes two or more quarriers (normally closely related, such as two brothers) would combine to work a quarry.[9] In addition to those owning or working in quarries, the Purbeck stone industry included two other groups: stonemasons and stone merchants. The stonemasons were employed on the surface, dressing the quarried stone blocks to whatever size and shape was required. However, quarriers and stonemasons did not form separate trades. The men who worked in the quarries were all skilled to some degree as masons, and many would move between the two activities during their working lives. The stone merchants were a small and powerful group who purchased the quarried and dressed stone from the quarriers and sold it on to buyers throughout England and Wales. This gave them effective control of the industry, though it also insulated the quarriers from fluctuations in the demand for stone. Merchants would frequently continue to purchase stone from the quarriers even when there was no immediate demand for it, storing it on a quay at Swanage (still called the 'stone quay') until buyers appeared.[10]

The Purbeck quarriers, masons and merchants were all required to be members of an institution known as the Company of Marblers and Stone Cutters.[11] The rules and organisation of the Company are reminiscent of those of medieval craft or trade guilds. Their basis was that employment in the Purbeck stone industry should be reserved to freemen of the Company and their apprentices. Freemen employing non-Company labour, or taking non-freemen as partners, were liable to fines and forfeitures. An apprenticeship lasted seven years, during which time the apprentice had to be lodged in the home of a freeman. In practical terms, by the nineteenth century this restricted apprenticeship to the sons or relatives of freemen.[12] Upon reaching the age of 21 years an apprentice was eligible to be enrolled as a freeman at the Company's annual meeting, held every Shrove Tuesday at Corfe Castle. An apprentice who wished to become a freeman had to demonstrate his ability as a stonemason by preparing an 'apprentice-piece'. Once this 'apprentice-piece' had been inspected and passed by the Wardens of the Company, he was admitted as a '"freeboy", and given a Certificate of Membership'.[13] The fact that all the members of the Company (even those who would work in quarries) had to be skilled as masons is of considerable importance in understanding their migration patterns.

Table 6.1 Occupational structure of stone-working parishes in the Isle of Purbeck, 1851

	Percentage of those stated to be employed		
	Langton Matravers	*Swanage*	*Worth Matravers*
Farmers	3	1	5
Farm workers	24	8	41
Trades and crafts	16	28	11
Maritime occupations	0	5	12
Professionals	3	5	3
Servants	10	10	6
Stone workers	42	36	22
Others	3	6	1
Total number employed	309	807	143
Employed as percentage of total population	40.8	39.6	36.7

Notes: 'Trades and crafts' includes both masters and 'journeymen'. 'Maritime occupations' includes coast guards (who were employed against smugglers). 'Professionals' includes landowners and other rich and/or educated persons.
Source: Census enumerators' books, 1851 (The National Archive HO 107/1856).

By the nineteenth century, the stone trade was largely confined to three parishes: Langton Matravers, Swanage and Worth Matravers. Their occupational structure in 1851 is shown in Table 6.1 where quarriers and stonemasons are treated as a single category of 'stone workers'.[14] In Langton Matravers, which was the most important quarrying parish by the mid-nineteenth century, more than two out of every five occupied males were in the stone trade. In Langton Matravers and Worth Matravers, agriculture was the other important occupation, whereas in the port and small town of Swanage, trades and crafts provided the main alternative source of employment.

The stone-working population displayed similar marriage and residential patterns to the general population.[15] However, this hides the fact that children aged 0–14 years constituted a higher proportion of the population in agricultural labouring households than they did in the stone-workers' households. Conversely, in the stone-workers' households, offspring aged 15 years and over were relatively more numerous. The difference is explained largely by the tendency for stone-workers' sons to remain at home and work in the stone trade, often in their fathers' quarries. By contrast, the teenage sons of agricultural labourers tended to be much more mobile, many leaving home to work elsewhere.

The birthplaces of the stone workers

Table 6.2 classifies the inhabitants of the three stone-working parishes in 1851 by occupation, and according to whether they were born in the parish where they were living in that year, in a nearby parish (within 8 km) or further afield. There was a major difference between the stone workers and the rest of the population: more than 87 per cent of stone workers had been born in the parish where they

Table 6.2 Occupied male population of three Purbeck stoneworking parishes in 1851 classified by place of birth and occupation

Occupational group	Langton Matravers		Swanage		Worth Matravers		Three parishes combined	
	Percentage native born	Percentage born within 8 km	Percentage native born	Percentage born within 8 km	Percentage native born	Percentage born within 8 km	Percentage native born	Percentage born within 8 km
Farmers	25	63	29	58	14	28	23	50
Farm workers	43	82	67	88	56	85	53	85
Trades and crafts	60	90	56	65	30	50	56	72
Stone workers	75	96	93	97	81	100	87	97
Others	53	67	54	67	18	35	51	65

Notes: 'Others' includes occupations related to the sea (mainly coast guards) and servants. Those classified as 'occupied' in this table are all those stated to be occupied in the 1851 census. This includes all but a handful of males aged over 15 years.
Source: Census enumerators' books, 1851 (The National Archive HO 107/1856).

were living in 1851, compared with only 53 per cent of agricultural labourers, 56 per cent of tradesmen and craftsmen and 51 per cent of those in 'other' occupations. This testifies to the efficacy of the restrictions on who could work in the stone trade, and to the strongly familial nature of the industry.[16]

The fact that only about half the workers in the remaining occupational groups (except for the small number of farmers) had been born in the parishes where they were living in 1851 also shows that there was a great deal of in-migration to these parishes, even during periods when overall net out-migration was occurring. In the case of farm workers, most in-migration was from nearby (with only about 15 per cent of farm workers in 1851 having been born more than 8 km from the parish where they were living in that year). For some other occupations, however, longer-distance migration was common. This is particularly the case with those in 'other' occupations in Worth Matravers. Many of these men were coast guards, employed to spy on smugglers. Locals were never engaged as coast guards to reduce the chance of conspiracy with fellow residents to turn a blind eye to smuggling activity (which, of course, could benefit them considerably). The farmers were the most mobile of all the occupational groups, although their numbers were small.[17]

The birthplaces of spouses and children recorded in the CEBs can reveal successive moves for a given family.[18] Elsewhere we have analysed the reported birthplaces in the 1881 census of those members of stone-workers' and agricultural workers' families in Langton Matravers who were born outside the Isle of Purbeck.[19] The differences between the stone workers and the agricultural labourers are striking. The latter had extensive links with the rest of Dorset but virtually no contact with other counties. Out of thirty-five members of agricultural workers' families who were born outside Purbeck, thirty-three were born in Dorset. In this they resemble agricultural workers throughout most of rural England in the late nineteenth century. The stone workers, on the other hand, appear to have had rather limited links with the rest of Dorset but quite strong links with certain other counties. Of forty-four members of stone-workers' families born outside Purbeck, only eleven had been born elsewhere in Dorset. This, in itself, is at one level not surprising, since stone workers might be expected to move to places where their skills were in demand, and these were few and far between in Dorset.[20] Nevertheless, the list of places where stone workers had previously lived is indicative of rather more than this, since most of these localities are known from other sources to have historical links with the Purbeck stone industry. They included Hampshire (seven members), Kent (five members) and the London area (five members), all of which were, or had been, major markets for Purbeck stone. Another county with which a connection existed was Lancashire. This probably came about through the London-based building contractor John Mowlem and Company, which was founded by a Swanage man and was being run by his nephew in 1881.

Out-migration

Out-migration has been, and continues to be, much harder to analyse than in-migration. There is no single source which will furnish information both on who moved away from a particular area and where they went, in the way that the CEBs will simultaneously assist the identification of who has moved in and where they came from (or, at least, where they were born). Investigators have until recently been confined to analysing who moved and who stayed, without being able to provide much information about where the out-migrants went. Even the analysis of movers and stayers is time-consuming, for it relies upon nominal record linkage of successive censuses and parish burial registers. This exercise allows the investigator to classify those resident in a parish at one census according to whether they were (1) still resident at the next census, (2) recorded in the Church of England burial register of the parish during the intervening period or (3) neither (1) nor (2). Persons in group (3) are assumed to have moved out of the parish between the two censuses.

Some extant work of this type begins with those who were resident in a parish at a particular census. The majority of these studies show that only about 40 per cent of persons in one census remained in the parish ten years later.[21] It is also possible to begin by identifying all those born in a particular parish within a specific period. This birth cohort is then traced for a number of years using the CEBs from successive censuses and the parish burial registers. It seems that the majority of those born in English villages during the mid-nineteenth century had left their native parishes before their twenty-fifth birthday. Not only were most migrants young, but most young people moved.[22]

Our investigation of out-migration begins with a study of the second type. Using the Church of England baptism registers and the census enumerators' books for the parish of Langton Matravers, we have identified as many boys who were born in the parish between 1841 and 1861 as we could.[23] These boys have then been searched for in subsequent censuses up to and including that of 1881, and in the parish burial register for the period between each boy's birth and the date of the 1881 census. The results enable us to identify the numbers of boys still living in the parish at each census after their birth, and the number who had died in the parish and been buried in the churchyard.[24] For the majority of boys, it also proved possible to identify their fathers' occupation (either from the baptism register or from the census enumerators' books), so we can examine persistence rates by occupational group.

The results confirm the conclusions of previous studies that most boys moved away from their parish of birth by the time they were 25-years-old. Only twenty-three out of 114 boys born between 1841 and 1851 were still living in Langton Matravers in 1871 (when they were aged 20–30 years). The corresponding proportion for the boys born between 1851 and 1861 (based on their place of residence in 1881) was forty-one out of 153. Since twenty-three members of the 1841–51 birth cohort had died in Langton Matravers by 1871, and twenty-seven members of the 1851–61 birth cohort had died in the parish before 1881, we estimate that 60 per cent (68/114) of the 1841–51 birth cohort and 55 per cent (85/153) of the 1851–61 birth cohort had moved away from the parish by the time they were about 25 years of age.[25]

The sons of stone workers were much less likely to leave the parish than other boys. Whereas fewer than one in five of the sons of farm workers remained in

Langton Matravers until they were in their twenties, between a quarter and a half of the sons of stone workers did so.

Destinations

Until recently, it was very difficult to trace out-migrants because no indication of their destinations is given in the CEBs. However, the recent growth of data storage and processing capacity has opened up new possibilities for the analysis of individual-level migration using census data. Now we can, in principle, find out fairly efficiently the place of residence in various census years of everyone who was alive and living in England and Wales.[26] This means that the study of out-migration from rural areas using record linkage methods can now be extended to include some analysis of destinations.[27] We shall still only observe transitions between the last date at which people were living in the study area and the census date which is the target of the search, rather than complete residential histories. However, out-migrants from any locality who were still alive at the target census date and who were living in England and Wales can be traced, and placed in context in the communities where they were living at that time.[28] One limitation of this method is that, for the most part, it can only be applied to males, since it requires linkage on the basis of surname, and this cannot be achieved for women who have married before the target census date.

We have performed a search for persons living in England in 1881 who were born in the three stone parishes of Langton Matravers, Worth Matravers and Swanage.[29] Because the stone trade was carried on in families, the great majority of stone workers had one of a relatively small number of surnames. Restricting attention to these few surnames vastly speeds up the searching process, and we have been able to search the 1881 data for a wide area of England for anyone with one of these surnames who was born in any of the three stone-working parishes of Purbeck.[30]

The geographical distribution of out-migrants among these stone-working families may be illustrated by considering just the 356 family members born in Langton Matravers whom we have traced in the 1881 census. Of these, 256 (or 75 per cent) were living in the parish where they were born. Of the remainder, twenty-four were living in the neighbouring parishes of Swanage and Worth Matravers, and only thirteen elsewhere in Dorset. The fifty-three who were living in other counties in 1881 were concentrated in Hampshire (fourteen), Surrey (sixteen), Middlesex (twelve) and Lancashire (five), all of which areas had connections with Purbeck through the stone trade. Some of those who left Purbeck moved around considerably. For example, Henry Edmonds, aged 54 years, was in 1881 living (rather appropriately) at 120 Dorset Road, Lambeth, Surrey with his wife, four children and one grandchild.[31] His eldest son, aged 20 years, had been born in Southsea in Hampshire, and his three younger children in and around Chatham in Kent. This appears to confirm that although out-migrant stone workers were highly mobile, they moved between places that had historical links with the stone trade. This was the case with both the Southsea area of Hampshire and the north Kent coast.

Stone workers who left Purbeck during the nineteenth century largely remained in the stone trade. Most of them became stonemasons in their new locations, an option open to them because of the requirement that a freeman of the Company of Marblers and Stone Cutters be skilled as a mason as well as a quarrier. Since masons were in general demand, a Purbeck worker who wished to leave the Isle was likely to find work in almost any reasonably populous place. Unlike workers in other extractive industries (for example the tin miners of Cornwall), therefore, the Purbeck stone workers were not constrained to migrate to areas where quarrying or mining was taking place.[32] Instead, they not unreasonably chose places where they had built up family or trade links.

The 1881 census listings reveal that it was common for out-migrants to head for places where previous out-migrants had gone. For example, at number one Trigon Road, Lambeth (part of the built-up area of London by the mid-nineteenth century), we find Henry Corben, a stonemason, born in Worth Matravers, with three sons and a daughter, all of whom had been born in Lambeth or elsewhere in London).[33] In the same street, at number twenty-one, is Joseph Saunders, also a stonemason. He himself was born in Portsea (the city of Portsmouth), in Hampshire, but his wife and eldest son were born in Worth Matravers.[34] Similarly, in the parish of Holdenhurst (Bournemouth) the families of Thomas Chinchen and John Bridle (both stonemasons, and both born in Langton Matravers) were living next door to one another in Terrace Road.[35] Finally, at fifteen St Stephens, Lambeth, we find Won. Wil. Bower (*sic*), a stonemason born in Portsmouth but whose wife was born in Langton Matravers. Described as 'boarders' in this household were Walter Nineham, aged 25 years, a stonemason born in Worth Matravers, and Samuel C. Clarke, aged 21 years, a stonemason born in Langton Matravers.[36] Since the Bowers' three children (aged 4, 6 and 8 years) were born in Lambeth, we can surmise that their movement there took place at least eight years before 1881. It is likely that the two boarders were more recent migrants, living temporarily with the Bowers while they gained a foothold in the Lambeth area.

Finally, return migration to Purbeck was common among the stone workers. Some young men left for a short period and then moved back. In other cases, members of stone-working families who were born outside Purbeck might move into the area. For example, Frederick Brown, a stonemason, was living in 1881 in Lambeth.[37] He had been born in Woolwich in north Kent. His wife, Alice, however, was born in Langton Matravers. With them in 1881 were their three sons: Arthur, aged 9 years, was born in Worth Matravers; Hubert, aged 6 years, was born in Lambeth; and Sidney, aged 1 year, was born in Worth Matravers. It appears, therefore, that, rather like James Carter, the subject of Christopher Ferguson's chapter, who moved several times between Colchester and London, the stone worker Frederick Brown had moved from Kent to Purbeck, then to Lambeth in Surrey, then back to Purbeck, and then to Lambeth once again.

Conclusion

An initial reading of the migration patterns of the stone workers might suggest a classic case of a declining rural industry leading to out-migration, mainly to large urban areas, and especially London, in much the same way that the decline of craft industries and rural trades elsewhere had been a major force driving people to leave the countryside.[38] Julia Neville's chapter on the country butchers of the Exe Valley illustrates how the decline of that particular way of combining the production and sale of meat drove several country butchers into the city of Exeter to open conventional retail shops, or out of the sector altogether and into other activities in urban areas (such as running public houses in expanding parts of London). This rural–urban movement was often self-perpetuating with others from specific rural localities following the paths taken by earlier migrants, a phenomenon known as 'chain migration'. The tendency for migrant stone workers from Purbeck to concentrate in a small number of urban areas, and to live in relatively close proximity to one another when they arrived in these towns, might also be interpreted as an example of this process. There also appears to be some evidence of the maintenance of kin networks in the destination areas. However, while each of these interpretations contains some truth, the real situation is more complicated.

The migration streams and networks that we have identified among the stone workers in the nineteenth century probably originated many centuries before. It is known that in medieval times masons from Purbeck went with their stone to London and elsewhere to work on cathedrals and churches.[39] This habit of working 'on site' continued into the eighteenth and nineteenth centuries, when it was known as 'following the tools'. Thus, out-migration among the stone workers was long established, and had originally been associated not with a contraction of the industry but with expansion. The men who left Purbeck in the nineteenth century should not, therefore, be seen primarily as economic refugees fleeing rural poverty. Indeed for many, returning to Purbeck was always a distinct possibility.[40]

The fortunes of the stone trade rose and fell over time. While stone merchants dampened the effect of variations in the demand for stone on the quarriers and their families, there were periods when some of those born into stone-workers' families would find employment in the trade hard to come by. Moreover, even in good times, the number of employees that the trade could absorb was limited, and carrying capacity was lower than the number of sons that stone workers were producing.[41]

Stone workers living in Purbeck who could not find work in the stone trade could either take up other occupations locally (agriculture or some other trade), or move away. Among the stone-working families of Langton Matravers, work in the agricultural sector in the same parish was very rarely chosen. This may have been because of a cultural aversion to working on the land. However, it is more likely that the low wages of agricultural workers made this occupation very unappealing (even if work was available). Moreover, as we have seen, stone workers had a ready-made escape route provided by their skills as stonemasons, and historical trade links with other parts of the country.[42]

Because of the long history of out-migration along well-defined paths, those wishing to pursue their trade outside Purbeck were likely to follow in the footsteps of their ancestors, and found assistance from Purbeckians already located in their destinations. This assistance probably occurred less because of kinship bonds and networks than as a result of shared membership of the Company of Marblers. Among the stone-working community in Purbeck, whereas kinship links *within* families were strong, links *between* families were relatively weak.[43] Moreover, out-migration of whole families was rare. A stone worker who arrived in, say, Lambeth in Surrey, therefore, might not find many members of his immediate family there, but he would meet other members of the Company of Marblers, who would not necessarily have any close family connection but would provide assistance in finding accommodation, and probably employment. Thus, we think that family and kinship networks played a smaller role in assisting integration of Purbeck stone workers into the destination community than they did, for example, among the migrants into the Lancashire town of Preston studied by Michael Anderson.[44]

A few members of stone-working families took up other trades and crafts in Purbeck. For example, one John Bower is described as a 'blacksmith' in the censuses of 1851 through 1881; and Ambrose Lander is described as a 'grocer and draper' in 1861, but a 'stonemason' in 1871, when his son Samuel is described as a 'grocer'.[45] But these were exceptions. The overwhelming impression given by the census data is that the Purbeck stone workers either worked in their trade locally, or, if that was not possible, pursued it elsewhere.[46] The family traditions were strong, and leaving the industry entirely was very unusual.

Thus, this occupation group did not exhibit the classic rural–urban migration patterns of a declining rural industry. They moved between countryside and town following long-established paths which were also two-way routes, leading from countryside to town and back again, sometimes several times in a man's working life. The peculiar history of the trade influenced how the urban part and the rural part of the trade interacted. The Purbeck stone-workers' story suggests that the traditional nineteenth-century model of a countryside being depopulated by people who were flooding into overcrowded cities with overstretched infrastructures is not universally applicable. Neither should we assume that stone workers inhabited a 'borderland', still bound to the traditions of rural life, yet changed forever by the experience of city life. They had never been fully integrated into agricultural Dorset, or 'bound to the soil', as Barbara Kerr suggests the agricultural labourers were.[47] Nor should we suppose that they were uncomfortable in the urban environments they had literally helped to build.

We should be wary, therefore, of over-generalisation about nineteenth-century migration patterns, and about the relationships between town and countryside. Aspects of the stone workers' relationships with urban areas were *sui generis*, but the same could be said of many other groups of rural workers. Even those described in a similar way in official records were in different positions in different regions (for example, an 'agricultural labourer' in Dorset did not have the same potential to move to an expanding city as his counterpart in the Yorkshire Dales). As this volume shows, there were many and varied relationships between countryside and city, each dependent on the history of the people and the communities involved, and on the local political economy.[48]

Finally, opportunities to study local migration patterns and rural–urban interactions will expand as more of the nineteenth-century censuses become available in machine-readable and searchable formats.[49] Researchers can currently access only the listings for whole towns and their surrounding rural areas for the 1881 census. Other censuses are likely to become available soon, which will open up new possibilities for detailed research into how 'easy' or 'uneasy' the relationship between town and countryside was, and how it evolved over time.

Acknowledgements

We wish to thank Reg Saville, Hon. President of the Langton Matravers Local History and Preservation Society, for information about the history of the stone trade. We are grateful to the participants at the Uneasy Neighbours conference held in Southampton in September 2013, and particularly Prof. Keith Snell, for their comments and suggestions. Michael Edgar's contribution to the research for this chapter was supported by grants from the Crowther Fund, the Parkes Foundation and the Roger Schofield Local Population Studies Research Fund. The staff of the Dorset Record Office (now Dorset History Centre) provided exemplary assistance with data collection.

Notes

1 Studies of migration among 'occupational communities' of this sort are quite rare in the literature. An important exception is H. R. Southall, 'The Tramping Artisan Revisits: Labour Mobility and Economic Distress in Early Victorian England', *Economic History Review*, 44 (1991), pp. 272–96. See also M. Jones, 'Combining Estate Records with Census Enumerators' Books to Study Nineteenth-Century Communities: the Case of the Tankersley Ironstone Miners, c. 1850', in D. Mills and K. Schürer (eds), *Local Communities in the Census Enumerators' Books* (Oxford: Leopard's Head Press, 1996) pp. 200–16; C. Leivers, 'The Modern Ishmaels? Navvy Communities in the High Peak', *Family and Community History*, 9 (2006), pp. 141–55; and R. Gant, 'School Records, Family Migration and Community History: Insights from Sudbrook and the Construction of the Severn Tunnel', *Family and Community History*, 11 (2008), pp. 27–44.

2 C. Pooley and J. Turnbull, *Migration and Mobility in Britain since the Eighteenth Century* (London: University College London Press, 1998).

3 The low wages of Dorset labourers were remarked upon by contemporaries such as J. Caird, *English Agriculture in 1850–51*, 2nd edn (London: Longman, Brown, Green and Longmans, 1852). On the causes of poverty in rural Dorset during the first half of the nineteenth century, see B. Kerr, 'The Dorset Agricultural Labourer 1750–1850', *Proceedings of the Dorset Natural History and Archaeological Society*, 84 (1962), pp. 158–77, on pp. 162, 171, 174–5.

4 For additional material on the history of the stone trade, see M. Edgar and A. Hinde, 'The stone workers of Purbeck', *Rural History*, 10 (1999), pp. 75–90.

5 We are informed by Mr R. J. Saville that the traditional boundaries of the Isle of Purbeck include the entire parishes of Arne, Church Knowle, Corfe Castle, Kimmeridge, Langton Matravers, Steeple, Studland, Swanage, Tyneham and Worth Matravers together with the extra-parochial place of East Holme.

6 E. Benfield, *Purbeck Shop: a Stone Worker's Story of Stone* (Cambridge: Cambridge University Press, 1940), p. 10; see also *Hutchins's History and Antiquities of the County of Dorset*, ed. W. Shipp and J. W. Hodson, 3rd edn, 4 vols (Westminster, 1861–70).

7 M. M. Crickland and C. H. Vellacott, 'Industries', in W. Page (ed.), *The Victoria History of the County of Dorset* (London: Archibald Constable, 1908), vol. 2, p. 337. See also Letter from Jn Bishop, 10 June 1771, Dorset Record Office D-RWR/E/107.

8 We use the term 'quarries' to describe what were in fact deep mines. They were usually described by those who worked in the industry as 'quarrs'. Quarrying stone using deep mines had not always been a feature of the Purbeck stone industry: in the Middle Ages open-cast mining had been practised. However, from the seventeenth until the twentieth centuries, it seems that deep mining was the norm.

9 Letter XXVIII, 'The stone quarries of Swanage', in P. E. Razzell and R. W. Wainwright (eds), *The Victorian Working Class: Selections From Letters to the Morning Chronicle* (London: Cass, 1973), p. 43.

10 Letter XXVIII, 'The stone quarries', pp. 45–7.

11 This Company was probably of medieval origin, although we have found no records confirming this. The earliest extant document seems to be a copy of the Company's ten Articles of Agreement dated 3 March 1651. The fact that merchants were required to be members of the Company was confirmed to us in correspondence by R. J. Saville.

12 In our analysis of the nineteenth-century records, we have failed to find any apprentice who was not the son of a stone worker.

13 R. J. Saville, *Langton's Stone Quarries*, 2nd edn (Langton Matravers: Langton Matravers Local History and Preservation Society, 1986), p. 26.

14 In addition to the fact that movement between these two activities was common, it seems likely that nineteenth-century census enumerators failed to distinguish consistently between the two.

15 See Edgar and Hinde, 'The Stone Workers of Purbeck'.

16 Jones, 'Combining Estate Records', p. 215 also found that a large proportion of the ironstone workers of Tankersley, in the West Riding of Yorkshire were locally born, a fact which he ascribes to the organisation of the industry.

17 For further information on the high mobility of farmers in southern England see, for example, A. Hinde, H. R. Davies and D. M. Kirkby, 'Hampshire Village Populations in the Nineteenth Century', *Southern History*, 15 (1993), pp. 140–61, on p. 150.

18 This type of analysis was pioneered by D. Bryant, 'Demographic Trends in South Devon in the Mid Nineteenth Century', in K. J. Gregory and W. L. D. Ravenhill (eds), *Exeter Essays in Geography in Honour of Arthur Davies* (Exeter: Exeter University Press, 1971), pp. 125–42.

19 Edgar and Hinde, 'The stone workers of Purbeck'.

20 The Isle of Portland was the other Dorset area where stone was quarried. However, it seems that there was no love lost between the quarriers of Purbeck and Portland during the nineteenth century, and contact between the two groups was limited.

21 See P. D. Howard, 'An analysis of migration in rural northern Hampshire 1841–1861' (MA dissertation, University of Southampton, 1996), p. 7; good individual examples are J. Robin, *Elmdon: Continuity and Change in a North-West Essex Village 1861–1964* (Cambridge: Cambridge University Press, 1980); B. Wojciechowska, 'Brenchley: a Study of Migratory Movements in a Mid Nineteenth Century Rural Parish', *Local Population Studies*, 41 (1988), pp. 28–40 (reprinted in Mills and Schürer, *Local Communities*, pp. 253–66); and C. French, 'Persistence in a Local Community: Kingston Upon Thames 1851-1891', *Local Population Studies*, 81(2008), pp. 18–36, on p. 22.

22 P. R. A. Hinde, 'The Population of a Wiltshire Village in the Nineteenth Century: a Reconstitution Study of Berwick St James, 1841–71', *Annals of Human Biology*, 14 (1987), pp. 475–85, on pp. 481–2.

23 The recording of births in Church of England baptism registers in the nineteenth century was usually much less complete than was the recording of deaths in the burial registers. We have tried to overcome this problem by adding into the sample of births all those who were aged under 10 years in the 1851 and 1861 censuses, whose birthplace was stated to have been Langton Matravers but who do not appear in the baptism register. Similarly, we have added in a few boys whose deaths are reported in the burial register, and whose age at death indicates that they were born within the period 1841–61 but for whom there is no

record in the baptism register. However, this will still not capture the births of boys whose baptisms are unrecorded, and who moved away from the parish prior to the subsequent census or their death. To this extent, the method will tend to underestimate out-migration.

24 A similar exercise for girls is much more difficult because they changed their names on marriage. In many cases their marriages took place outside the parish and so their married name is unknown. As the focus of this analysis is on the different migration networks of stone workers and others, and these are revealed principally by the experience of males, we have not analysed female migration.

25 In fact, these percentages are slight underestimates, since we have classified a number of return migrants as if they had remained in the parish throughout the period. If the return migrants are included with the out-migrants, the percentages who had never left Langton Matravers by their twenty-fifth birthday increase to 62 per cent for the 1841–51 birth cohort and 58 per cent for the 1851–61 birth cohort.

26 A range of databases can be used to search the census data. These include UK Census Online (http://www.ukcensusonline.com/index.php), and the genealogical electronic data bases of Ancestry (http://www.ancestry.co.uk/), Genes Reunited (http://www.genesreunited.co.uk/), and Find My Past (http://www.findmypast.co.uk/). The National Archive also has an entry point into some of these data bases: (http://www.nationalarchives.gov.uk/records/census-records.htm). A challenge to using these genealogical data bases for academic research is that they are optimised for searching for individuals. Searching for all the members of a particular social or occupational group is therefore still very tedious, and hardly possible unless the name of each member is known. The exception is the 1881 census, the whole of which has been rendered machine readable and downloadable from the United Kingdom Data Archive at the University of Essex: see K. Schürer, *1881 Census for England and Wales, the Channel Islands and the Isle of Man* (study number 4177), (Colchester: UK Data Archive, 2000).

27 For examples of work of this type, see Leivers, 'The modern Ishmaels?'; G. Nair and D. Poyner, 'The Flight from the Land: Rural Migration in South-East Shropshire in the Late Nineteenth Century', *Rural History*, 17 (2006), pp. 167–86; J. Fripp, 'Mobility in Victorian Dorset', *Proceedings of the Dorset Natural History and Archaeological Society*, 129 (2009), pp. 39–47; and C. Bailey, ' "I'd Heard It Was such a Grand Place": Mid-19th Century Internal Migration to London', *Family and Community History*, 14 (2011), pp. 121–40.

28 Intermediate moves can sometimes be ascertained from the birthplaces of spouses and children.

29 The search is much easier for the 1881 census than for other censuses because of the existence of the machine-readable transcript of the whole 1881 census (see Schürer, *1881 Census*).

30 The surnames we searched were as follows: Benfield/Bonfield, Bower, Bridle, Chinchen, Corben, Edmonds/Edmunds, Lander, Phippard, Saunders/Sanders, Vye and Webber. Eight out of every nine stone workers recorded in the six censuses of Langton Matravers between 1841 and 1891 inclusive had one of these eleven surnames (see The National Archive [hereafter NA]: CEBs for Langton Matravers, 1841 (NA HO 107/278/2), 1851 (NA HO 107/1856), 1861 (NA RG 9/1343), 1871 (NA RG 10/1992), 1881 (NA RG 11/2098) and 1891 (NA RG 12/1641)).

31 NA RG 11/603.

32 For example, several Cornishmen were to be found in the lead mining parish of Sheldon in Derbyshire in the mid nineteenth century (NA HO 107/2149, NA RG 9/2539 and NA RG 10/3627).

33 NA RG 11/602.

34 NA RG 11/602.

35 NA RG 11/1195.

36 NA RG 11/603.

37 NA RG 11/604.

38 See J. Saville, *Rural Depopulation in England and Wales, 1851–1951* (London: Routledge and Kegan Paul, 1957), pp. 20–30.

39 G. D. Drury, 'The Use of Purbeck Marble in Medieval Times', *Proceedings of the Dorset Natural History and Archaeological Society*, 70 (1948), pp. 74–98, on pp. 78, 97–8.

40 The aforementioned John Mowlem, who eventually founded a large construction company that is still in existence, records in his diary that when he started work as a foreman in London: 'I was put over men old enough to be my father. It is true I knew but little, but I moved upwards, knowing I could any day go back to the bankers [the piles of stone stored either at the quarry head or at the stone quay at Swanage prior to shipment].' See *John Mowlem's Swanage Diary, 1845–1851*, ed. D. Lewer (Dorchester: Dorset Publishing Co., 1990), p. 17.

41 Stone workers tended to have large families, with six and seven children being common. Assuming that half of these were males, and even allowing for a fairly high rate of child mortality, for all sons born to stone workers to have been absorbed by the industry, the number of workers would roughly have had to double every 25–30 years. This did not happen. The number of persons described as stonemasons or quarriers in Langton Matravers was 132 in 1851, 93 in 1861, 105 in 1871, 145 in 1881 and 68 in 1891 (NA HO 107/1856, NA RG 9/1343, NA RG 10/1992, NA RG 11/2098 and NA RG 12/1641).

42 See M. Moore, 'Stone Quarrying in the Isle of Purbeck: an Oral History' (MA dissertation, University of Leicester, 1992), p. 70. We are grateful to Prof. K.D.M. Snell for drawing our attention to this thesis, and kindly allowing us to see a copy of it.

43 See Edgar and Hinde, 'The stone workers of Purbeck' for more discussion of this issue.

44 M. Anderson, *Family Structure in Nineteenth-Century Lancashire* (Cambridge: Cambridge University Press, 1971).

45 NA HO 107/1856, RG 9/1343, RG 10/1992 and RG 11/2098.

46 In the five censuses from 1851 to 1891, in Langton Matravers, we found only seventeen members of the eleven main stone-working families described as tradesmen or craftsmen.

47 See B. Kerr, *Bound to the Soil: a Social History of Dorset 1750–1918* (London: John Baker, 1968).

48 The chapters on Doncaster and Exeter, for example, show how the relationship between these towns and their rural hinterlands was affected by the impact of local politics on the construction of markets. In Doncaster there was a unified commitment to building a market to allow the town to compete with neighbouring urban areas. In Exeter, intra-urban rivalry led to the division of effort and the construction of two markets, neither of which was successful.

49 See, for example, the Integrated Census Microdata project at the University of Essex (https://www.essex.ac.uk/history/research/icem/default.htm).

Part III

The impact of modernity on rural life

7 'Life in our villages is practically no life at all'

Sketching the rural–urban shift in nineteenth-century depictions of Wales

Michelle Deininger

With its dramatic scenery, distinctive culture and ancient language, Wales has long provided the travel writer and amateur sketcher with a rich canvas to survey. Outsider perspectives, such as those of Daniel Defoe, William Gilpin and the more idiosyncratic George Borrow, in his popular travel text, *Wild Wales* (1862), have had a long-lasting impact on the way in which Wales and the Welsh have been depicted and imagined. To delve further into the complexities of cultural and social shifts, however, there are other avenues to explore. Of the many excellent and worthwhile digitisation projects currently being undertaken in Britain, *Welsh Newspapers Online*, which encompasses publications in both Welsh and English from the early 1800s to 1919, has the potential to transform understanding of many aspects of nineteenth-century Welsh life.[1] With new titles being added regularly, the capacity of this resource to provide a more nuanced and comprehensive understanding of lived history in Wales is unparalleled. For the purposes of this chapter, the aspect of Welsh cultural history explored in some detail is the way the shift from rural to urban living was articulated and scrutinised in the popular press. What comes to light as more titles are added to *Welsh Newspapers Online* is that this shift was registered in a multitude of different ways, ranging from the way day-to-day life was changing in rural areas to gossip columns which focused on slips in moral judgement in newly established industrial towns.

Given the generic make-up of newspapers, with their eclectic mix of articles, letters, advertisements, gossip columns and literary pieces, they provide an unusually vibrant cross-section of the most pressing social issues, anxieties and preoccupations. Because *Welsh Newspapers Online* covers diverse titles, from national dailies to weekly local papers, the range of available texts is especially broad. There is often an intriguing overlap between the literary and the factual in many of the newspaper extracts discussed in this chapter, especially regarding wider generic links with the sketch, travel writing and the short story. These interrelated yet distinct genres are underpinned by a recurring preoccupation with ethnography, a discipline which informs both insider and outsider accounts of Wales. The writing explored here forms part of a wider network of ethnographic writing, which was extremely popular across Europe in the nineteenth century, and went some way, I would argue, towards defining the nation both within and without.

Modern ethnography has been defined as a discipline which 'takes the position that human behaviour and the ways in which people construct and make meaning of their worlds and their lives are highly variable and locally specific'.[2] In the nineteenth century, an amateur ethnographic approach structures numerous texts which focus on Welsh life and has many similarities with colonial travel writing of the period – writing which seeks to examine, categorise and contain difference.

The main trope which links articles taken from newspapers and other 'sketches of Wales and the Welsh' is the figure of the participant-observer narrator, the data-gatherer of ethnographic studies, who is both inside and yet subtly removed from the action he or she describes. In modern ethnography, researchers 'learn through systematic observation in the field by interviewing and carefully recording what they see and hear, as well as how things are done'.[3] In the nineteenth century, elements of this approach are clearly traceable, but the participant-observer can be prone to bias, misunderstanding and cultural imperialism. Written from a somewhat distanced perspective, these kinds of text attempted to identify essential aspects of Welsh life and cultural traditions. However, rather than simply describing or containing elements of Welsh life which were different or unfathomable, the work of the participant-observer narrator can be more that of a facilitator. Sandra A. Zagarell's definition of the genre known as 'narrative of community' is especially relevant as she makes specific reference to the participant-observer narrator as a figure of mediation between a way of life that is swiftly disappearing and a new world order. This genre is 'concerned with continuity', Zagarell contends, attempting to

> represent what gives the community its identity, what enables it to remain itself. The approach is imbued with a concern for process. Writers understood communities to take form through negotiation among diverse, often recalcitrant components – people living at distances from each other; sometimes reluctant individuals; scarce resources; values, practices, and lore that are threatened by time and change; a harsh physical environment – and they foregrounded the specific dynamics through which these elements are continuously reintegrated.[4]

Having roots in texts such as Maria Edgeworth's *Castle Rackrent* (1800), which used the vernacular to represent folk culture, the genre flourished in the nineteenth century and encompasses other well-known texts such as Mary Russell Mitford's *Our Village* (1824–32), Elizabeth Gaskell's *Cranford* (1851–3) and Sarah Orne Jewett's *The Country of the Pointed Firs* (1896). In Wales, Sara Maria Saunders' 'Welsh Rural Sketches', which regularly appeared in *Young Wales* between 1896–9, have a similar flavour. Forming what is ostensibly a short-story cycle, these sketches explore the complex interactions between the characters of a community on the cusp of change, especially in terms of religion and gender hierarchies.[5]

This chapter weaves together elements of genre and travel writing theory in order to examine the way rural life is depicted in English-language regular columns which bear a distinct generic resemblance to earlier sketches, travel literature and short stories, often emphasised by titles such as 'Tales and Sketches of Wales', 'Sketches of Welsh Life' and 'Sketches from the Country'. At the same time, it seeks to examine how newspaper representations and their literary antecedents oscillate between realist observations, which focus on the difficulties facing communities in the wake of increased industrialisation, and a nostalgic, idealised portrayal of a way of life which was beginning to be lost.

Inspecting Welsh life and traditions

Sketches and travel writing which focus on Wales not only shape the way the country's topography is imagined but also inform political discourses concerning national identity, the characteristics of its people, language, customs and traditions. From the mid-nineteenth century, these aspects of Welsh life and traditions were under particular scrutiny, not least because of the Chartist rising in Newport in 1839, and the Rebecca Riots of the early 1840s, which stemmed from high rises in toll gate taxes. As a result of this period of discontent in Wales, the now infamous *Reports of the Commissioners of Inquiry into the State of Education in Wales* (1847) were compiled, which crystallised many ill-informed and erroneous assumptions regarding cultural and linguistic difference in Wales. While they were commissioned specifically to examine 'the means afforded to the labouring classes of acquiring a knowledge of the English language', the *Reports* actually recorded far more than this, including opinions concerning moral standards and supposed lack of chastity, particularly among women.[6] Besides these outcomes, the *Reports* also document elements of Welsh culture, including local customs and agricultural practices, which often feature in travellers' accounts and in later Welsh-based newspaper articles. As the commissioners were themselves unable to speak Welsh but were examining men and women who could only speak that language, the *Reports* were, unsurprisingly, extremely negative, and found that standards in education were 'deplorably low, particularly with regard to the teaching of English'.[7] The *Reports*, which became known as 'The Treason of the Blue Books' due to their distinctive blue binding, linked, as Jane Aaron has argued, this 'lack of educational access to English civilisation with what it claimed to be the barbarity and primitive backwardness of the population'.[8]

One particularly eloquent response to the *Blue Books* came in 1848, from Jane Williams, using her bardic name of Ysgafell, who argued that they had

> done the people of [Wales] a double wrong. They have traduced their national character, and in doing so, they have threatened an infringement upon their manifest social rights, their dearest existing interests … their local customs, and their mother tongue.[9]

In many ways, the newspaper columns and articles explored here focus on these same aspects of Welsh culture that the *Reports* represented so negatively. While they cannot necessarily be regarded as a direct response to the *Reports*' findings, they seem to highlight some of the fault lines in perspectives of Wales, especially in respect of rural poverty.

While the 1830s was a period of 'marked political turbulence in Wales', as Jane Aaron has commented, many mid-nineteenth-century texts portray a Wales which is, on the surface, far from unrest and turmoil.[10] Indeed, the novelist Anne Beale (1815–1900), who was born in Somerset but moved to Wales in 1841, opens her 1844 hybrid travelogue-novel, *The Vale of the Towey; or, Sketches in South Wales* (a text which was repeatedly reprinted throughout the 1850s and 1860s, partly in response to the *Blue Books*), by focusing on 'tranquil vales and mountains' rather than 'descriptions of stirring events, and portraitures of a people of a determined, if not of a turbulent and rebellious character'.[11] The text continually reassures the reader of female propriety, in the form of a recurring character, Rachel, who is virtuous, hardworking and keeps a clean house but also exhibits unease in the portrayal of itinerant female characters, such as the homeless 'Mad Moll' and a travelling pedlar.

The examples from mid-nineteenth century sketches and travel writing discussed below are taken from the writings of Catherine Sinclair and Amy Lane, and tend to emphasise the authoritative view of the upper-class visitor, as a participant-observer narrator, entering a lower-class domain. By the time of the examples in Welsh newspapers from the later decades of the nineteenth century, the vestiges of this narrative position can still be detected. However, the focus and readership of material concerning Wales and the Welsh had shifted significantly – from outsiders lapping up tales of strange and somewhat exotic customs and places, to Welsh readers keen to understand how the world around them was changing. While Beale's novels, with their focus on women's domestic and romantic lives in rural settings, were popular in their time, they would have appealed to a select, mainly middle-class, female audience. Literacy levels during the nineteenth century increased significantly, making the demographic of readership for newspapers in particular much more inclusive.[12]

While the *Reports* criticised Welsh-language culture as a whole, the effect they had on perceptions of Welsh women was particularly damaging because they depicted them as promiscuous and morally lax. In a section entitled 'Morals in Brecknockshire', David Griffiths, a 'working-man at Builth', stresses that young women are 'unsteady', and that 'nothing is thought of having a bastard, and, when in the family-way, they walk as publicly as a married woman'.[13] In 'Morals in Radnorshire', a local magistrate reports that 'Unchastity in the women is, I am sorry to say, a great stain upon our people'.[14]Although it was not just women who were accused, the taint of moral permissiveness was damning for women in towns, but especially for those in close-knit rural areas. Ultimately, the *Reports* haunt many later Welsh texts, not least those by women. The language used in gossip columns, such as 'Aunt Maria's Diary of the Doings Round the Towns', discussed below, continues to voice anxieties about the appropriateness of female behaviour in a swiftly changing, increasingly urbanised world.

Wales in sketches and travel writing

If we pause briefly to explore some nineteenth-century sketches and travel writing, it is possible to chart specific strategies and methods commonly deployed in depictions of Wales and Welsh life which foreground the authority of the participant-observer narrator. Catherine Sinclair's *Hill and Valley; or, Hours in England and Wales* (1838) is especially valuable as an example of how class was constructed in outsider accounts of rural areas. Sinclair (1800–1864) is significant as a self-styled 'home tour' writer who travelled extensively around Britain, including several tours of her native Scotland. Her Scottish and Welsh travel narratives were originally published in Edinburgh, suggesting that they were aimed at a Scottish audience, but later editions of her Welsh travels were published in London. She revelled in traversing the most remote and underdocumented areas of the British Isles, and was able to comment from both an insider and outsider perspective – as British, but decidedly not Welsh. Although extremely popular in her lifetime, Sinclair's travel writing has been neglected, with recent attention focused mainly on her children's novel, *Holiday House: A Series of Tales* (1839).

For the modern reader of *Hill and Valley*, it is striking that it takes Sinclair nearly a fifth of the lengthy narrative to reach Wales from Scotland, despite making use of newly established railways. When she finally reaches North Wales, however, it seems worth the arduous journey:

> Everyone continues partial to the first new country in which he [sic] has performed a tour; but certainly for richness of scenery, natural grandeur, and real antiquity, I have seen no place which can excel Wales, where we had already enjoyed some pleasant excursions, and were now preparing to climb up real undeniable mountains, to see the inhabitants living on Welsh mutton and Welsh rabbits, dressing in Welsh flannel and Welsh wigs, and listening to Welsh harpers, the older the better.[15]

While the key imperialistic tropes commonly found in travel writing that Mary Louise Pratt has identified in *Imperial Eyes* are clearly at work in this description, Sinclair's emphasis on the almost overwhelming vibrancy of the landscape she surveys and on the authenticity of the history, traditions and customs, make the tone comic and somewhat mocking.[16] The repetition of 'Welsh' certainly suggests that Sinclair is making fun of this search for 'authentic' culture.

Significantly, descriptions which focus on domestic details, such as women's clothes, diet and housing seem to concentrate on the lower classes in rural areas, suggesting that authenticity is most manifest among these people. Sinclair writes that '[a]ll women among the lower orders in Wales wear men's hats over muslin caps, and a long blue cloth cloak, which gives them, at some distance, the air of ladies a moment before dismount[ing] from horseback'.[17] She also notes that the diet the 'common-people indulge very largely' in, of 'ale, butter toast, and bacon', makes them 'grow enormously fat'.[18] During a rain shower, Sinclair takes refuge in a cottage where she is addressed in Welsh. Although she 'return[s] thanks in English', she makes the point that 'there is a universal language of courtesy which can never be misunderstood when kindness is intended on both sides', suggesting the similarities between Welsh and English-speaking cultures.[19] However, she returns to the position of the knowledgeable, educated observer as she examines the room and begins to underline the class differences apparent in the scene. Surveying the 'clean and comfortable room', replete with 'dog, cat, poultry, and pigs, exhibiting a great appearance of cheerfulness and plenty', she 'observe[s] a broad flat loaf of brown bread, like a tea tray, suspended from the roof, with a carving-knife dangling beside it, wreaths of onions, and graceful draperies of herrings'.[20] While an earlier panoramic scene in Bangor is compared to landscape paintings by Thomson and Turner, this domestic interior is 'quite a study for Ostade or Teniers' – Dutch artists who both were known for rustic paintings of the intimacies of rural peasant life.[21] Sinclair's closely observed account of rural life, then, is underpinned by the desire to turn the people and landscape into a palatable, aestheticised and, therefore, comprehensible product to be consumed by her readership.

In contrast to Sinclair's wit and humour, Amy Lane's somewhat self-important *Sketches of Wales and the Welsh* (1847) explores the relationship between England and Wales, as well as rich and poor, in some detail. Apart from biographical snippets which indicate Lane's Welsh heritage, as well as detailed knowledge of Welsh customs embedded within the text, nothing is known about Lane's life. The volume appears to have only had one modest print run but includes 'Her Most Gracious Majesty Adelaide, the Queen Dowager' and Lady Charlotte Guest as subscribers.[22]

'Remarks', a sketch which concerns the general manners, habits and customs of the Welsh, provides another ideologically inflected depiction of rural life. Lane writes:

> Among the popular literature of the present day, that which describes the scenery of Scotland and Ireland, with the manners and customs of the interesting inhabitants, ha[s] been so ably written, that I have regretted that a people so peculiar in their habits and opinions as are the Welsh, – having resisted any amalgamation with the English for so many centuries, viewing them as their conquerors, and affecting to despise their superior civilization, – should have so long lacked a narrator of their remaining peculiarities.[23]

This reiterates a similar concern found in *Hill and Valley*, when Sinclair notes that 'Travellers may go farther and fare worse than in Wales, so it is surprising that while many libraries boast of possessing "England and the English", or "Germany and the Germans", no author has yet favoured the world with "Wales and the Welsh."'[24] This suggests that by the time of Lane's *Sketches of Wales and the Welsh*, published nearly a decade after the first edition of Sinclair's text, manners, customs and ways of life in Wales were still assumed to be underdocumented. The fact that such 'sketches of Wales and the Welsh' were still regularly appearing in print throughout the nineteenth century suggests a reading public still hungry for this type of writing. Having discussed a substantial amount of detail, ranging from child-rearing to the discipline of servants, Lane continues: 'It will be understood that these observations regard the country people; the Welsh gentry are, as other gentry, adopting habits of civilization.'[25] Lane distances herself somewhat from the position of competent narrator, remarking: 'I could wish to draw the attention of some able writer to this subject before these ancient habits are obliterated.'[26] Yet, at the same time, she seems to strive for a kind of narrative mastery over details pertaining to the poor – the use of the term 'civilisation' suggests that the lower classes are being associated with savagery.

Wales and the Welsh in the press

Close analysis of the examples given in these albeit selective examples from the 1830s and 1840s can provide us with a much clearer understanding of the way in which Wales has been represented and imagined. More importantly, they also enable us to begin tracing links between the ways in which rural life is constructed in these texts. The extracts from newspapers discussed in the second half of this chapter are, I would argue, directly influenced by the tone and style of writers such as Beale, Sinclair and Lane. In an 1869 piece written for the regular column 'Tales and Sketches of Wales', in the *Pembrokeshire Herald*, for example, we find this kind of description:

> Amongst the wilds of the Welsh mountains many an incident of romantic interest is buried, and only to be exhumed either by the wanderer who, pedlar fashion, gathers up village gossip, or by the sage antiquary. [27]

In the opening of *The Vale of the Towey*, Beale describes at length the mountain views which are 'sublimely grand and fitted to elevate the mind to high and noble thoughts'.[28] She then changes her focus to what is effectively gossip, describing how a 'little incident was narrated to me connected with these Beacons which it may not be out of place to introduce here'.[29] The tale she relates concerns a young woman who is being wooed by two men. Both suitors fall to their deaths on the mountainside while trying to win the young woman's affections. In the *Herald* piece, which is even more dramatic, the author tells the story of another young woman, Ellen, who gets her revenge on the man who killed her brother. Ellen takes part in an archery competition, disguised as a man, and shoots her brother's murderer (dead) but gets away with it. The article continues:

> Forthwith, she cast away all adornments, and robed herself in masculine attire, as men's clothes are snobbishly called, and found herself, after a little experiment or two, transferred into a very passable Welsh-man, and quite stalwart enough to keep brawlers at a distance, whether countrymen or Normans.[30]

This particular example is a little out of the ordinary in that it crosses many types of boundaries, including notions of proper dress and the role of women, as well as perhaps echoing the subversive Rebecca Rioters who donned women's clothing to disguise themselves during assaults on turnpikes. Yet it gives some indication of the complex generic interplays that take place in these kinds of regular columns and articles. In many ways, these texts, which describe themselves as 'tales and sketches' of authentic Welsh life are, in fact, made of up hearsay, local folklore and gossip.

In another example, from a series entitled 'Sketches of Welsh Life', taken from the *Llangollen Advertiser* of 1894, the author is at great pains to underline the extent to which the village of Llandawel has been untouched by modernity.

> The village of Llandawel lies hidden among the hills of North Wales. It is not disturbed by any rush of commercial life ... Quietly and calmly its period of existence passes by. Llandawel retains all its rural charms, despite the squire's many efforts to introduce un-needed changes under the name of 'modern reforms.' ... The simplicity of [the villagers'] country homes characterises their lives too. Day by day passes by with scarce an incident demanding notice. No doubt there are little tragedies and comedies enacted within these humble cottages, but somehow *they are hidden from the public gaze and are not seen except by those who act them.* [31]

The way the village is described has strong links with the generic features of 'home tour' writing, a genre which has been explored in fascinating detail by Zoë Kinsley in *Women Writing the Home Tour* (2008). Resonating strongly with the 'tales and sketches' found in newspapers, the tropes Kinsley identifies in this kind of writing include the recurrence of paradisiacal imagery in descriptions of landscape and lifestyles.[32] In the *Llangollen Advertiser* example, paradisiacal may be a stretch too far, but the village is described as somewhere almost perfect, untouched by time or modern ways of living. Of course, in this particular case the participant-observer narrator does not have an omniscient gaze, suggesting that there has been a slight shift away from earlier models of narrative such as in Lane and Sinclair.

In a series entitled 'Sketches from the Country' in the *Aberystwyth Observer*, another example emphasises the innocence and purity of rural inhabitants. Country folk are as untouched as the buildings and landscapes of those in Llandawel:

> I propose now and then to send you some notes and sketches from the country. Country life and habits are quite different in many respects from those of a town, therefore perhaps it will interest many of your town readers to have a glimpse now and then of country life among the mountains and valleys of Wales. All notes will be the fruits of observation ... There are few places where human nature can be better studied than in the country for there you see the circle of the individual's life thoroughly ... In the town far more people are seen, but far fewer known. The country folk are ignorant of what are termed the laws of modern decorum. They have never read any publications on etiquette, and have never mixed in society, such as is meant by the word at the present time. Nature has been their own only educator, and I am glad to testify that many of them have been true to her. [33]

Reading 'Sketches from the Country', we can perhaps detect traces of the noble savage in the descriptions of the Welsh; there is certainly a focus on the 'natural', tabula rasa state of the people observed, who have not been tainted, as it were, by the rules and conventions of polite society. The narrative voice is once again the authoritative participant-observer narrator who makes a direct reference to 'notes' and 'observation', suggesting the language and framework of the ethnographer or anthropologist, although the use of the word 'glimpse' once again suggests a partial view.

A little earlier, in 1887, the *Cardiff Times* features a particularly perceptive regular column, entitled 'Rural Life', which focuses on the changes made to farming by modernisation and increased industrialisation.

> Every day something new is introduced into farming, and yet the old things [i.e. traditional farming equipment] are not driven out ... All the old things remain on the farm, but the village is driven out – the village that used to come as one man to the reaping. Machinery has not altered the earth, but it has altered the condition of men's lives, and as work decreases, so men decrease. Some go to the cities, some emigrate; the young men drift away, and there is none of that home life that there used to be.[34]

The use of machinery, rather than older techniques which involved the whole community, has had an increasingly negative impact on social cohesion in rural communities. Rural areas are, of course, more likely to be fractured by these changes, and this is reflected in the increased migration towards urban centres.

A few years later in the *South Wales Star*, in 1891, another article under the heading of 'Rural Life' looks in a little more detail at the impact of changes to local demographics and compares Wales' situation with that of the depopulation of the home counties, commenting on the 'sad – almost hopeless – condition of the agricultural labourer':

> It is a fact that cannot be denied that our rural population is decreasing year by year. Especially is this the case in Wales. The last census shows us a decrease in every agricultural county in Wales, and a tremendous increase in the population of our towns. The depopulation of the country districts is a great danger – indeed, it is about the greatest danger which England will have to face.[35]

The article goes on to examine why rural communities are moving towards urban centres, suggesting a number of valid reasons which underline issues not just in Wales but across Europe:

> Why is it that our rural population migrate to the towns? It is because the people have learned that vigorous health and strong arms are better valued in the towns. Education has given them ideas which cannot be attained in the country, and the multiplicity of railways tempts them to seek their fortune from home. Life in our villages is practically no life at all.[36]

This last example cites compelling reasons for losses to rural communities, not least through the advent of an accessible and affordable rail network, coupled with increased educational opportunities. While education in late nineteenth-century Wales was relatively basic and varied considerably between boys and girls, the 1889 Education Act, which demanded English-language schooling, further fuelled the exodus from Welsh-speaking rural areas. In the *South Wales Star* example, the loss of an older way of life, as described by Zagarell, is very apparent, and may also encompass language loss. Here, unlike the previous example from the *Cardiff Times*, there is no 'I' of the participant-observer narrator to intervene or explain – it is the role of everyone, the communal 'we', to understand how and why life has changed.

From rural to urban: life in Welsh towns

The authoritative voice of the participant-observer narrator can still be traced in writing which is focused fully on the town. In a particularly venomous yet witty regular column, which concentrates mainly on the urban areas around Barry in south Wales, a superficially light-hearted impression of Welsh life is depicted in comparison to the sorrow and loss evoked by 'Rural Life' or 'Sketches from the Country'. Written under a female pseudonym and entitled 'Aunt Maria's Diary of the Doings Round the Towns', the column reports scandal, gossip and local developments. Barry had become, by the late nineteenth century, a hub of industrial life. With its excellent transport links and expanding population, the town was rapidly changing. Then part of Glamorganshire, Barry was itself a town 'blasted out of ... the last shuddering explosion of British industrialisation' with the creation of Barry Docks, which opened in 1899.[37] The former villages surrounding Barry Docks, including Barry itself, Merthyr Dyfan and Cadoxton, have histories which can be traced back to the medieval period. With the establishment of the docks came a massive shift in the way people lived and worked, moving from agricultural to industrial occupations. The tattling, spiteful Aunt Maria is, in many ways, foregrounding the same concerns with the loss of the old ways of life repeated in many of the other examples in Welsh newspapers of the period by continually commenting on modern developments, including the way people interact, socialise, travel, dress and work.

The column is particularly illuminating for tracking the changing face of leisure and transport in newly urbanised areas. One issue the town faced was the problem of electrifying its tramway, itself a marker of how much travel had changed in a short space of time. Aunt Maria notes: 'It is a pity that the Barry Company cannot work their tramway by electricity, all because another party object. It will now have to be worked either by steam or horse power.'[38] By this point, steam and horsepower were beginning to seem outmoded in contrast to the new, more efficient, and cleaner form of energy offered by electricity. The tramway development was part of a wider project to 'render [Barry Island] a most attractive seaside resort' for holiday visitors.[39] 'Aunt Maria's Diary' is in fact a continuation of another column, entitled 'Round the Towns by "Gadabout"', published in the same newspaper. The fascination with developments in transport technology can also be traced in the original 'Gadabout' column. In an example from just before the handover to Aunt Maria, Gadabout notes that 'Mr William Saunders, of Cadoxton, has applied for a patent for his improved method and means of simultaneously locking and unlocking railway carriage doors throughout a train.'[40] That this kind of detail is published alongside gossip and tittle-tattle gives us some indication of the changing preoccupations of modern life.

Yet what is especially significant is the huge stress laid on appropriate behaviour and appearances, especially for women, which seems to return full circle to the moral criticisms found in the *Blue Books*. Aunt Maria reports, during a walk through the former village of Cadoxton:

> I sometimes go for a walk on Cadoxton Common, and in spite of all the Commoners, say I maintain that I have a right to do what I like there. The dear little misses in the building close by also think the same, and I noticed last week two of them were enjoying the sunshine with a male teacher between them. How they were walking I could scarcely see, but I heard it suggested that there was a link of love. But is not there an old saying that 'two is company three is none?'[41]

The partially obscured vision of the participant-observer narrator is once again at play, filling in the blanks with rumour and hearsay. In her very first instalment, Aunt Maria had already set her sights on women in the South Wales industrial areas, commenting that: 'Any little item of news which you have I shall be pleased to deal with, and now my dear little Misses just look out.'[42] The power of this column over the inhabitants of the area becomes very clear in an extract from later that same year where Aunt Maria, in her assumed position as moral guardian of the community, threatens to expose a woman who has overstepped acceptable moral codes: 'There is a certain party in the particular neighbourhood [of Barry Dock] who is very fond of enticing respectable young men to stay there at night time, and if they do not drop enticing young men I shall have to publish names.'[43] There is also a sense that the shift from rural to urban living has actually made it easier to survey the behaviour of a town's population, and that the press is taking on a role that would have been more readily associated with the chapel. Aunt Maria notes: 'It is a well-known saying that a city on a hill cannot be hidden. Such is the case with Penarth. It is so elevated that all the doings of the inhabitants are known.'[44] Aunt Maria seems to be directly contradicting the commentary of the *Aberystwyth Observer* here, emphasising that people in urban areas are, in fact, known. The column acts as a kind of narrative of community itself, ensuring that social cohesion is retained, while still underlining the compressed and now highly visible nature of social relations.

Conclusions: *Welsh Newspapers Online* in the future

This chapter has attempted to open up discussions of the rural–urban shift in the nineteenth century in Wales. Studying newspaper columns in relation to connections with literary genres may seem, at first sight, an unusual approach, but the episodic nature of many of the columns discussed, alongside titles which suggest some kind of shared, ethnographic genealogy, allows for a meaningful exploration of generic similarities. Zagarell's concept of narrative of community would seem all the more translatable to a non-literary text in this context. The titles of many of the articles and regular columns now digitally available suggest a recurring preoccupation with defining Wales and Welsh culture in a time of immense changes – not to outsiders but to a home audience. The role of the participant-observer narrator, a key figure in Zagerell's theory, has only been lightly sketched out in the examples discussed, yet this authoritative narrative voice, which is both inside and outside, seems especially fitting considering that the material discussed is in the English language. In the nineteenth century, Welsh still had a large Welsh-speaking population, and this narrative position may well be a means of bridging the gap between the two aspects of the culture.

While an overarching understanding of the rural–urban shift can only be glimpsed at this stage, it is significant that articles which focus on the rural exodus are, for the most part, centred around South Wales, while pieces which depict idyllic village life tend to be located in North or West Wales.

It is to be hoped that *Welsh Newspapers Online* will, in future, form the basis for more comprehensive redefinitions and rereadings of our understanding of Welsh urban and rural culture from the inside. For too long our understanding has been dominated by accounts of Wales as wild or purely picturesque. *Welsh Newspapers Online* offers the opportunity to construct a far more inclusive and accurate understanding of the impact of urbanisation and industrialisation on Welsh life – not just for the literary scholar but for the historian, the sociologist and modern ethnographer. Ultimately, it promises to open up a much more nuanced dialogue between these long forgotten voices and those of the outsider perspectives which have dominated understandings of the social and cultural complexities of Welsh life in the nineteenth century.

Notes

1 See http://welshnewspapers.llgc.org.uk/en/home. All references to newspaper articles and columns in the chapter are taken from this resource.
2 J. J. Schensul and M. D. Lecompte, *Designing and Conducting Ethnographic Research* (Walnut Creek, California: AltaMira, 1999), p. 1.
3 Schensul and Lecompte, *Designing and Conducting Ethnographic Research*, p. 2.
4 S. A. Zagarell, 'Narrative of Community: The Identification of a Genre', *Signs*, 13.3 (Spring, 1988), pp. 498–527, on p. 520.
5 See, for example, S. M. Saunders, 'The Courtship of Edward and Nancy', *Young Wales*, 1897, pp. 28–32.
6 William Williams, quoted in J. Aaron, 'Introduction: Chartism, Nationalism and Language Politics', in J. Aaron and U. Masson (eds), *The Very Salt of Life* (Dinas Powys: Honno, 2007), pp. 3–14, on p. 6.
7 Aaron, 'Introduction', p. 6.
8 Aaron, 'Introduction', p. 6.
9 J. Williams, Ysgafell, 'Artegall, or Remarks on the *Reports of the Commissioners of Inquiry into the State of Education in Wales*', in Aaron and Masson, *The Very Salt of Life*, p. 18.
10 Aaron, 'Introduction' p. 3.
11 A. Beale, *The Vale of the Towey; or, Sketches in South Wales* (London: Longman, Brown, Green & Longman, 1844), p. vii.
12 Across England and Wales, literacy rates were around 60 per cent male and 40 per cent in females. By 1891 this had risen to 94 and 93 per cent respectively. See S. Eliot,

'From Few and Expensive to Many and Cheap: The British Book Market 1800–1890', in S. Eliot and J. Rose (eds), *A Companion to the History of the Book* (Chicester: Wiley-Blackwell, 2009), pp. 291–302, on p. 293.

13 *Reports of the Commissioners of Inquiry into the State of Education in Wales, Part II: Report on the Counties of Brecknock, Cardigan, Radnor, and Monmouth* (London: HMSO, 1847), p. 58

14 *Reports of the Commissioners*, p. 60.

15 C. Sinclair, *Hill and Valley; or, Hours in England and Wales* (New York: Robert Carter, 1838), p. 80.

16 Pratt suggests three strategies at work in the rhetoric of travel writing 'which create qualitative and quantitative value for the explorer's achievement'. She argues that the landscape is aestheticised, as in a painting. Secondly, the landscape is described through a high level of adjectival modifiers to create an over-abundance of description. Finally, the landscape is perceived in terms of a power relationship between the viewer and the landscape being viewed in which Pratt uses the term 'master-of-all-I-survey'. See M. Pratt, *Imperial Eyes: Travel Writing and Transculturation* (London: Routledge, 1992), p. 204–5.

17 Sinclair, *Hill and Valley*, p. 115.

18 Sinclair, *Hill and Valley*, p. 96.

19 Sinclair, *Hill and Valley*, p. 118.

20 Sinclair, *Hill and Valley*, p. 118.

21 Sinclair, *Hill and Valley*, p. 118.

22 See A. Lane, 'Subscriber's Names', in *Sketches of Wales and the Welsh* (London: Hamilton & Adams, 1847), v–ix.

23 Lane, *Sketches of Wales*, p. 71.

24 Sinclair, *Hill and Valley*, p. 2.

25 Lane, *Sketches of Wales*, p. 74.

26 Lane, *Sketches of Wales*, p. 71.

27 'Tales and Sketches of Wales: A Welsh Heroine', *Pembrokeshire Herald*, 10 December 1869, p. 3.

28 Beale, *The Vale of the Towey*, p. 4

29 Beale, *The Vale of the Towey*, p. 5.

30 'Tales and Sketches of Wales: A Welsh Heroine', *Pembrokeshire Herald*, 10 December 1869, p. 3.

31 'Sketches of Welsh Life: God's Poor', *Llangollen Advertiser*, 28 December 1894, p. 8. Emphasis added.

32 See Z. Kinsley, *Women Writing the Home Tour, 1862–1812* (Aldershot: Ashgate, 2008), p. 155.

33 'Sketches from the Country', *Aberystwyth Observer*, 9 February 1889, p. 5.

34 'Rural Life', *Cardiff Times*, 20 August 1887, p. 1.

35 'Rural Life', *South Wales Star: Barry, Cadoxton and Penarth Edition*, 28 September 1891, p. 4. See Barry Sloan's chapter below for a discussion of reactions to rural depopulation in England.

36 'Rural Life', *South Wales Star: Barry, Cadoxton and Penarth Edition*, 28 September 1891, p. 4.

37 D. Smith, 'Barry: A Town out of Time', *Morgannwg*, 29 (1985), 80–85, on p. 80.

38 'Aunt Maria's Diary of the Doings Round the Towns', *South Wales Star*, 24 March 1893, p. 8.

39 'Electric Tramway to Barry Island', *Evening Express*, 14 October 1892, p. 3.

40 'Round the Towns [by Mr Gadabout]', *South Wales Star*, 10 February 1893, p. 8.

41 'Aunt Maria's Diary', *South Wales Star*, 7 April 1893, p. 8.

42 'Aunt Maria's Diary', *South Wales Star*, 24 March 1893, p. 8.

43 'Aunt Maria's Diary', *South Wales Star*, 28 July 1893, p. 8.

44 'Aunt Maria's Diary', *South Wales Star*, 24 March 1893, p. 8. Penarth is a town adjacent to Barry which had its own thriving docks by the end of the nineteenth century.

8 The early popular press and its common readers in nineteenth-century *fin-de-siècle* Prague[1]

Jakub Machek

Introduction

This chapter focuses on the emerging Czech popular press in the period of rapid urbanisation and population movement at the turn of the twentieth century, and on the experience of its readers, who found themselves caught between their traditional, rural mindset and the modernity of the city. The newcomers to urban areas needed a replacement for their oral traditions of sharing news and entertainment and were searching for a different cultural identity. The sensational illustrated press became not only a guide to life in the new environment but helped readers to develop a shared sense of urban selfhood.[2] The discussion that follows examines the specific way the Czech sensational press blended traditional folk culture with modern urban popular culture to attract its new audience. The key examples include *Illustrirtes Prager Extrablatt* (1879–1882), which was influenced by early print culture, such as murder ballads and popular fiction; and *Pražský Illustrovaný Kurýr* (*Prague Illustrated Courier*) (1893–1918) which, unlike other contemporary Central European sensational press publications, positioned itself between the rural and the metropolitan, the traditional and the modern. The latter will be discussed through analysis of its content as well as its illustrations, and by undertaking a comparison with other Central European press publications.

Although educated Czechs welcomed the arrival of technological innovation in Prague in the late nineteenth century, the nationalist and mostly conservative elite was wary of foreign intellectual and cultural influences, and particularly hostile to urban popular culture represented by the sensational press. This is reflected in the words of the editor of the democratic weekly, *Pochodeň* (*Flambeau*), who characterised the *Courier* as a 'paper that … can satisfy only perverted people, who are aroused by horrible daubs depicting various murders and spectacles in gaudy manners and whose thirst for sensation could only be satiated this way'.[3]

According to Peter Fritsche, the crisis of cultural authority precipitated by modernity resulted in the liberal bourgeoisie losing its dominance over accepted moral values, and over ideas on the future of society.[4] Their reaction to this loss of cultural authority was to rail – like the editor of *Pochodeň* – against the predominantly urban mass culture, which, instead of encouraging the wider population to subscribe to approved bourgeois ideals, offered them an unauthorised sensational stream of information, ideas and interpretations with no apparent hierarchy of values.[5] Crucially, events that were considered important by elite culture and the serious press were replaced by sensationalism. Following earlier examples from abroad, popular newspapers headlined crime, affairs and gossip, while the political or economic events valued by the serious press were relegated to inside pages and submerged among short telegraph messages. Political articles and speeches were mostly rejected. The sensational press also ceased to promote self-improvement and focused on entertainment and popular culture rather than 'high art'.

Because of its increasing importance in this critical period of change, the emerging popular press can fruitfully be analysed both for its social influence and as a marker of modern Czech urban experience. Its significance is reinforced further because of the rarity of sources such as diaries and memoirs referring directly to the life of lower class urban migrants – a situation which differs from the United Kingdom, as Michelle Deininger and Christopher Ferguson show in their chapters in this volume. Even official documents of the period often omitted discussion of lower-class life, whereas popular culture, although produced by the elites, addressed ordinary people and offered them a set of meanings relevant to their lives. This chapter therefore explores further the origin of the Czech popular press, how it became representative of the masses and why it was so attractive to the urban newcomers.

Central European urbanisation in the nineteenth century and the transformation of society

Martin Conboy has argued that the development of printed materials played a crucial part in the transition from pre-capitalist folk culture to modern popular culture.[6] Furthermore, the commercial imperative of print culture encouraged entrepreneurial initiatives to win lower-class audiences by appealing to widely held traditional beliefs and opinions within an environment increasingly shaped by key features of urban life: materialism, mechanisation, new forms of work, social mobility and greater freedom and scope for entertainment. The success of popular culture and its capacity to speak to ordinary people was thus bound up with its ability to incorporate elements of tradition into the new cultural environment, and the press was particularly effective in achieving this. As people moved from the countryside to the city, they were forced to acquire new behavioural patterns, to adapt to different forms of social organisation and to confront unfamiliar ways of thinking and a new range of experiences. In these circumstances, the cultural influence of the cities increased while that of the provinces and rural areas declined.[7]

Prague's rapid urban population growth mirrored that of other major European cities in the late nineteenth and early twentieth centuries. In the 1840s, urban dwellers comprised only one fifth of the society of the Czech lands; in 1880 this reached one third and in 1910 almost 50 per cent.[8] In the most intensive phase, the urban population doubled between 1869 and 1930.[9] The metropolitan area of Prague (which, until 1918, was split into several municipalities) saw a record population rise of 25.7 per cent during the 1890s.[10] In 1900, 60 per cent of the Prague metropolitan population had been born outside the area, but 95 per cent came from Bohemia and only 2 per cent from Moravia and Silesia. Hence, Prague functioned as a migration destination for its region only because the German-speaking population of Bohemia tended to move increasingly to Vienna.[11] The most rapid growth was to be observed in the suburbs, where the majority of incomers settled in newly constructed and mostly small flats.[12] These reflected the living standards not only of newcomers but of the population as a whole – three-quarters of Prague households had no servants. Prague had a relatively high number of state and land officials but also a large percentage of industrial workers, petty artisans, subaltern clerks and unskilled staff.[13] On their arrival in the city, many of the latter shared one rented room with the whole family and possibly also with apprentices.[14] The most skilled, such as iron workers, rollers, printers and typesetters, usually occupied a whole flat, including a kitchen and one room.[15] These, then, were the people whom the popular press sought as an audience; and as they increasingly benefited from rising standards of education, better economic prospects and new possibilities for political involvement, they soon became targets for existing as well as newly formed political parties who used the new mass media as an ideal platform to capture support among the expanding electorate. As had happened earlier elsewhere, the cultural dominance of the upper class was gradually eroded with the increase of commercially produced and distributed cheap books, newspapers and magazines which had to be circulated on a mass scale to guarantee profit. Publishers therefore adapted the content, form and political stance of their productions to suit ordinary people, who had minimal experience of elite culture. Thus, print culture itself ceased to belong exclusively to the elites and gradually became accessible to a broader audience.

The cheap sensational press

The growth of the sensational press, especially in its illustrated variants, reflects this shift from a political press designed for specific educated readers to urban newspapers providing the general public with information and entertainment. In the 1830s in New York, *The Sun* had been launched as the first penny paper and its immediate success encouraged other publishers to follow its example. In Central Europe, Vienna was a pioneer in developing a cheap illustrated paper in the 1870s with *Illustrirtes Wiener Extrablatt*, and this served as a model for the Czech publishers to launch their own illustrated newspaper. (The popularity and commercial rewards of the penny press are reflected in the fact that, after the turn of the century, this type of publication was even launched in the Galician local metropolis, Kraków.)

The penny press covered its production costs by advertising: in the *Prague Illustrated Courier*, the most common advertisements were for books and magazines, food and drink, clothes and fabrics, and medical services. Illustrations became the main selling feature of the sensational press, as they were intelligible to less literate readers and also appealed to those from the lower strata of the population, who had never seen anything like them. The engravings themselves followed the conventions and iconography of elite culture but in a less elaborated, simplified form.[16] The most frequent title illustrations depicted various crimes, police actions, criminals and their victims. These account for about one fifth of all the illustrations. Another fifth can be described as representations of miscellaneous curiosities and another fifth show diverse disasters and accidents. Other popular subjects include homicides and suicides which constitute about 15 per cent of the illustrations, and more serious pictures of festivities, processions and parliamentary sessions. Portraits, however, formed only about 8 per cent of all cover illustrations.[17]

In Prague, the first successful illustrated daily went on sale in 1893 under the name of *Pražský Illustrovaný Kurýr* (*Prague Illustrated Courier*). By this stage Prague's economic development had reached the point at which the necessary conditions to sustain a cheap press – a critical mass of urban dwellers, with enough purchasing power and sufficient leisure time to read newspapers – had been achieved. This situation contrasts with the circumstances that had led to the collapse of *The Courier*'s earlier unsuccessful antecedents. Between 1874 and 1879, for example, the Czech National Conservative Party published a non-illustrated but popular and sensational daily, *Brousek* (*Whetstone*). Although it had a circulation twice as high as that of the existing serious press, like the publication of its rival party *Obrana* (*Defence*), it had to be subsidised by its publisher. A similar situation arose later when a private publisher tried to break into the market. These cases illustrate the indispensable importance of the right social and economic conditions for the cheap press to become commercially successful.

Regular news for almanac readers

The first illustrated Prague-based newspaper was the *Illustrirtes Prager Extrablatt*, published by J. B. Brandeis between 1879 and 1882. Initially published in German, the newspaper was most likely aimed at the German and Czech middle- and upper-class residents of the city, who were accustomed to reading in that language (the publication also included advertisements for Czech theatre performances).[18] The majority of cover illustrations depicted significant residents of Prague or members of the Austrian emperor's court. However, in January 1881, a markedly more sensational Czech supplement was added, most likely aimed at the lower, predominantly Czech-speaking, classes. This Czech supplement was rather unusual and entirely atypical for a newspaper of the time.

While it was a newspaper in form it was not so in its content, which was more closely related to productions of early print culture, such as chap books and almanacs, or prints of murder ballads than to the composition of a modern urban newspaper. It followed the formal pattern of the *Illustrirtes Wiener Extrablatt*, which inspired the Czech publisher not only by its concept and name but also by its graphic layout. This is most clearly visible in the design of its cover pages, where the main article accompanied by a large illustration was particularly controversial, given that in Austria selling newspapers by calling out the headlines on the street was formally illegal. The cover stories were often fantastic and thrilling tales disguised as regular news with headlines such as '*Heartbreaking aerial ride*' (a story about a horse drawn carriage ride through the air), '*Fight in the air*' (a story about a fight between two winged men), or '*Crucified by madmen*', referring to a story about a host who was nearly killed by his guests who were infected with rabies. The headline stories started with deliberately vague information about dates and times, and featured protagonists with names of equally uncertain geographical origin (e.g. Broven, Jar, Taner, Taller, Tegler, Seran, Velvik), which were typical features of popular fiction.

Sometimes, a story would begin by introducing a real time and place, as in the article '*Dreadful Night*', which carries the subtitle: '(*The Latest Event in the Church of Skeletons in Sedlec/Kutná Hora*).[19] It then makes a more vague reference to 'three students well known in their county' (although the county is not named) who went on holiday and spent a dreadful night in the ossuary in Kutná Hora.[20] Finally the article ends on even more uncertain terms, pushing the story back into the indefinite, long-ago past: 'That well-meaning sacristan had, to this day no idea what had really happened in the church and if a good friend of our paper Mr. Kaftan, now living in Vienna, had not told us the story, we would have never found out.'[21]

Editors also often compromised the previously alleged novelty and originality of their news items, when, at their conclusion, they would state a source for it (e.g. 'a certain American newspaper' in the case of an article that began as a story about a well-known inhabitant of 'our' town); or they might even call into question the truthfulness of the entire story.[22] Nevertheless these texts were supposed to be taken as real news, and were published without attribution, as was customary for news articles of the period. Fictional contributions, on the other hand, had designated authors whose names were found inside each issue of the *Prager Extrablatt*.

Even the cover illustrations of the Prague paper were different from those of the *Wiener Extrablatt* and other illustrated newspapers of the period. Although both were printed using engraving technique (used for copying line drawing and photography), those in the *Prager Extrablatt* seemed to imitate the style of the less sophisticated woodcut illustrations to be found in almanacs and chapbooks. The specific character of the cover illustrations can be seen in the following example (8.1) of the cover page of the *Illustrirtes Prager Extrablatt* from 7th of July 1881 (the headline for the story is: 'Cannibals!').

Editors also employed seemingly archaic language reminiscent of traditional chapbooks that had been reprinted without changes for centuries. This is evidence of their efforts to address the cultural habits and rural origins of their lower-class readers, whom they supposed to be more accustomed to the older forms of printed material familiar in the countryside where they had previously lived, and not yet ready to embrace the format of the modern sensational newspapers. This conservatism of the Prague-based readership has been observed by Martin Sekera, who also highlights the rejection of a new method of reproduction – zincography – introduced in the popular magazine *Květy* (*Flowers*) in the 1860s.[23]

Číslo 128. Ročník III.

Přiloha k časopisu

V Praze 7. července 1881.

Extrablatt.

Jednotlivá čísla 3 kr.

Lidožrouti!

Figure 8.1 Cover page of *Illustrirtes Prager Extrablatt*, 7 July 1881. Author's collection.

Thus, the publisher of *Illustrirtes Prager Extrablatt* was, on the one hand, inspired by the modern sensational illustrated press and eager to imitate its techniques, but on the other hand, he understood the need to temper these innovations to the needs of a readership who were still insufficiently assimilated into their new environment to comprehend and feel at ease in urban popular culture. He assumed the population of Prague to be unprepared to read only about everyday events from around the world and therefore offered them a compromised blend of traditional folk and modern urban culture. This blend included fantastic stories instead of fresh news, a traditional format of graphic representation instead of a 'realistic' depiction of events, and an old-fashioned form of written language instead of a written variant of the language of contemporary everyday speech. Yet although the circulation of *Extrablatt* was considerable (it came second in Prague and accounted for two thirds of all newspaper sales), this does not appear to have been enough to make the business profitable.[24] The publisher of *Extrablatt* tried to promote the newspaper by promising attractive and tempting serial fiction such as a translation of Émile Zola's novel *Nana*, or a novel about the arsonist who destroyed the National Theatre only a few days after the fire took place. Often, however, these promises were not kept. Other promotional attempts included inviting the reportedly famous mesmerist, Hansen, to present a private performance 'for supporters and friends of the newspaper'.[25] Compared to the later publication, *The Courier*, the *Extrablatt* included markedly less advertising, possibly because of its numerous lower-class readers who were not considered sufficiently affluent to be consumers of goods and services.

Prague citizens and the *Illustrated Courier*

Pražský Illustrovaný Kurýr (*Prague Illustrated Courier*), published between 1893–1918, can be regarded as the first successful Czech illustrated daily newspaper. It was established as a picture supplement to *Hlas národa* (*Voice of the Nation*), the official newspaper of the Staročeská strana (Czech National Conservative Party), and, in contrast to the *Prague Extrablatt*, was similar to its illustrated sensational press counterparts in Vienna or Berlin.[26] The *Courier* was originally launched in order to improve the circulation of the main paper as the publisher was suffering economic hardship, but owing to its immediate success it was produced as a separate, independent publication from the beginning of 1893 onwards. The *Courier* cannot be described as a strictly partisan publication, such as the *Voice of the Nation*, although it mostly supported the point of view of Czech nationalists who were opposed to Germans and to social-democratic policies, rather than agitating against rival Czech political parties.

Like other Central European press publications of its kind, the *Courier* was aimed at new readers from the lower classes rather than existing readers of serious newspapers. As I have shown elsewhere, its typical reader would have come from a family of small artisans, retailers, state employees, clerks or skilled workers.[27] The news reports were tailored to such people, covering, for example, topics to do with trade associations, changes affecting clerks, officials and some skilled workers. Analysis of the paper's advertisements – particularly the small ads – confirms the low social status of many of the readers, but there is also evidence of an appeal to the middle-class aspirations of better-paid skilled workers and artisans.

The key distinguishing mark of the *Courier* was its large cover illustrations, often taking up the whole page, and the popularity and appeal of these are shown in a grotesque and unexpected way through a court report from a rival daily paper, *Národní politika* (*National Policy*). Recording the case of a 19-year-old accountant who shot and wounded his beloved in a suburban forest, the report continues:

> He left for Prague, visited the music hall *Varieté* and then he messed around in cafés. He waited for the morning issue of the *Illustrated Courier*. There, he found a report of his crime but he looked in vain for an illustration of the event. Disappointed, he came to the police station to turn himself in.[28]

The paper's content included references to sensations, spectacles and important personalities, as well as serialised fiction and picture riddles. In effect, therefore, it adapted many aspects of the content of the daily bourgeois press, adding a twist of sensationalism and drama to subjects such as government policy and social commentary to engage the attention of its lower-middle and upper-working-class readers. Editors also shaped their readers' understanding of the meaning of particular news items by mythologising them. For example, rather than formally reporting events, news items were framed and categorised as tragedies, horror stories or comedies by accentuating the good and the evil. This style of reporting was used by other newspapers of the period, but the *Courier*'s editors employed it by far the most often and with particular extravagance, as the following example taken from a report of events during a parliamentary session shows:

> [MP Wolf] roared with his shrilly annoying and repugnant voice. Others guffawed in the face of Prince Lobkovic with impudent mockery. German MPs remained close together, heckled and behaved like rascals indeed.[29]

The commentaries and captions linked to title illustrations were often given tragic overtones or evoked ideas of an unfortunate shocking event, as the next example demonstrates:

> A cruel, horrible love drama. So curious and unusual that we look in vain in the rich chronicle for an example quite like it. Something dreadful is emanating from this picture, which announces that fate has chosen a strange way to plan its attack.[30]

Wit and humour, too, were used on occasion. Thus, in an article about conflict between tenants in a tenement house and a poisoned cat found in the courtyard there is a witty, colloquial, pun that can be roughly translated as 'Amina [the name of the cat] ceased to be Amina'.[31] But when comedy was used in reports on the regular clashes between groups of social and national democrats, it was commonly criticised by other newspapers for trivialising things that were important, as can be seen in this expression of anger by young leftist activists: 'At the same time we condemn the *Illustrated Courier* for cheaply sensationalising recent serious events.'[32]

The *Prague Illustrated Courier* also functioned as a platform for promoting a sense of the life shared by the residents of the city. It did this on the one hand by publishing detailed reports of mundane local news as well as sensational events. There were accounts of small injuries, street accidents, misfortunes and petty crimes; reports about associations and from entertainment venues like popular theatres and music halls; and listings of funerals, bankruptcies and voluntary contributions. On the other hand, the paper assisted in shaping the collective imagination by including news of 'serious' events not only in Prague but from the rest of world. As these were not separated out within the layout of the paper, they created a kind of counterpoint to the previously mentioned examples of urban everyday life. Nevertheless, even serious political news was not spared from being depicted as spectacle and was placed alongside reports of bloody crimes, disasters and riots. Reports from Parliament were a favourite, as the Czech and German nationalist MPs regularly launched into quarrels and brawls, which the *Courier* anticipated before the session had even started, as in the following example:

> A Czech MP seized him and threw him off the table into a row of chairs. MP Mayer rose again and ran, with his fists clenched, among the Czech MPs, followed by MPs Dr Herold from Most and nobleman Dr Kriegelstein and nobleman Stransky... MP Schreiter *appeared with a piece of wood among the German MPs, but one of the Czech deputies pounced on him and snatched the piece of wood with such violence that MP Schreiter's finger was ripped apart* [sic] *by a splinter.* [emphasis in original] Ceaseless whistling and pounding on tables.[33]

As events like these were a regular occurrence, they fitted easily into the mosaic of everyday reports of urban life.

Although the *Courier*'s success proved to be limited and temporary – it is thought to have reached its highest market share in 1898 and was in decline after 1908 – the scale of its readership confirms that during a particular period its aim and content suited its readers, who chose it as their main means to access information on their new environment as well as to gain information about the wider world.[34]

Prague as a big neighbourhood

In this way, therefore, the popular press reflects the dialogue between tradition and modernisation in turn-of-the century Prague. Compared to the sensational press of other Central European cities, the *Courier* and other examples of the Prague-based press offered their readers a less exclusively metropolitan view of life in the rest of the world. On the contrary, the extensive and specific detail with which the editors of the *Courier* reported on local events can be read as a surviving remnant of the oral transmission of news in rural communities, as the following example, which appeared under the heading, '*Accidents*', suggests:

> Yesterday, Anna Řadová, the 59-year-old wife of a mill worker in Klecany, was picking plums in order to make dumplings. She fell from the ladder and broke her arm. Constable Václav Melichar, who was picking walnuts, endured a similar injury. He fell from the tree and injured himself. Yesterday, 14-year-old student Jindřich Fehrer from Ústí n. L., living in Jungmann Street in Karlín, broke his leg on the playground.[35]

This kind of reporting on persons known to the majority of the readers living in a small area was a standard feature of the provincial press, and may be compared with the reports of 'Aunt Maria' in the *South Wales Star* discussed by Michelle Deininger. It also highlights a significant contrast with the impersonality of metropolitan life.

The persistence of reports in this style in the Prague press may be understood as a sign that the largest part of the population continued to perceive their surroundings and their own lives primarily as if they were located in a small town, or even in the countryside, rather than identifying themselves with the anonymity of city life.[36] It appears to be as a result of this mentality that the kind of detailed and personal news typical of the provincial press continued to be so important for the *Courier* readers in Prague. As Michel de Certeau noted, memories which interconnect dwellers with their places are personal, and may be of little interest to anyone else, but they provide a neighbourhood with character.[37] We can thus think of *fin-de-siècle* Prague as one large neighbourhood in the eyes of its inhabitants which they found represented in the *Courier*. As the suburbs of Prague grew, becoming in themselves major population centres, and as opportunities for gossip and the exchange of information in markets or at public pumps and fountains declined for increasing numbers of people, the *Courier* and other papers provided an alternative means of preserving the sense of a neighbourhood community.

This situation contrasts with the practices of the press in cities such as Berlin or Vienna, where ordinary citizens were only mentioned by name if they had accomplished some extraordinary deed or suffered a tragedy, and where everyday news reports were reserved for the likes of prominent residents and significant court or theatre celebrities. In time, however, even in Prague news coverage increasingly concentrated on events and individuals in the city and its suburbs, and less attention was paid to reports from the rest of Bohemia and Moravia. This development is indicative of the declining interest of the former newcomers to the city in their places of origin, and of the growing strength of their ties to the urban community in which they were now living. Places where the *Courier* and other illustrated popular press publications were displayed and sold became gathering points for people keen to discuss the lurid illustrations and the latest news whether from home or abroad. For the crowds who regularly met in this way, the newspaper was an important agent in sustaining a sense of community because it provided a focus for people to share their interests and concerns. As one of the illustrators remembered, the latest issue of the *Courier* with its large title illustration of some kind of disaster or murder outshone other newspaper titles and Prague citizens would look curiously at it and start a discussion with others who were on their way to work.[38] Thus, the *Courier* is an important example of a paper whose editorial policy was based on a shrewd understanding of its readers' expectations and habits in a period of cultural change, and which found an effective way of satisfying these through a skilful combination of traditional and modern news reporting.

Nationalist rather than interurban tendencies

According to research undertaken by Peter Fritzsche and Nathaniel D. Wood, the popular press in Berlin and Kraków became an important guide to life in the city as it helped its readers to recognise themselves as a part of a larger metropolitan public.[39] Popular urban newspapers were so much favoured by their metropolitan readers that they completely overtook their more serious competitors, including the socialist press. Illustrated newspapers were simultaneously a local as well as an interurban phenomenon. Their mix of local news and foreign spectacles was also part of an international network of sharing news and sensational stories. While the depiction of metropolitan culture itself was interpreted variously in different cities, their citizens nevertheless read the same stories while performing the same urban rituals such as sitting in cafés, travelling by tramway or promenading in the streets. Although the inhabitants of rather provincial Central European cities such as Prague or Kraków had only limited possibilities to sample the more exotic and extreme experiences and sensations associated with metropolitan centres such as Paris or Berlin, their daily papers shared enough common ground with the French and German press to stimulate readers' interest in stories from such very different locations. As a consequence, Central European urban readers felt themselves to be part of a wider interurban network of news as well as members of a specific city, and they consciously began to differentiate themselves from their rural neighbours. Moreover, they felt that their self-consciously urban identity linked them to modern city-dwellers everywhere, and was different from their sense of local or national identity. This particular awareness of a common urban identity was, according to Wood, stronger than the developing attraction of nationalism, even in the case of the provincial metropolis Kraków which was significantly smaller than Prague.[40] As Wood notes, 'Even in an era of intense nationalism, the popular press and its average readers were more concerned on a daily basis with urban issues rather than national ones.'[41]

However, analysing the content of the *Courier*, we can see a rather different picture. While there was less interest in foreign news and fewer images of metropolitan life in its columns, there was a significant interest in politics and especially in militant nationalism. The rhetoric of the paper was strongly nationalistic, and the German population was described as the enemy. This played to the prejudices of many of its Prague readers, as a significant section of Prague citizens, ranging from apprentices and students through to workers, small artisans and traders (i.e. typical *Courier* readers), regularly took part in nationalist riots.[42]

National identity was a major preoccupation of these activists, and it probably overshadowed their awareness of or interest in a more inclusive interurban identity of the kind mentioned above. Instead, a strong sense of nationhood, shared by the Czech rural population, fuelled the agenda in the nationalist fight against the Germans in their midst. The significance of nationalist concerns can be observed in the regular and detailed reporting of national and language-related injustices caused by the Germans (and, by implication, in the silencing or glorification of those injustices perpetrated by Czechs). These issues prompted nationalist rallies and outbreaks of violence incited by a sense of solidarity with the Czech population living in areas with a German majority (e.g. Sudetenland and Vienna). However, the *Courier*'s heightened concern with political and nationalist issues ceased to be as appealing after the turn of the twentieth century when papers with socialist sympathies – especially the social-democratic *Právo lidu* (*People's right*) – adopted a more sensational style and probably took away a significant number of the *Courier*'s readers. This contrasts sharply with the fate of the socialist press in other Central European cities where circulation figures plummeted as working-class readers turned increasingly to sensational news publications.

Conclusion

At the turn of the twentieth century, the sensational pictorial press was the main feature of Central European urban popular culture. Its emergence was related to the formation of new urban areas, and especially to the rapid growth of metropolitan centres. During the period of the most rapid urbanisation, which was inseparably linked to the advance of industrialisation, a substantial stream of newcomers from rural areas came to the cities to find a better place to live with greater employment opportunities, higher wages and more scope for entertainment. The move from the countryside to the inner city or the suburbs necessitated the migrants' discovery of a culture that differed from that of their rural origins. Sensational illustrated newspapers helped them with this by acting not only as guides to life in the new environment but also through assisting their readers in developing a shared sense of urban identity. Their success in doing so derived from the Central European publishers' ability to adapt global patterns found in the successful mass daily press to address their local audience's specific beliefs, values and desires. In the case of the Prague-based popular press, this involved modifying the newspapers' content so that it combined elements of the rural with the metropolitan, and of the traditional with the modern. The process was further complicated, as the example of *Pražský Illustrovaný Kurýr* shows, because editors also had to compromise the typically interurban character of illustrated daily papers to retain readers whose top priority had become the narrower concerns of Czech nationalism.

Notes

1 This study was supported by the project *The Emergence of Popular Culture in the Czech Lands* (GP13-39799P) sponsored by the Czech Science Foundation (GAČR).

2 The role of the local press as a moral guardian of the urban community is discussed in Michelle Deininger's chapter.

3 *Pochodeň*, 14 July 1914, p. 2.

4 P. Fritzche, *Reading Berlin 1900* (Cambridge, Mass.: Harvard University Press, 1996), p. 185.

5 Fritzche, p. 178.

6 Martin Conboy, *The Press and Popular Culture* (London: Sage, 2002), pp. 23–25. Conboy's work builds on Peter Burke, *Lidová kultura v raně novověké Evropě* (Praha: Argo, 2005).

7 P. Horská, E. Maur and J. Musil, *Zrod velkoměsta, Urbanizace českých zemí a Evropa* (Praha, Litomyšl: Paseka, 2002), pp. 8, 11.

8 The common term 'Czech Lands' is used to describe the area of today's Czech Republic, which includes former parts of the Austro-Hungarian Empire – the Kingdom of Bohemia, Margraviate of Moravia and a major part of Austrian Silesia.

9 Horská, Maur and Musil,, pp. 197–202, 220.

10 Horská, Maur and Musil, p. 201.

11 G. B. Cohen, 'Society and Culture in Prague, Vienna, and Budapest in the Late Nineteenth Century, '*East European Quarterly*, 20,4 (1986), pp. 467–484, on p. 469.

12 L. Fialová et al., *Dějiny obyvatelstva českých zemí* (Praha: Mladá Fronta, 1996), p. 397.

13 Horská, Maur and Musil, pp. 206, 7.

14 J.Machačová and J.Matějček, *Nástin sociálního vývoje českých zemí 1780–1914*, p. 428.

15 Horská, Maur and Musil, p. 223.

16 P. Anderson, *The Printed Image and the Transformation of Popular Culture: 1790–1860* (Oxford: Oxford University Press, 1991), p. 43.

17 J. Machek, 'Pražský illustrovaný kurýr. Masový tisk jako obraz světa obyčejných lidí' (PhD Dissertation, Charles University, Prague, 2012), p. 168.

18 The Prague German population was predominantly of middle and higher class. The lower class was predominantly Czech, and there was only a gradual growth of higher-class families using Czech as a public language during the nineteenth century.

19 There is a famous baroque ossuary in Sedlec near Kutná Hora.

20 'Strašlivá noc', *Illustrirtes Prager Extrablatt*, 21 July, 1881, p. 1.

21 'Strašlivá noc', *Illustrirtes Prager Extrablatt*, 21 July 1881, p. 2.

22 'Boj ve vzduchu', *Illustrirtes Prager Extrablatt*, 10 July 1881, p. 2.

23 M. Sekera, 'Podíl Grégrů na rozvoji novinářství a politické publicistiky', in M. Řepa and P. Vošahlíková (eds), *Bratři Grégrové a česká společnost v druhé polovině 19. století* (Praha: Eduard Grégr a syn, 1997), pp. 29–37, on p. 31.

24 J. Dorčáková, 'Počátky senzacechtivého tisku v českých zemích' (MA Dissertation, Charles University in Prague, 2010), p. 68.

25 *Národní listy*, 28 February 1880, p. 4.

26 The (Czech) National party was established in 1848 as the first Czech political party. After the secession of the Young Czechs (National Liberal Party), it was later known as the Czech National Conservative Party and gradually lost its influence as well as seats in the Imperial Council after the 1891 election. However, because of a Census suffrage in the Bohemian Diet as well as in the Prague municipality, the Old Czech Party still played a certain role in local policymaking since it was the party of the Czech-oriented nobility, the most significant landowners and the bourgeoisie.

27 J. Machek, 'Pražský illustrovaný kurýr', p. 114.

28 *Národní politika*, 28 October 1896, p. 2.

29 'Z Říšské rady', *Pražský Illustrovaný Kurýr*, 15 January 1908, p. 3.

30 'Kruté, hrozné drama lásky', *Pražský Illustrovaný Kurýr*, 13 February 1898, p. 2.

31 'Kočka a myš (Drama tichého domu)', *Pražský Illustrovaný Kurýr*, 17 March 1898, p. 4.

32 O. Kodetová, *Prameny k revolučnímu hnutí a ohlasu ruské revoluce, sv. I., Rok 1905* (Praha: Nakladatelství ČSAV, 1959), p. 365.

33 'Velká bouře na sněmu království českého', *Pražský Illustrovaný Kurýr*, 25 September 1908, p. 2.

focus of this case study is the piney woods of Mississippi and the adjacent coastal meadows. The coastal meadows occupy a very narrow swath of land, perhaps twenty miles in width that stretches northward from the shallow passes and sounds of the Gulf of Mexico. The region's two main river systems, the Pascagoula and Pearl, form in the central part of the state and flow south some 200 miles to the Gulf of Mexico, dissecting first the Jackson Prairie and then the more expansive shortleaf and longleaf pine forests. Along these routes, narrow but fertile bottomlands populated by a tenuous band of hardwoods are commonly found. These rivers flow at a roughly ninety-degree angle to the coastline, a spatial pattern which served to both encourage and inhibit travel. The waterways enabled travel in the antebellum period by providing effective routes to transport heavy materials, and increasing the mobility of those who wished to journey along a north to south route. The rivers served as a barrier, however, to east-west mobility, as travelers had to negotiate multiple portages and fords to reach their destination. Once away from the narrow band of the coastal meadows and the river floodplain, longleaf and other species of pine proliferated. Covering the sandy soils of the rolling hills of the region, these conifers formed a canopy over a sea of wiregrass. This physiographic region developed differently from other regions of the state because in general its soil is not ideal for plantation agriculture and the production of cotton. While this stunted the growth of the region in the antebellum period, new technologies to exploit its vast forest resources, combined with low land prices, lured capital and people there after 1865.[2]

In the early nineteenth century, towns and villages were scarce in the piney woods. Geographer Howard Adkins notes: 'Before 1840 ... minor trade centers and county seats constituted almost the entire urban fabric of Mississippi.'[3] Trading towns and county seats evolved to service the economic and bureaucratic needs of the largely rural population. Most were small villages located along the banks of the slow, meandering river systems utilised to move goods to coastal markets. Augusta, Mississippi, is typical of these early settlements. Founded in 1812 and situated on the banks of Leaf River, Augusta served two important functions: as the county seat of Perry County from 1818 to 1906 and as a United States Land Office from 1819 to 1860. In 1841 it consisted of a town square dotted with a dozen structures, including a tavern, courthouse, clerk's office, the county jail, and ten to twelve homes. Archaeological excavations reveal no real town plan or grid pattern to the streets. The Leaf River, a tributary of the Pascagoula, offered access to the Gulf of Mexico. The lower Pascagoula represented a vital link in the transportation system, as, according to one local resident in 1829, 'the largest kind of vessels can come in'.[4] Despite being the centre of county government for eighty years, Augusta declined quickly when the railroad bypassed it in 1898 on the south side of the Leaf River. The lack of a railroad linkage caused immediate decline and in 1906 the courthouse moved two miles south to the nascent town of New Augusta, ultimately causing the extinction of old Augusta.[5]

Corn, cattle, cotton, pigs, sheep, lumber, and turpentine were the primary products of the piney woods in the antebellum era. Limited population growth occurred as settlers instead flocked to the prime agricultural lands along the

Mississippi Yazoo delta and the Tombigbee River in the western and north-central portion of the state. Overall, Mississippi before 1860 was a state dominated by the plantation cotton economy, based on slave labour. The piney woods were atypical, however, because the sandy soils in their ecosystem discouraged the development of large-scale plantation agriculture. The region, therefore, did not develop the cotton economy that characterised other physiographic sections of the state. The depression of 1837–1849, in which cotton prices dropped from a high of 25 cents per pound to a low of 5 cents per pound, influenced many farmers and planters statewide to grow both subsistence and cash crops. According to John Hebron Moore, many of the planters in the state 'lost their aversion for importing food stuffs, livestock, and manufactured goods from the Upper Mississippi Valley once they had cash in their pockets'.[6] A 1997 study by Bradley G. Bond supports this theory, arguing that instead of following the safety first strategy of growing enough staple crops on which to subsist, and only then producing for economic gain, between 1850 and 1860 residents in the piney woods counties of Covington, Jones, and Perry deliberately aimed at production for market.[7] Some yeoman farmers followed the more conservative path of planting both cash and subsistence crops. Cotton was still an important cash crop in the pine barrens, but the sandy soil exhausted quickly and produced limited yield. Corn served as both a subsistence and cash crop, and was the most popular crop in the pine belt because of its versatility. While the pine belt certainly engaged in agricultural activity similar to other regions of the state, the content and quality of the soil forced farmers to make choices about the types of crop that matched the climate and local markets. This resulted in a diminished reliance on cotton as a cash crop in the region, which in turn made farmers less likely to import slaves to the piney woods to engage in large–scale cotton production. While most of the population of the state as a whole in 1860 was slaves, the piney woods maintained a free white majority.

Livestock raising was also an important economic pursuit in the piney woods in the antebellum period. In 1841, J. F. H. Claiborne commented on his visit to Greene County: 'Many of the people here are herdsman, owning large droves of cattle, surplus increase of which are annually driven to Mobile. These cattle are permitted to run in the range or forest.'[8] Brooks Blevins notes the region offered the 'ideal environment' for cattle herders, with an open range, warm climate, adequate forage, and a lack of underbrush to hinder control and management of the herd.[9] These circumstances led to large cattle herds, with beef sold in the nearby New Orleans and Mobile markets. The piney woods' cattle industry was a precursor to the open-range grazing which later occurred in Texas and more broadly in the American west in the latter half of the nineteenth century.[10] Frank Owsley in his classic 1949 work on plain folk contends that the lack of large landowners in the piney woods of Mississippi in 1850 can be directly attributed to the availability of free range in the region and the large numbers of small landowners engaged in herding cattle as their means of livelihood.[11] Agriculture, however, whether farming or herding, dominated life in the piney woods region until the American Civil War.

Before the war, slavery provided a steady labour force for agriculture in Mississippi. After it ended in 1865, cotton remained the primary cash crop of the agricultural economy in the state. The basis of the postwar agricultural economic system shifted from slavery to the sharecropping or tenant farming system. Worried about retaining a steady labour force, landowners enacted a crop lien system which worked in tandem with tenant farming to create a stable workforce. For many rural Mississippians, land ownership became the exception rather than the norm. By 1910, tenants operated 66 percent of Mississippi's 274,000 farms. While whites composed only 44 percent of Mississippi's overall population, they comprised 75 percent of farm owners. In contrast, nearly 77 percent of the tenants were black, and blacks owned a meagre 25 percent of owner-operated farms. The end of slavery did not bring autonomy to many rural blacks, and acquiring land was a particular difficulty. The piney woods' population, however, differed from prevailing demographic patterns in the state. In contrast to the state as a whole, whites composed a distinct majority of the overall population in the region, and represented between 63 to 72 percent in a six-county population sample. Likewise, tenant farming was less pervasive. In Lamar County, for example, only 22 percent of farmers were tenants, and in Jones County the tenancy rate was 36 percent. Whites comprised the majority of both farm owners and tenants in the pine belt. Blacks were equally likely to own their farms instead of sharecropping, a fact Neil McMillen attributes to the marginal quality of land in the region.[12] The primary reason for this demographic variation between the region and the state was the quality of the soil: the sandy soil of the pine uplands was unsuitable for large-scale, long-term cotton monoculture. The low rates of sharecropping reflect the limited profitability of cash crop agriculture. This dearth of large-scale agriculture allowed blacks and whites of lesser means to purchase and retain plots of farmland in the pine barrens. While the piney woods remained rural with an agricultural economy in the late nineteenth and early twentieth centuries, a new path to economic freedom emerged to tempt workers to leave the farm for the city.

The introduction of the railroad to the region altered patterns of human-environmental interaction, serving to reorient the geography of the region and to create fledgling urban areas. William Harris Hardy played a significant role in this shift. In 1868, Hardy foresaw the potential economic impact of a railroad connection between Meridian, Mississippi and New Orleans which would link the southern interior with the port city. Hardy moved to Meridian and acted on his vision to secure a charter for a rail line linkage with New Orleans. In the late summer of 1880 while surveying the southern section of the proposed tracks of the New Orleans and Northeastern Railroad, Hardy had an epiphany. Stopping for a noontime rest on a creek near the Leaf River, Hardy took time to contemplate the geography of southern Mississippi in relation to his proposed railroad line. As he studied the topography, he realised that a locale very near the spot in which he was relaxing was the logical choice for the intersection of any future route built from the Mississippi Gulf coast to the state capital.[13]

True to his vision Hardy located a station in the area, just south of the confluence of the Bouie and Leaf rivers. In 1882, he purchased the land which would become the heart of the future city of Hattiesburg. While surveying the rail lines he also established the cities of Laurel, Mississippi and Slidell, Louisiana, and erected the first bridge across Lake Pontchartrain, the longest railroad bridge in the United States. Hardy overcame both financial difficulties and environmental challenges in completing the line. This pattern of town formation in conjunction with the establishment of railroad lines was a common global phenomenon in the nineteenth and early twentieth centuries.[14]

Hardy did not fare so well with his second project: a railroad to connect the Gulf Coast with Jackson, Mississippi. The Gulf and Ship Island Railroad would link Jackson with Hattiesburg and a new port city Hardy named Gulfport. The project ran into major financial difficulty in the late 1890s, and was eventually taken over and completed by Joseph T. Jones, a wealthy businessman who made his post-Civil War fortune in the Pennsylvania oil fields. It was Jones's ambition as a builder not only to complete the Gulf and Ship Island but also to develop Gulfport as a deep-water harbour to provide access to the Gulf of Mexico. The importance of the port was clear to a group of Mississippi businessmen who met in Hattiesburg in 1898 to express support for federal funds to dredge a deep-water channel to provide access to the gulf. The body resolved that: 'this road would run through a portion of the State now destitute of road or water transportation, embracing about one-third the area of Mississippi, with a population of about 400,000, who depend entirely upon agriculture for support'.[15] The resolution was part of a government report which documented how the proposed channel and harbour would benefit agriculture and open the door for industrial development of the 160 mile north–south corridor. The completion of the line from Gulfport to Jackson in 1900 and the dredging of the deep-water port on the Gulf of Mexico in 1902 offered a direct outlet for regional timber products to international markets.[16] The opening of the harbour spurred the economic development of the region by giving rural farmers engaged in agriculture an outlet for their crops, and provided new opportunities for industrial workers in the sawmills adjacent to the Gulf and Ship Island tracks.

A passion for progress and love of the region in which he lived inspired W. H. Hardy to build railroads which profoundly altered Mississippi's piney woods. The railroad and industrial revolution caused a reorientation of both human and spatial geography in the region, changing the relation between humans and space and place. As Allen Trachtenburg has noted, 'the railway journey produced novel experiences—of self, of fellow-travelers, of landscape, of space and time'.[17] Likewise, railroads compressed time and space and created new towns and urban landscapes with which rural residents were at first unfamiliar. Indeed, the process changed political geography as railroads created new towns and bypassed older, established ones, often leading to their decline. An example of this is Gainesville, Mississippi. Founded in 1810 as a planned community and located on the eastern bank of the Pearl River, Gainesville was one of a handful of south Mississippi towns incorporated in this period. It served as a regional trading town, was the county seat of Hancock County from 1837 to 1857, and contained one of the largest lumber mills in the South in the antebellum era. At the time of the construction of the New Orleans and Northeastern Railroad through the region in the early 1880s, it was the primary trading town in the vicinity, and contractors building the railroad received many of their supplies from Gainesville by wagon. Yet when the railroad bypassed it by ten miles, the city dwindled as the new railroad village of Picayune siphoned off trade and industry. By 1906 the population of Picayune was twice that of Gainesville.[18] Other antebellum piney woods towns suffered the same fate. In 1904, a fire destroyed the Covington County Courthouse in the county seat of Williamsburg. Founded at the formation of the county in 1819, Williamsburg typified communities in antebellum Mississippi, and serviced the surrounding region as a centre for agricultural trade and a seat of government. First bypassed by the railroad, Williamsburg's consequent loss of its courthouse proved fatal. In 1906, a new county courthouse opened in nearby Collins, a railroad boomtown and home to several sawmills. Across the piney woods, this pattern repeated itself in the postbellum era as older antebellum centres declined and were replaced in the hierarchy of urban importance by upstart railroad towns based on the influx of technology and industry.[19]

The new urban life in the piney woods is best examined through a brief portrait of its leading city, Hattiesburg. W. H. Hardy purchased the first 160 acres of land in the city proper, and was responsible for the sale of the initial lots. Hattiesburg was incorporated shortly after the completion of the New Orleans and Northeastern Railroad in 1884, and quickly grew into a thriving market town: the population in 1890 was 1,172, grew to 4,175 in 1900, and by 1910, had reached 11,733.[20] As the legal description that created the municipality indicates, the geographic centre of Hattiesburg was the New Orleans and Northeastern Depot. West of this location, a planned grid of streets marked the downtown business section. East of this area, toward the Leaf River, residential neighbourhoods dotted with churches took hold. By 1910 the major business section was near the intersection of Front and Main Streets. Clustered along Mobile Street was a second area of businesses for the African-American residents. Segregation was both the custom and the law. As a result, there were separate areas of black business and residence. Jesse McKee's examination of patterns of African-American residence in Hattiesburg identified three main areas with an African-American majority: Mobile Street, Tipton-Currie, and Dabbs-Royal. Utilising city directories and census data, McKee discovered that the African-American residential areas were settled principally between 1895 and 1905, and that in them the 'residential mixing of Negroes and whites within the same block existed only to a small extent'.[21] African-Americans were also limited to the most dangerous and low-paying jobs in the industrial economy. For example, sawmill work was hazardous and blacks often did manual labour, moving logs and lumber, while white workers occupied the skilled positions. From 1880 to 1910, Mississippians moved from the farm to the factory to enhance their economic opportunities. Blacks, however, failed to find the type of freedom they yearned for and the rigid Jim Crow laws and a strictly enforced system of de facto segregation prompted many African-Americans to leave the south after 1910, resulting in the massive migration of the Great Diaspora.[22]

The New Orleans and Northeastern Depot marked not only the geographic centre of town but was also an important point of reference for both residents and visitors. As Jeffrey Richards and John M. MacKenzie observe, 'There is perhaps no more potent or dramatic symbol of the Industrial Revolution than the railways. The Victorians equated railways with progress and civilization.'[23] Created as a railroad town, by 1910 Hattiesburg boasted links with all points of the compass, and life in the city centred on its downtown stations and loading docks. Direct connections hurried passengers and freight to Jackson, Natchez, New Orleans, Gulfport, Mobile, Meridian and points beyond. The New Orleans and Northeastern remained the city's most important rail line, and became a part of the larger Queen and Crescent route connecting Chattanooga and Cincinnati in 1895.[24] However, much of Hattiesburg's early growth was prompted by the smaller regional railroads which extended into its hinterlands. The Gulf and Ship Island Railroad linked Gulfport on the Gulf of Mexico to the growing state capital at Jackson, and Hattiesburg was an important intermediate passenger and freight depot on the line. The Mississippi Central Railroad connected Hattiesburg to Natchez in 1908, and this route provided a link to more than two dozen sawmills in southwestern Mississippi. The Mobile, Jackson, and Kansas City Railroad, completed to Hattiesburg in 1902, gave the city a direct link with the nearby port city of Mobile.[25] The intersection of these four rail lines made Hattiesburg the central town in the pine belt's timber-based economy, so that it eventually outpaced Laurel for economic dominance over southeastern Mississippi.

The result of a contest sponsored by the Hattiesburg Commercial Club in 1912 to create a slogan for the city reflects the residents' recognition of its importance as a railroad centre for the timber industry: Hattiesburg was dubbed 'Hub City,' and the Henry L. Doherty Company paid $3,000 for the erection of a 42-foot-high sign. Paul Vasselus, a Greek immigrant who arrived in the city in 1915, recalled 'the first thing I saw was a beautiful sign over the Ross Building ... a giant of a sign. It read Hattiesburg: The Hub.'[26] The tricoloured sign displayed the city's new moniker and carried the names of the six major cities to which it was connected by rail. Placed in a highly visible position near the intersection of the downtown railroad tracks, the sign illuminated the night with some 1,142 lights and symbolized both the success of the growing city and the residents' optimism about its future.[27]

The results of the timber boom in south Mississippi were astounding. Pine belt counties were among the fastest growing in the state between 1900 and 1910, exceeding the 15 percent rate of population growth for Mississippi as a whole. In a region once isolated because of poor roads and shallow waterways, the railroad now created opportunities for movement of both people and resources, and the once-insulated dominion of the yeoman farmer, the livestock herder, and the solitary turpentine worker reverberated with the mechanical shriek of the steam whistle and the clatter of mill machinery, particularly in the newly formed municipalities of the region, where population multiplied dramatically. In 1890 one incorporated city existed in what would become Lamar County with a total municipal population of 287. By 1910 three municipalities existed with a total population of 4,893 residents, or 42 percent of the population of the entire county. In other piney wood counties, results were similar. In Forrest County 56 percent of county residents lived in Hattiesburg. In Covington County, 29 percent of county residents resided in one of the five new municipalities incorporated after 1902. In Jones County 43 percent of the population lived in eight incorporated locations.[28] Sawmills, cottonseed mills, and the forest products industry created jobs, and residents of the pine belt flocked to towns to acquire them. For at least a portion of Mississippi, the transformation into a 'New South' began as the piney woods changed from a rural, agrarian domain to a place punctuated by small towns and villages filled with wage labourers. The majority of the residents of these new communities were migrants from inside the state or from other deep-south states. Although some skilled sawmill labourers, managers, and owners migrated from established timber production regions in Pennsylvania and Wisconsin to exploit the fresh supply of forest products, most migrants moved to the industrialising municipalities to replace an agricultural lifestyle for one of wage labour.

Some migrants were professionals who sought economic gain in more lucrative markets. The photographer D.B. Henley left Thomasville, Alabama for Hattiesburg after a disastrous fire burned his home and studio in 1902. He opened on Railroad Street, and developed a thriving business taking individual and family photographs and selling his images of the city on picture postcards.[29] The city also attracted a small number of foreign immigrants. One of Henley's main competitors, George Papson, also known as Papodopolo, emigrated from Smyrna, Turkey, Americanised his name, married the daughter of a local farmer and set up a portrait studio on Main Street advertising 'High Art Photos'.[30]

Not everyone in the region perceived urbanisation and industrialisation as either practical or useful. Whereas farmers relied on the railroads both to move their crops to market and to receive manufactured goods from across the nation, many rural Mississippians were sceptical about them and their powerful and mainly northern owners who quickly acquired vast holdings of land at rock-bottom prices, especially after a national depression in 1893 constricted southern capital and gave northern financiers control of the majority of piney woods lines. The aforementioned Joseph T. Jones took over the Gulf and Ship Island in 1895, while the New York financier J. P. Morgan purchased an interest in the New Orleans and Northeastern the same year. Fenwick Peck, a Pennsylvanian, constructed and controlled the Mississippi Central Railroad, a Hattiesburg to Natchez route completed in 1908.[31] Railroads came to epitomise corporate culture in Gilded Age America, and cattle owners frequently filed suit for loss of livestock killed in railroad collisions. One study estimates that the most frequent cases involving open-range laws were those involving damages for cattle.[32] Likewise, northern lumber interests purchased vast areas of prime timberland beginning in the 1877. Delos Blodgett of Michigan and Edward Hines of Chicago alone controlled nearly 1 million acres of timberland in the piney woods. Harsh taxation laws created a cut out and get out mentality, which resulted in deforestation, the temporary exhaustion of forest resources, and job losses as sawmills suspended operations.[33]

Despite these many changes, the piney woods in 1910 remained overwhelmingly rural. Increasingly, however, the rural population identified themselves in relation to the hamlets, villages, and towns of the region, creating what C. Phythian-Adams terms 'cultural provinces'.[34] The new rail networks facilitated the flow of rural products, including corn, cotton, and vegetables while the development of regional transportation spurred the expansion of the forest products industry. This process created numerous cities, towns, and villages like Collins and Picayune. Although the Industrial Revolution came late to the area, it uprooted families and prompted internal migration from farm to factory. While farming and herding remained key methods of economic livelihood for a majority of the population in Mississippi's piney woods, poor soil, the declining size of the average farm, the arrival of the boll weevil, and the desire to escape tenant farming accelerated the shift from rural to urban. By 1910, steam engines and sawmills were as familiar a sight as ploughs and mules. Jack Temple Kirby argues that the true transformation in the South occurred between 1920 and 1960, but it is clear that the process of industrialisation and rural to urban migration began much earlier and contributed directly to the creation of uneasy relationships between the rural and urban populations.

What lessons can we take away from this case study? First, region is a useful tool to develop geographical, historical, and sociological models of interpretation. Researchers define regions by many different types of boundaries: economic, environmental, political, and social are but a few examples. The concept of region as an academic methodology to study rural and urban relationships dates back over a hundred years to the work of the sociologists Patrick Geddes and Benton MacKaye. Both proposed early models of the life cycle of city and hinterland using regionalism as a model, although they drew different conclusions about how the two interacted.[35] Still, they also contended that rural and urban must be understood in relation to one another within a region to fully explain the dynamics of human society. This line of thinking led to the blossoming of regionalism as a methodology in the decades before and after World War Two. The two most influential thinkers in this period, Howard W. Odum and Rupert Vance, utilised regionalism to describe the southern United States. Odum's *Southern Regions of the United States* (1936) and Vance's *Human Geography of the South* (1932) are classic works which focus on the South as a case study. Odum's encyclopedic work sought both to understand the south as a region and to emphasise the importance of the connections between regions of the United States. Vance's work focused on how humans and nature interact to create unique and identifiable regions.[36] Modern studies utilising region stress individual factors which identify a region or subregion. David Goldfield, writing in 1997, proposed ruralism, race, and colonialism as the 'three general factors which have characterized the historical growth of the South'.[37] These three factors are clearly evident in the piney woods as a subregion, but on their own they are not sufficient to explain the complex workings of regional history.

Second, regions can be further defined by studying the interaction of man with nature in the field of environmental history. Although most experts pinpoint the early 1970s as the birth of American environmental history, sociologists, ecologists, and geographers were already employing the holistic approach of studying man and nature. Through the lens of environment, it is possible to draw conclusions about the historical development of broader conceptual regions, such as the South and the American west, as well as smaller bioregions. Albert Cowdrey uses a conceptual framework in *This Land, This South: An Environmental History* (1983) in which he presents an environmental history of a region defined by the 'landscape of the mind'.[38] Others outline regional boundaries via nature. Rupert Vance recognised the piney woods as a distinct biotic region of the South.[39] Jack Temple Kirby's *Poquosin: A Study of Rural Landscape and Society* (1995), defines his study utilising river basins in the area between Virginia's James River and North Carolina's Albermarle Sound.[40] Dan Flores takes another view, contending that defining an area as a bioregion to explore its unique patterns of human and environmental interaction can be an effective interdisciplinary methodological approach.[41] In *This Delta, This Land: An Environmental History of the Yazoo-Mississippi Floodplain* (2005) Mikko Saikku also uses the river basin to define a subregion, embracing both Flores' call for bioregional history and offering an interpretation of the Yazoo-Mississippi Delta via Fernand Braudel's *Histoire de la longue durée.*[42]

Like Saikku's work, this study narrows the focus from the South to a specific bioregion, but the two differ in their timescales. While longer timeframes are preferable to show interactions between humans and nature, it is possible to draw conclusions about the past of a bioregion utilising a shorter timespan, in this case roughly the long nineteenth century. Adding bioregion as a factor tightens the scope of the work but still allows for comparison with other similar regions.

Interregional connections directly impact both man and nature, and no bioregion exists in a vacuum. Regions connect over time and space, and as humans migrate they bring with them new technologies which reshape both nature and humans' conception of the region. In the piney woods, the arrival of a new transportation technology, the railroad, clearly impacted the biological balance of the region and reoriented human spatial patterns. In *The Railway Journey* (1986), Wolfgang Schivelbusch illustrates the importance of railroads in the United States, stating that they created traffic by 'opening up the wilderness to civilization and economic utilization' via an 'effective transport system'.[43] Kenneth Noe recognised a similar pattern in 1850s' southwestern Virginia: 'Rural Americans suddenly connected to wider markets through transportation technology, eventually railroads, and embraced not only the wider market but the wider world'.[44] Claiborne's 1876 call to bring the piney woods closer to the gulf also recognised that technology was essential to transport the forest resources to a port on the gulf which would offer access to world markets.[45] Railroads commercialised the region. Mark Wetherington, in his study of the piney woods of Georgia, contends that the railroad changed the lives of the small farmers and herders in the region by ending their isolation and promoting their integration into national commercial networks.[46] Therefore, technology represents a fifth important factor used to interpret regional identity.

This study attempts to bridge the divide between urban and rural studies. These five factors—ruralism, race, colonialism, bioregion, and technology—offer a useful framework to describe the piney woods, and should be considered by those seeking an interpretive method to describe rural and urban relationships. Scholarship on the American South often focuses either on the rural or the urban rather than on their symbiotic relationship. For example, the primary work on rural history in America, David Danbom's *Born in the Country* (2006), paints a broad picture of the factors driving the southerner out of the country as agriculture floundered during the late nineteenth and early twentieth centuries but contains few mentions of specific subregions, such as the piney woods, or of how rural–urban interactions worked in tandem to change the lives of those who left rural life, whether voluntarily or of necessity.[47]

In conclusion, the piney woods constitute a unique bioregion in Mississippi which developed at a distinct chronological pace and with different rural and urban patterns to the rest of the state. The pine belt remained sparsely settled in the antebellum period due to its unsuitability for large-scale plantation agriculture and its focus on livestock herding. After 1865, growth accelerated as technology enabled the harvesting of its natural forest resources and the amelioration of its transportation challenges. The formation of cities, towns, and villages literally changed the map of the region, reorienting it from a river-based to a railroad-based economy which was integrated into national and international commercial networks. The region also saw an intense, but temporary, shift to urbanisation beginning in 1880 which was atypical of the state. This brought rural migrants to the city, and often resulted in an uneasy relationship between town and country as industry and agriculture competed for labour. Unlike Mississippi as a whole, the piney woods did not develop a high rate of tenant farming, and the white native population remained a majority of the rural population. In the end it remained a part of the South, marked by ruralism, colonialism, and race; yet the unique ecology of the piney woods' ecosystem contributed to the region's divergent patterns of development. Mikko Saikku noted that 'natural environment is seen as an active and often decisive factor in human history, influencing the economic options available and shaping the developmental paths taken'.[48] This chapter's regional approach, incorporating specific environmental factors and applying a synthetic multidisciplinary framework, both reinforces the relevance of Saikku's words to the Mississippi piney woods, and suggests a productive methodology for understanding the past.

Notes

1 J.F.H. Claiborne to General West, May 6, 1876, in *Report of Mississippi State Board of Centennial Managers* (Jackson, MS: Clarion Steam Printing Establishment, 1877), p. 29.

2 E.W. Hilgard, *Report on the Geology and Agriculture of Mississippi* (Jackson, MS: E. Barksdale, 1860), pp. 348–62; L.S. Early, *Looking for Longleaf: The Fall and Rise of an American Forest* (Chapel Hill, NC: University of North Carolina Press, 2004), pp. 1–4, 109.

3 H.G. Adkins, 'The Geographic Base of Urban Retardation in Mississippi, 1800–1840', *Studies in the Social Sciences*, 12, 1973, pp. 34–48, on p. 47.

4 Matthew Carter, Jr. to Griffin Mizell, 7 June 1829 in B. Bond (ed.), *Mississippi: A Documentary History* (Jackson, MS: University Press of Mississippi, 2003), pp. 46–7.

5 J.F.H. Claiborne, 'A Trip Through the Piney Woods', in Franklin Riley (ed.), *Publications of The Mississippi Historical Society*, Volume IX (Oxford, MS: Mississippi Historical Society, 1907), pp. 518–520; A.L. Young and R.S. Kidd, 'Some Eight to Ten Miserable Tenements: Archeological Investigations at Old Augusta, Perry County, Mississippi', *Mississippi Archeology*, 33:1 (1998), pp. 21–7.

6 J.H. Moore, *Agriculture in Ante-Bellum Mississippi* (Columbia, SC: University of South Carolina Press, reprint edition, 2010), p. 182.

7 B.G. Bond, 'Herders, Farmers and Markets on the Inner Frontier: The Mississippi Piney Woods, 1850–1860', in S.C Hyde (ed.), *Plain Folk of the South Revisited* (Baton Rouge: Louisiana State University Press, 1997, pp. 71–89; V. Bynum, *The Free State of Jones: Mississippi's Longest Civil War* (Chapel Hill: University of North Carolina Press, 2001), pp. 53–6.

8 J.F.H. Claiborne, 'A Trip Through the Piney Woods,' p. 521.

9 B. Blevins, *Cattle in the Cotton Fields: A History of Cattle Raising in Alabama* (Tuscaloosa, AL: University of Alabama Press, 1998), p. 15.

10 J.D.W. Guice, 'Cattle Raisers of the Old Southwest: A Reinterpretation', *Western Historical Quarterly*, 8:2 (Apr., 1977), pp. 167–87.

11 Frank L. Owsley, *Plain Folk of the Old South* (Baton Rouge: LSU Press, reprint 2008), p. 165.

12 N.R. McMillen, *Dark Journey: Black Mississippians in the Age of Jim Crow* (Urbana, IL: University of Illinois Press, 1989), pp. 111–53.

13 T. Hardy, *No Compromise With Principle: Autobiography and Biography of William Harris Hardy* (New York: American Book-Stratford Press, Inc., 1942), pp. 218–31.

14 D.E. Nye, *America as a Second Creation: Technology and Narrative of New Beginnings* (Cambridge, MA: MIT Press, 2003), pp. 163–7.

15 *Annual Reports of the War Department: for the Fiscal Year Ended June 30, 1899: Report of the Chief Engineers Part II* (Washington, DC: United States Government Printing Office, 1899), p. 1801.

16 *Gulf and Ship Island Minute Book*, 1887–1907, Hattiesburg, MS, University of Southern Mississippi Special Collections; M. Rowe, *Captain Jones: Biography of a Builder* (Hamilton, OH: The Hill-Brown Printing Company, 1942), pp. 201–23.

17 A. Trachtenberg, 'Foreword', in W. Schivelbusch, *The Railway Journey: The Industrialization of Time and Space in the 19th Century* (Berkeley: University of California Press, 1986), p. xiv.

18 S.G. Thigpen, *A Boy in Rural Mississippi* (Picayune, MS: S.G. Thigpen, 1966), pp. 97–101; J. H. Napier III, 'The Gilded Pearl: From Settlers to Sawmill Hands', *Gulf South Historical Review* 10:1 (Fall 1994), pp. 113–15; M.R. Herring, *Way Station to Space: A History of the John C. Stennis Space Center* (Washington, DC: National Aeronautics and Space Administration, 1997), pp. 19–21.

19 D. Rowland, *Mississippi: Comprising Sketches of Counties, Towns, Events, Institutions, and Persons, Arranged in Cyclopedic Form* Volumes I and II (Jackson, MS: Mississippi Department of Archives and History, 1907: reprint, Spartanburg, SC: The Reprint Company Publishers, 1976), pp. 470–1, 971; H.G. Adkins, 'The Historical Geography of Extinct Towns', in P.W. Prenshaw and J.O. McKee (ed.), *Sense of Place: Mississippi* (Jackson, MS: University Press of Mississippi, 1979), pp. 131–3, 144–5.

20 A. English, *All Off For Gordon's Station: A History of the Early Hattiesburg, Mississippi Area* (Baltimore, MD: Gateway Press, Inc., 2000), pp. 55–8.

21 J.O. McKee, 'The Residential Patterns of Blacks in Natchez and Hattiesburg and Other Mississippi Cities' (PhD Dissertation, Michigan State University, 1972), pp. 84–5, 99.

22 J. Gregory, *The Southern Diaspora: How the Great Migrations of Black and White Southerners Transformed America* (Chapel Hill: University of North Carolina Press, 2005), pp. 23–4.

23 J. Richards and J.M. Makenzie, *The Railway Station: A Social History* (Oxford: Oxford University Press, 1986), p. 1.
24 B. Davis, *The Southern Railway: Road of Innovators* (Chapel Hill, NC: University of North Carolina Press, 1985), pp. 182–7.
25 J.R. Skates, 'Hattiesburg: The Early Years,' in K. G. McCarty (ed.), *Hattiesburg: A Pictorial History* (Jackson, MS: University Press of Mississippi, 1982), pp. 9–10.
26 Oral History Interview with Paul Vasseulus, quoted in O. B. Caudill (ed.), *Hattiesburg: the First Hundred Years An Oral History* (Hattiesburg, MS: The Mississippi Oral History Program, 1982), p. 39.
27 *Hattiesburg News*, 29 November 1912.
28 United States Department of Commerce, Bureau of the Census, *Thirteenth Census of the Unites States, 1910*.
29 *Thomasville Echo*, 19 June 1902; E. Ayers, *The Promise of the New South: Life After Reconstruction* (Oxford: Oxford University Press, 1992), pp. 55–6.
30 *Hattiesburg American*, 24 May 1918; National Archives of the United States, Washington DC, *World War I Selective Service Registration Cards, 1917–18*, M1509.
31 J.F. Stover, *Railroads of the South: A Study in Finance and Control* (Chapel Hill: University of North Carolina Press, 1955), pp. 254, 281.
32 J.C. King, Jr. 'The Closing of the Southern Range: An Exploratory Study', *The Journal of Southern History*, 48: 1 (February 1982), pp. 53–70, on p. 62.
33 Napier, 'The Gilded Pearl', p. 112.
34 B. Reay, *Rural Englands* (New York: Palgrave Macmillan, 2004), p. 17; C. Phythian-Adams, in *Societies, Cultures and Kinship, 1580–1850* (London: Leicester University Press, 1993), pp. 9–18.
35 P. Geddes, 'Civics: As Applied Sociology, Part 1', *Sociological Papers, 1904* (London, 1905), pp. 103–38; B. Mackay, 'End or Peak of Civilization?' *Survey Graphic*, LXVII (October 1932), pp. 441–44; D. Goldfield, *Region, Race and Cities: Interpreting the Urban South* (Baton Rouge, LA: Louisiana State University Press, 1997), pp. 17–22.
36 Goldfield, *Region, Race, and Cities*, pp. 25–32; H.W. Odum, *Southern Regions of the United States* (Chapel Hill, NC: University of North Carolina Press, 1936); R.B. Vance, *Human Geography of the South* (Chapel Hill, NC: University of North Carolina Press, 1932). pp. 109–44.
37 Goldfield, *Region, Race and Cities*, p. 40.
38 A. Cowdrey, *This Land, This South* (Lexington, NY: University Press of Kentucky, 1983), p. 7.
39 Vance, *Human Geography of the South*, p. 109.
40 J.T. Kirby, *Poquosin: A Study of Rural Landscape and Society* (Chapel Hill, NC: University of North Carolina Press, 1995), p. xi.
41 D. Flores, 'Place: An Argument for Bioregional History', *Environmental History Review*, 18:4 (Winter 1994), pp. 1–18.
42 M. Saikku, *This Delta, This Land: An Environmental History of the Yazoo-Mississippi Floodplain* (Athens, GA: University of Georgia Press, 2005), pp. 7, 25; F. Braudel, 'Histoire et sciences sociales: La longue durée', *Annales E.S.C.*, XIII, 4, 1958, pp. 7–37.
43 Schivelbusch, *The Railway Journey*, p. 90.
44 K.W. Noe, *Southwest Virginia's Railroad: Modernization and the Sectional Crisis in the Civil War Era* (Urbana, IL: University of Illinois Press, 1994.), p. 3.
45 J.F.H. Claiborne to General West, 6 May 1876, p. 29.
46 M. V. Wetherington, *New South Comes to Wiregrass Georgia, 1860–1910* (Knoxville, TN: University of Tennessee Press, 1994), pp. 302–3.
47 D. Danbom, *Born in the Country: A History of Rural America*, 2nd Ed. (Baltimore, MD: Johns Hopkins University Press, 2006).
48 Saikku, *This Delta, This Land*, p. 11.

Part IV

Social mobility and anxiety

10 The urbanisation of James Carter

Autobiography, migration and the rural–urban divide in nineteenth-century Britain

Christopher Ferguson

The title of this chapter alludes to one of the most celebrated nineteenth-century autobiographies, *The Education of Henry Adams* (1907). Scholars have long argued that Adams employed his own life history to engage in more general reflections on the history of nineteenth-century modernity.[1] The same assertion is made here about the comparatively less celebrated autobiographical writings of the English tailor, James Carter (1792–1853).[2] Though neither formally educated nor a trained historian like Adams, in his two-volume *Memoirs of a Working Man* Carter engaged in a similar reflective exercise, accompanying the narrative of his life with many general 'observations…upon men and things'.[3]

James Carter was born in Colchester, Essex, in 1792, trained as a tailor and moved to London in 1810. During the next two decades he moved regularly between London and Colchester, before settling in the metropolis permanently in 1836. He began writing in the 1830s, publishing at least fifty poems and seven books, including his autobiography. After his death he was forgotten and most of his publications were regularly misattributed, usually to 'Thomas Carter'. Nevertheless, during his lifetime Carter's writings were widely available and frequently praised, and therefore deserve serious scrutiny. Taken collectively, these constitute one man's sustained attempt over two decades to make sense of the revolutionary changes unfolding in the Britain he inhabited, with urbanisation foremost among them.[4]

Urbanisation was a foundational element in both the history of nineteenth-century Britain, and the 'making of the modern world', involving the integration of country and city and the unification of the nation into a single society.[5] Because Carter witnessed, participated in and responded to this revolutionary development, his autobiography represents a particularly rich vista from which to consider how urban expansion altered the customary relations believed to exist between the country and the city in nineteenth-century Britain.

Given his frequent movements between Essex and the capital, discussions of the country and the city are understandably prominent in both Carter's account of his own life experiences and his wider reflections on 'men and things'. His copious and carefully catalogued reading likewise predisposed him to evaluate the relative costs and benefits of urban and rural life and equipped him with a literary vocabulary influenced by contemporary Romantic poetry, eighteenth-century poems in the Georgic tradition and the more urbane essays of *The Spectator* and *The Tatler*, all of which engaged in comparing and contrasting country and city life. As an inhabitant of both environments accustomed to meditating on their relative strengths and weaknesses, conceptualising the rural–urban nexus and the rural–urban divide was an understandably recurring topic in Carter's *Memoirs*.

In particular, Carter's autobiography demonstrates the pivotal role rural–urban migration played in shaping the man he had become by the 1840s. Despite his repeated moves between the country and the city, Carter claimed that his initial exposure to London life left an indelible impression on his behaviour and worldview. His own personal transformation into a 'city man' paralleled his country's transformation into a nation of city-dwellers during the same period. Thus, while at his birth less than 30 per cent of Britons lived in cities, by the time of his death more than 50 per cent of the population inhabited urban areas.[6] His metamorphosis, however, like his country's, was also incomplete. A vestige of Carter's prior identity as a 'countryman' continued to inform his own sense of self and his perceptions of Britain's increasingly urban society.

The countryman in London

In 1814, the London illustrator George Cruikshank produced a comic engraving entitled *The Countryman in London*. In it, a baffled-looking bumpkin inquires of a fashionable London dandy, 'Which be my way to St. Paul's?' The city-dweller replies with a lengthy series of directions, that if followed, would lead the naive countryman on a wild goose chase through various neighbourhoods of the metropolis, before depositing him in St. Giles's (the notorious slum) by which time it 'will be quite dark', and where (the dandy claims), 'any body will shew you the way to St. Paul's'.[7]

There is no evidence that James Carter ever saw this satire, or any of the other works Cruikshank produced addressing similar subjects.[8] Nevertheless, this image offers a particularly useful entry point for thinking about the tailor's own experiences of (and in) London during the same decade, and what these suggest about the way urbanisation was transforming Britain.

First, Cruikshank's cartoon replicated a dominant motif informing British culture in the nineteenth century – one also addressed in several chapters in this collection: the contemporary belief in a dichotomous relationship existing between the city and the country; and, as Barry Sloan and Mary Hammond likewise note, between the city- and country-dweller in particular.

For Carter and countless Britons of his generation, the city was everything the country was not. If for the tailor, London was 'a scene of noise and turmoil, and mere worldliness', the country represented 'rural quiet and beauty'.[9] The 'comparative quietude' of 'a country life', he asserted, made it a place of seclusion conducive to intellectual and spiritual contemplation, whereas the city was a 'restless … resort and mart of all the earth', characterised by crowds, commerce and conversation – 'a vast and widely-varied multitude', 'derived from almost

Figure 10.1 George Cruikshank, The Countryman in London (London: R Harrild [1814]),

every region of the inhabited earth', and 'drawn together by that powerful and ever-working impulse, which…leads man to seek the society of his fellow-man'.[10] Carter found mingling with the London crowd as often prompted feelings of 'loneliness' and 'vexation' as of 'amusement' and 'pleasure', while in the solitude of the country he 'felt nothing of loneliness', having 'learned to hold converse with scenes and objects … of either sublimity or beauty'.[11]

Cruikshank's satire invoked a similar binary vision. His city- and countryman are defined by a series of related contrasts: the bumpkin is innocent, stout and unfashionably dressed – a 'timeless' character much like the 'timeless' environment from which he hails – while the Londoner is 'knowing' and manipulative, skinny and dressed *à la mode,* right down to his fashionable 'Hessian' boots. The Londoner's cane contrasts with the countryman's simple staff which testifies to his natural, rustic way of life. These iconic 'props' were commonly employed to designate city or country status in contemporary visual culture which often offered humorous representations of innocent, bumbling, rotund countrymen being abused or robbed by fashionable Londoners.[12]

Humorous likenesses of the 'Countryman' and the 'Londoner' also invoked serious political debates about the country and the city, and, in particular, about rural life as a bastion of moral virtue and social stability.[13] In positive accounts of rustic life the relationship between city and country was likewise defined in conflicted and binary terms. Indeed, Cruikshank's puzzled 'Countryman' is almost a spitting image of the traditional farmers – the hearty men, well fed on 'bread, beef and beer', celebrated in the writings of the journalist and farmer-politician William Cobbett –whose inattention to fashionable attire represented a moral virtue rather than their timeless, 'bumpkin' status.[14]

Thus, in James Carter's Britain the city was perceived as the country's 'other', and the tailor's own writings reiterated this dichotomous vision of urban–rural differences, which was famously expressed in William Cowper's oft-quoted maxim, 'God made the country, and man made the town'.[15] In fact, much of Cowper's poem *The Task* (1785) was concerned with addressing the characteristics he believed differentiated the city from the country and, like his contemporaries, Carter quoted liberally from it when composing his own meditations on the state of British society roughly half a century later.[16] Carter's description of London as the 'resort and mart of all the earth', for example, was a direct quotation from the poem's third book.[17] Shortly before his death, the tailor also quoted Cowper's verse, 'the country wins me still', as an expression of his own preferences.[18] The frequency with which Carter asserted such views throughout his writings makes them somewhat problematic because by the time Carter penned them, he had lived a substantial portion of his life in London. In fact, he copied the line from Cowper while residing there. This disjunction between a poor tailor 'hymning' the virtues of the country, while inhabiting one of the least rural places in the world bears further scrutiny.[19]

Carter's claims to be a 'countryman' reared in a 'rustic village' might likewise be viewed with some scepticism.[20] Although in his autobiography the tailor endeavoured to strike a strong contrast between the unnatural, 'brick-walled'

London environment and the 'sight-refreshing green' of his native Colchester (again, the images are borrowed from Cowper), the emphasis on these differences was more indicative of his choice of reading than of the realities of the milieu in which he spent his early years and much of his adult life.[21] At the beginning of the nineteenth century, Colchester may have been a 'very delightful locality' on account of its 'many picturesque scenes and objects' as Carter claimed, but it also was a growing town of some 12,000 persons, whose buildings and popular culture exhibited less of the traditions of 'Old England' and more of the eighteenth-century 'Urban Renaissance'.[22] In like manner, while the youthful Carter worked for a short time minding horses and had delighted in wandering the fields, few of his experiences bore any resemblance to agricultural pursuits. In fact, as a child his poor health frequently kept him at home. Later he spent several years attending the town's charity school, and, after the age of twelve, worked as an apprentice in a tailor's shop, where continual employment left him little time for engaging with the natural world.[23]

If closer consideration of Carter's claims to have lived a life structured around, and informed by, a compartmentalised city and country divide makes them look more complex, the same is true of Cruikshank's satire on 'The Countryman in London'. As with Carter's *Memoirs*, a deeper reading of this image significantly complicates the rural–urban distinction Cruikshank invoked. What is particularly notable is that the directions the London dandy offered the countryman were incorrect. Cruikshank probably intended this to be indicative of a prank – a view supported by the fact that he published a second engraving to accompany it entitled 'The Londoner in the Country', in which the countryman has his revenge by providing a metropolitan visitor with equally problematic (mis)directions.[24]

Contemporary sources suggest that another interpretation was available to the nineteenth-century viewer: that the London dandy himself did not know the answer to the countryman's question. In the first half of the century, writers regularly emphasised how the scale and frenetic activity of the metropolis combined with perpetual changes to its built environment to ensure that large sections of it remained unknown even to its life-long inhabitants.[25] In preparing his work *The Great Metropolis* (1837), for example, the journalist James Grant noted he had 'in several instances, visited places, and mixed with classes of men, before unknown to him'.[26] Early nineteenth-century accounts of London routinely claimed that it was unknowable and confusing to 'strangers' and 'inhabitants' alike.[27] Even the self-styled expert on 'life in London', Pierce Egan, complained that it was impossible to know in its entirety.[28]

Regardless of which meaning the viewer attached to Cruikshank's engraving, the implications upset the assumed city–country binary. Where did morality reside, if city-dweller and countryman were equally manipulative when offered the opportunity? What did it mean to claim to be a 'Londoner' if even a resident of the capital could not provide directions to its most famous landmark? In which category did an individual like Carter belong, having lived nearly equal parts of his life in London and the provinces, and when and how did he shift from one identity to the other?

Grant wondered if such a person as a 'native' Londoner existed: 'Take any fifty grown-up individuals with whom you happen to be in company, and the probability is you will not find more than one or two who first drew their breath in London.'[29] The work of historical demographers supports such an impression, emphasising both the character of the metropolis as a massive 'revolving door' through which substantial sections of the population passed at different points in their lives, and the fact that high levels of infant mortality ensured that its spectacular growth during the first half of the nineteenth century – like that of every other major British city – continued to be generated primarily by in-migration.[30] London more than doubled in size between Carter's first visit to the metropolis and the year he died (from roughly 1,327,000 persons to 2,685,000).[31] Demographers estimate that as much as three-quarters of this growth was generated by migration, placing the relationship between the 'Londoner' and the 'countryman' in a very different perspective.[32]

Before the 1850s, most adult Londoners had been country-dwellers during some previous phase of their lives. Furthermore, given the frequency with which the city changed inhabitants, many were likely to become country-dwellers again after a sojourn in the metropolis. London, Grant asserted, was 'like a great vortex, drawing persons from all parts of the world into it, and after whirling them about a short time, again throwing them out', and Carter's life trajectory exemplified this larger contemporary pattern.[33]

Given this extensive movement between city and country, one is tempted to conclude that the urban–rural divide that so preoccupied contemporary Britons was largely illusory. Yet, their emphases on rural–urban distinctions should not be too quickly dismissed. There were real differences – social, spatial and sensory – between rapidly growing urban areas and the rest of the country. No city exemplified these differences more than London. If, at the beginning of the twenty-first century, Mumbai represents 'the future of urban civilization on the planet', as Suketu Mehta contends, then London was the Mumbai of the nineteenth century.[34] A city of unprecedented size and modernity, London's rapidly growing population, impoverished masses, crowded streets, magnificent shops and seemingly endless 'wilderness' of brick houses, inspired awe and horror in equal part.[35]

When Carter moved from Colchester to London in 1810, he joined a community more than one hundred times larger than his native town – indeed, more than five times the size of the entire population of his home county of Essex.[36] At that time there was no place in Colchester where one could stand outside and not see trees and fields. Such was certainly not the case in London. Contemporary accounts dwelled at length upon the absence of flowers, trees and shrubs in London's streets and squares. Grant observed that the stranger in London 'fancies himself in a vast world of houses, out of which there is no escaping'.[37] The differences between city and country life in Carter's day were real, and although by the end of the nineteenth century Britain had become the most urbanised civilisation in history, we should not forget that it had a rural majority when the century opened.

Furthermore, the evidentiary record – especially the prevalent motif of country–city difference in the poetry, fiction and autobiographies produced by Britain's labouring classes – suggests that the notion of a rural–urban dichotomy in early nineteenth-century Britain ought to be perceived as a distinctive, fundamental element of the culture of the day.[38] While this belief in a city–country binary was informed by a genealogy of ideas stretching back to classical times, as Raymond Williams demonstrated[39], it was also indicative of the specific conditions at work in British society in that period, and, above all, of the transformative impact of rapid urbanisation.[40] In this context, imagery of the urban–rural divide provided an essential language to express the liminal state produced by the widespread movement in and out of Britain's cities in which individuals had no clearcut identity either as 'city' or as 'country' men and women.

Countryman to Londoner

Let us return to the relationship between James Carter and the characters portrayed in Cruikshank's cartoon. When he moved to London in 1810, Carter intended his relocation to be permanent, but it lasted less than six months. Over the subsequent twenty-six years, he moved between these two communities five more times, before settling in London in 1836. Considered within the context of this personal history, the meaning of Cruikshank's satire on the inhabitants of city and country becomes particularly unstable, for it requires us to acknowledge that at different points in his life trajectory, Carter might have been either character.

Describing his first move to London some thirty years later, Carter noted that, although he did not expect to find 'streets…paved with gold or with penny loaves', he was nevertheless unprepared 'to witness so great a contrast as was here presented to all that I had been accustomed to see in my native place'.[41] Shortly after arriving, he likewise 'contrived to see something of the metropolitan curiosities in the mornings and evenings of the six working-days, as also on the Sundays', and thereby, 'caught a glimpse of the principal public buildings', St. Paul's Cathedral and Westminster Abbey foremost among them.[42] Thus, by his own account, Carter's experience replicated the standard narrative of the 'Countryman in London', involving liberal doses of both disorientation and sightseeing. This narrative was replicated not only in visual satires like Cruikshank's but in other sectors of British culture, including popular songs and the children's literature produced by Carter's fellow Colcestrians, Ann and Jane Taylor.[43]

Other contemporary autobiographical writing reproduces features of Carter's account of his initial exposure to London life, most notably the seventh book of William Wordsworth's *The Prelude*. Both the published 1850 version of the poem, which appeared after Carter's *Memoirs,* and its earlier, unpublished 1805 iteration, shared the tailor's emphasis on the disjuncture between the city as imagined and actually experienced, the importance of visits to metropolitan landmarks and the frenzied tenor of urban life which alternately stimulated and assaulted the senses. This not only suggests that both men's initial experiences in London had much in common but also that they drew on a similar stock of cultural imagery: Wordsworth – like Carter – had been a 'countryman' in London.[44]

Half a year later, however, Carter's role in Cruikshank's cartoon could have been reversed. By this time, the tailor claimed to have become a savvy Londoner, 'sauntering' through the streets and analysing the appearances of his fellow pedestrians, much like Baudelaire's 'painter of modern life'.[45] He recalled, for example, being able to easily identify the 'class of sturdy and clamorous mendicants', from those 'hapless beings' in the London crowds who were actually impoverished. In fact, Carter asserted that the city streets had become for him 'an open book, upon whose broad and diversified pages, even he who ran might see inscribed many an instructive lesson of practical knowledge'.[46] The tailor even owned a pair of Hessian boots![47] Thus, within a few short months, the countryman seemingly had become a seasoned Londoner.

If this transformation occurred remarkably quickly, it was also far from complete. Shortly after the end of his first London 'Season', Carter found himself unemployed, and took to wandering the streets. In Fleet Street his 'attention [was] arrested by a large map of [his] native country', hanging in a shop window. This sight caused him to be 'attacked by that very powerful disorder of the fancy called the "home-sickness"'.[48] He immediately settled his 'little affairs', and 'left the metropolis, with all its attractions', to return to 'fresher and fairer scenes', fully intending never to return.[49]

Seen from this perspective, Carter's altered relationship to London seems more like a momentary flirtation than a sustained commitment – a brief tour rather than an act expressive of the process of urbanisation. In his autobiography, however, Carter asserted that the transformation had been both significant and permanent – 'whether it were for good or evil', he claimed, 'the change was made', and its consequences could not be 'altered or obviated'.[50] In Carter's mind, therefore, the brief experience of London life in the 1810s had been a defining moment in his life that played a crucial role in shaping the man he had become by the 1840s. The very structure of his *Memoirs*, which like many working-class autobiographies drew upon the well-established conventions of religious autobiography, also encouraged the reader to understand his first encounter with London as a sort of conversion experience or a decisive turning point in his existence. This pattern, as Hammond notes, also later informed the fictional life trajectory of Philip 'Pip' Pirrip, the hero of Charles Dickens's *Great Expectations*.[51] What had this transformation entailed?

The tailor's description of how he spent his Sundays during his first year in London is particularly instructive. 'Sunday', he recalled, 'was my most interesting time – my true holiday – when I felt at liberty to go where I pleased.'[52] Though he had been raised as a Dissenter, in London, Carter noted, 'I did not restrict myself to any one sect of professing Christians.'[53] Freed from parental and community oversight, he attended worship at a variety of different churches and chapels, noting that he even 'frequently joined' in the services of 'the National Church Establishment' with 'unaffected satisfaction', despite having been raised to view it 'unfavorably'.[54] In fact, he emphasised that in London in general, 'I had no restraint upon my movements ... consequently, I was left perfectly free to choose for myself.'[55] Like the young Wordsworth, in the capital Carter was free to follow his 'unchecked fancy'.[56] He ranged widely from his lodgings, 'in order that I might see something new', and read copious publications in coffee houses or from bookstalls.[57]

If the contrast between the unnatural and the natural dominated the tailor's account of the city and the country, so also did the belief that the city represented a superior space for personal education. Carter repeatedly emphasised the 'knowledge' and 'instruction' provided in the 'powerfully impressive' lessons of London's 'much-thronged avenues' and other urban 'spectacles', and the relative dearth of such '*living* lessons' in the country.[58] Metropolitan bookstalls loomed especially large in this respect, and he noted that he 'took care to avail' himself of them 'as often, and for as long a time, as possible; and from these out-of-door libraries picked up a few – perhaps a good many – scraps of useful and amusing information'.[59]

Carter had discovered what so many nineteenth-century critics of the city lamented – that anonymity bred autonomy, of both mind and action. If for some late-nineteenth-century writers, as Sloan notes, the shift to city life seemed to threaten the physical health of the population and the strength of national traditions and values, in Carter's day the primary spectre it raised was of its insurrectionary potential as a social milieu that bred personal and political independence – and the tailor's recorded activities suggest such fears were not misplaced. Upon his return to Colchester, Carter bridled under parental and government authority. In fact, he avoided his parents' company entirely, choosing to retire to 'my garret, where I employed myself in either reading or working'.[60] After less than 'seven weeks with my parents', Carter was back in the capital, having fled there to evade service in the militia.[61] In London, he had learned that he 'felt it to be impossible to be a party-man', a stance that proved deeply divisive in the compartmentalised community of Colchester.[62]

Though he would return to live there on two more occasions, he found it impossible to be anything but a disruptive presence in his hometown. He married a Londoner without the knowledge of his parents.[63] He successfully represented a combination of tailors in a wages dispute that ultimately proved successful.[64] He engaged in religious freethinking, first leaving his family's Dissenting congregation for the Methodists, and then leaving the Methodists to join the Church of the New Jerusalem, becoming a Swedenborgian.[65] When asked to serve on a jury, he infuriated the summoning officer by demonstrating a superior knowledge of English law, and for protesting against the custom of 'treating' jury members with alcohol. The officer understandably 'never again gave [Carter] a summons'.[66]

Although other scholars have characterised Carter as the very essence of the 'deferential working man', his own descriptions of his behaviour have much more 'defiance' than 'deference' about them, and they exemplify how the experience of urban life had transformed the tailor's fundamental attitude toward authority.[67] 'I did not want to work as a journeyman', Carter admitted, when narrating his third return to Colchester in 1819, because he no longer wished to be beholden to any 'master' but himself.[68] This claim about his relationship to his primary trade paralleled the attitude he exhibited in general toward the rest of his native community, attesting to the altered perspective a London education had instilled in the mind of the 'humble' country tailor.

The country, the city and the borderland

We have noted that in the 1780s, William Cowper bemoaned the fact that increasingly 'the town has tinged the country', and deplored the negative changes in the rural world caused by the arrival of London clothing, crime and customs.[69] Roughly a century later, Thomas Hardy similarly lamented the extension of London's influence into the deepest reaches of the English countryside in his Wessex novels of the 1870s and 1880s, in which metropolitan fashions, books and ideas also invaded the material and cultural universe of rural life.

Carter also bore witness to these changes, albeit through his own ideas and attitudes. After 1810, in his independence of thought and action, as in his knowledge and attitudes, the tailor exhibited the 'tinge' of the metropolis. His record of his time in and out of London demonstrates that urbanisation involved more than simple population movement. Physical migration may have been impermanent, but its effects on the personality, behaviour and worldview of migrants were lasting. Carter's account of the abiding impact of rural–urban migration on his life and perceptions, and on his interactions with his family and the inhabitants of his native town, occupies the midpoint of the era stretching between Cowper's lament for a countryside 'tinged' by the city and Hardy's depictions of a near-fully urbanised nation where the 'existence of the town masses is more and more the existence of the rural masses'.[70] The tailor's writings also attest to the same revolutionary shift in the complexion of British social and cultural life wrought by urbanisation.

These same writings also remind us that the transformation engendered by the experience of modern urban life was never total. Until the day he died, many of Carter's default modes of thought remained implicitly or explicitly rural in nature. His defence of the benefits of early rising published shortly before his death in 1853 exemplified this tendency. 'No one', Carter claimed, 'except by personal experience, can adequately understand either the nature, the variety or the extent of this pleasure.'[71] Of what did this 'pleasure' consist? 'To walk abroad in the early hours of the morning; to inhale the fresh and refreshing morning air; to smell the fragrance of plants and flowers; to survey the beautiful verdure of the fields and meadows; to see the shepherd tending his flock, or the farm-labourer at his work.'[72]

Such pleasures, however 'delightful', were not available to the city-dweller. Carter lamented this reality elsewhere in the same essay, observing that: 'Modern habits of living are, indeed, unfavourable to these wholesome practices, especially as respects the inhabitants of large towns.'[73] Nevertheless, the fact that he still universalised these country images after almost two decades of uninterrupted life in the largest city in Europe, exposes the limits of the transformation London had wrought upon his worldview. In view of this, at first glance Carter's decision to narrate his secular transformation in the crucible of British modernity within the established rhetorical framework of the religious conversion narrative seems a poor choice, given his incomplete transition from a countryman into a city-dweller. To interpret it in such a fashion, however, risks missing a singularly important aspect of the lesson Carter's autobiography offers on the meanings of urbanisation in nineteenth-century Britain.

Carter's move to London in 1810 had transformed him, not from a countryman into a Cockney but into something in between. Amid the heightened migration that characterised his time, this hybrid state was an important category of identity in its own right, and one that became the inheritance of an increasingly large swathe of the population. Hardy was himself acutely aware that this was the case. Raymond Williams observed that while Hardy's Wessex novels are often portrayed as being dominated by a tension between timeless rural traditions and urban modernity, their central conflicts stem not from London clothes and books but from people who previously left the country for the city and returned home.[74] Despite their different titles, Williams argued that all of these novels addressed the same problem of the 'return of the native' – and the 'exceptionally complicated' relations between 'the migrant and his [or her] former group'.[75] Such individuals' migrations left them stuck in an eternal 'border' region, in which the emotional bonds of memory and family linked them forever to a place where they no longer felt fully at home. Arguably, Hardy himself was such an individual, having moved from his native Dorsetshire to London in 1862. Though he returned to the countryside in 1867 and celebrated scenes of rural life in his fiction, after his time in London Hardy remained largely an outsider in his native county, avoiding even his closest relatives. He was thus himself an inhabitant of the very borderland his novels sought to describe.[76]

After 1810, James Carter also inhabited this same socio-cultural borderland. Indeed, as Williams and others have observed, the changing rural world Hardy described was not that of his own day but of Carter's - a world of 'railways, the penny post, mowing and reaping machines, union workhouses, lucifer matches, labourers who could read and write, and National school children', all developments that occurred during the tailor's lifetime.[77] The evidence of autobiographies like Carter's reminds us that Hardy (and Williams) had grasped something that most demographic histories of rural–urban migration rarely acknowledge. While these histories emphasise the importance of 'two-channel' migration – of continuous, parallel movements between countryside and city and city and countryside – their authors assert that the frequency of such moves meant that they were socially and psychologically easy and stress-free, and that emotional and familial networks helped to make them this way.[78] Hardy knew that this was not the case, observing in 1883 that the 'varied experience' facilitated by migration, while making men and women 'shrewder and sharper' and 'more wide awake', came at the cost of the loss of 'individuality' and of 'local feeling or manner'.[79]

Accounts like Carter's demonstrate the truth of such assertions, providing evidence that the encounter with the modern city was not easily brushed aside. One could physically return to the country, but one could never really go home again, a notion that also informed Dickens's account of Pip's movement from the country to London. Carter returned to Colchester, to a family, a church and a community he no longer found congenial, and when the time came to start a family of his own, he chose as a mate, not an inhabitant of his hometown but a native Londoner. His repeated moves from Colchester to London and London to Colchester between 1810 and 1836 are indicative of a man of unsettled disposition whose physical wanderings were only brought to a halt by economic necessity and increasing physical debility. Carter exhibited the 'instability' that Victor Turner famously associated with liminal states – with those individuals who had passed out of one established social category (in Carter's case that of the 'Countryman') but failed to enter into another such category at the end of the process.[80]

In the nineteenth century, urbanisation created communities of individuals whose experiences represented a mixture of both city and country life. The inability to accommodate these men and women within the existing cultural system – one exemplified by the problems posed in attempting to square the evidence of Carter's autobiography with the visual iconography of Cruikshank's engraving – left many Britons in the same unstable state as Carter, contributing to the palpable sense of disruption and disorientation that characterised much of British society during the first half of the century. For the remainder of his life, the tailor physically and mentally wandered both fields and streets, never entirely at home in either. Carter's transformation into an inhabitant of this border country, a mental and cultural space inhabited by countless Britons of his day, was thus indicative of the changing society he lived in, one that was neither fully rural nor urban, neither a modern society nor an *ancien régime,* but someplace on the road between the two.

Notes

1 J. Gooder, 'Introduction', in H. Adams, *The Education of Henry Adams* (London: Penguin, 1995), pp. ix–xii; J. C. Rowe, *Henry Adams and Henry James: The Emergence of a Modern Consciousness* (Ithaca: Cornell University Press, 1976).

2 J. Carter, *Memoirs of a Working Man* (London: Charles Knight and Company, 1845); J. Carter, *Continuation of the Memoirs of a Working Man* (London: Charles Cox, 1850).

3 Carter, *Continuation of the Memoirs of a Working Man*, p. 11.

4 C. Knight, *Passages of a Working Life during a Half a Century*, vol. 3, pp. 12–14; 'Obituary: Mr. James Carter', *Gentleman's Magazine*, 49 (1853), pp. 96–97; Archives of the Royal Literary Fund, *Registered Case File, vol. 25, no. 813: Mr. James Carter, a Tailor of Colchester*, British Library Add MS RLF 1/813/1-60; F. Boase, *Modern English Biography: Containing Many Thousand Concise Memoirs of Persons Who have Died since the Year 1850* (Truro: Netherton and Worth, 1892), vol. 1, p. 561.

5 S. Gunn and J. Vernon, 'Introduction: What was Liberal Modernity and Why was It Peculiar in Imperial Britain?', in S. Gunn and J. Vernon (eds), *The Peculiarities of Liberal Modernity in Imperial Britain* (Berkeley: University of California Press, 2011), p. 3; C. A. Bayly, *The Birth of the Modern World, 1780–1914* (Malden, Mass.: Blackwell, 2004), pp. 170–198.

6 R. Woods, *The Population of Britain in the Nineteenth Century* (London: Macmillan, 1992), pp. 35–36.

7 G. Cruikshank, *The Countryman in London* (London: R. Harrild, [1814]).

8 G. Cruikshank, 'Picture of London', in *The Metropolis of England Displayed; or, A Pilot Thro' London* (London: G. Smeeton, n. d.); G. Cruikshank, *Looby Lump's Life in London* (London: George Humphrey, 1822).

9 Carter, *Memoirs of a Working Man*, p. 198.

10 Carter, *Memoirs of a Working Man*, pp. 160–161, 143.

11 Carter, *Memoirs of a Working Man*, pp. 140–143; Carter, *Continuation of the Memoirs of a Working Man,* p. 58.

12 M. D. George, *Catalogue of Political and Personal Satires in the British Museum* (London: British Museum, 1978), vol. 9, pp. 475–476; George, *Catalogue of Political and Personal Satires*, vol. 8, pp. 315, 502–503.

13 I. Dyck, 'The Town and Country Divide in English History', in M. Chase and I. Dyck (eds), *Living and Learning: Essays in Honour of J. F. C. Harrison* (Aldershot: Scolar

Press, 1996), pp. 81–102; A. Bermingham, *Landscape and Ideology: The English Rustic Tradition, 1740–1860* (London: Thames and Hudson, 1987), pp. 73–83.

14 I. Dyck, *William Cobbett and Rural Popular Culture* (Cambridge: Cambridge University Press, 1992), pp. 47–49, 54–58, 114, 131–132.

15 W. Cowper, *The Task* (1785), I: 749, in J. D. Baird and C. Ryskamp (eds), *The Poems of William Cowper: Volume II, 1782–1785* (Oxford: Clarendon Press, 1995), p. 136.

16 C. Ferguson, 'Inventing the Modern City: Urban Culture and Ideas in Britain, 1780–1880' (PhD Dissertation, Indiana University, 2008), pp. 299–301.

17 Carter, *Memoirs of a Working Man*, p. 161; Carter, *Continuation of the Memoirs of a Working Man*, p. 78; Cowper, *The Task*, III: 835.

18 J. Carter, *Thoughts on Several Subjects* (London: Charles Cox, 1852), p. 82; Cowper, *The Task*, IV: 694.

19 Carter, *Memoirs of a Working Man*, p. 111.

20 Carter, *Memoirs of a Working Man*, p. 50.

21 Carter, *Continuation of the Memoirs of a Working Man*, p. 90; Carter, *Memoirs of a Working Man*, pp. 121, 198; Cowper, *The Task*, 4:759, 771.

22 Carter, *Continuation*, p. 49; B. R. Mitchell, *British Historical Statistics* (Cambridge: Cambridge University Press, 1988), p. 26; S. D'Cruze, *A Pleasing Prospect: Social Change and Urban Culture in Eighteenth-Century Colchester* (Hatfield: University of Hertfordshire Press, 2008), pp. 24–30, 101–126; J. Borsay, *The English Urban Renaissance: Culture and Society in the Provincial Town, 1660–1770* (Oxford: Clarendon Press, 1989), pp. 111, 148, 237.

23 Carter, *Memoirs*, pp. 22–24, 42–61, 68–70, 111–114.

24 George, *Catalogue of Political and Personal Satires*, vol. 9, p. 476.

25 Ferguson, 'Inventing the Modern City', pp. 46, 141–142.

26 J. Grant, *The Great Metropolis* (New York: Saunders and Otley, 1837), vol. 1, p. iii.

27 Ferguson, 'Inventing the Modern City', pp. 56–57.

28 P. Egan, *Life in London* (London: Sherwood, Neely and Jones, 1822), p. 2.

29 Grant, *The Great Metropolis*, p. 16.

30 J. Langton, 'Urban Growth and Economic Change from the Seventeenth Century to 1841', in P. Clark (ed.), *The Cambridge Urban History of Britain, 1540–1840* (Cambridge: Cambridge University Press, 2000), pp. 453–490; P. Sharpe, 'Population and Society, 1700–1840', in P. Clark (ed.), *Cambridge Urban History of Britain* (Cambridge: Cambridge University Press, 2000), pp. 491–528; R. Lawton, 'Population Mobility and Urbanization: Nineteenth-Century British Experience', in R. Lawton and R. Lee (eds), *Urban Population Development in Western Europe from the Late-Eighteenth to the Early-Twentieth Century* (Liverpool: Liverpool University Press, 1989), pp. 149–177; C. G. Pooley and J. Turnbull, *Migration and Mobility in Britain since the Eighteenth Century* (London: UCL Press, 1998), pp. 84–85, 93–94, 307; I. D. Whyte, *Migration and Society in Britain, 1550–1830* (Basingstoke: Macmillan, 2000), pp. 90–91, 143, 146–147.

31 Mitchell, *British Historical Statistics*, p. 25.

32 Lawton, 'Population Mobility and Urbanization', p. 157.

33 Grant, *The Great Metropolis*, p. 17.

34 S. Mehta, *Maximum City: Bombay Lost and Found* (New York: Alfred A. Knopf, 2004), p. 3.

35 Ferguson, 'Inventing the Modern City', pp. 237–239.

36 Mitchell, *British Historical Statistics*, pp. 25–26, 30.

37 Grant, *The Great Metropolis*, vol. 1, p. 1.

38 Dyck, 'Town and Country', pp. 94–95; P. Joyce, *Democratic Subjects: The Self and the Social in Nineteenth-Century England* (Cambridge: Cambridge University Press, 1994), pp. 53–56; O. Ashton and S. Roberts, *The Victorian Working-Class Writer* (London: Cassell, 1999), pp. 11–14, 32–35, 78, 100–101; P. Gurney, 'Working-Class

Writers and the Art of Escapology in Victorian England: The Case of Thomas Frost',
Journal of British Studies, 45: 1 (2006), pp. 51–71.

39 R. Williams, *The Country and the City* (Oxford: Oxford University Press, 1973).

40 Dyck, *William Cobbett and Rural Popular Culture*, pp. 126, 138, 147; Ferguson,
'Inventing the Modern City', pp. 293–302.

41 Carter, *Memoirs of a Working Man*, p. 117.

42 Carter, *Memoirs of a Working Man*, pp. 125–127.

43 'The Countryman in London', *The Universal Songster; or, Museum of Mirth* (London:
John Fairburn, 1825), vol. 1, pp. 294–295; [A. Taylor and J. Taylor], *City Scenes; or,
A Peep into London for Good Children* (London: Darton and Harvey, 1809).

44 William Wordsworth, *The Prelude* (1805) and *The Prelude* (1850), 7: 58–140, 595–607,
659–663, 702–705, in Jonathan Wordsworth, M. H. Abrams and Stephen Gill (eds),
The Prelude 1799, 1805, 1850 (New York: W. W. Norton, 1979), pp. 226–267.

45 Carter, *Memoirs of a Working Man*, p. 134; C. Baudelaire, *The Painter of Modern Life
and Other Essays,* trans. J. Mayne (New York: Phaidon Publishing, 1964), pp. 4, 9.

46 Carter, *Memoirs of a Working Man*, pp. 142–143.

47 Carter, *Memoirs of a Working Man*, p. 150.

48 Carter, *Memoirs of a Working Man*, pp. 134–135.

49 Carter, *Memoirs of a Working Man*, p. 135.

50 Carter, *Memoirs of a Working Man*, pp. 118–119.

51 D. Vincent, *Bread, Knowledge and Freedom: A Study of Nineteenth-Century Working
Class Autobiography* (London: Methuen, 1981), pp. 14–19; E. Griffin, *Liberty's
Dawn: A People's History of the Industrial Revolution* (New Haven: Yale University
Press, 2013), p. 47.

52 Carter, *Memoirs of a Working Man*, p. 128.

53 Carter, *Memoirs of a Working Man*, pp. 128–129.

54 Carter, *Memoirs of a Working Man*, p. 129.

55 Carter, *Memoirs of a Working Man*, p. 130.

56 Wordsworth, *The Prelude* (1850), 7: 75.

57 Carter, *Memoirs of a Working Man*, pp. 128–131.

58 Carter, *Memoirs of a Working Man*, pp. 142–143, Carter's italics.

59 Carter, *Memoirs of a Working Man*, pp. 131–132.

60 Carter, *Memoirs of a Working Man*, p. 135.

61 Carter, *Memoirs of a Working Man*, p. 137.

62 Carter, *Memoirs of a Working Man*, p. 129.

63 Carter, *Memoirs of a Working Man*, p. 206; London Metropolitan Archives, *Saint Paul,
Covent Garden, Westminster, Transcript of Baptisms, Marriages and Burials, 1819
Jan–1819 Dec*, no.158, LMA 098/018.

64 Carter, *Memoirs of a Working Man*, p. 169.

65 Carter, *Memoirs of a Working Man*, p. 224; Carter, *Continuation of the Memoirs of a
Working Man*, pp. 66–67; 'Review: James Carter, *Two Lectures on Taste,*' *Intellectual
Repository and New Jerusalem Magazine*, 30: 34 (1835), p. 543.

66 Carter, *Memoirs of a Working Man*, pp. 218–220.

67 J. Burnett, D. Vincent and D. Mayall (eds), *The Autobiography of the Working Class:
An Annotated, Critical Bibliography* (New York: New York University Press, 1984),
vol. 1, p. 60; N. Hackett, *XIX Century British Working-Class Autobiographies: An
Annotated Bibliography* (New York: AMS Press, 1985), pp. 64–68; A. F. J. Brown,
Essex People, 1750–1900: From Their Diaries, Memoirs and Letters (Chelmsford:
Essex County Council, 1972), p. 104.

68 Carter, *Memoirs of a Working Man*, p. 207.

69 Cowper, *The Task*, 4: 553.

70 T. Hardy, 'The Dorsetshire Labourer' (1883), in H. Orel (ed.), *Thomas Hardy's
Personal Writings: Prefaces, Literary Opinions, Reminiscences* (Lawrence: University
of Kansas Press, 1966), p. 182.

71 Carter, *Thoughts on Several Subjects*, p. 141.
72 Carter, *Thoughts on Several Subjects*, pp. 141–142.
73 Carter, *Thoughts on Several Subjects*, p. 136.
74 Williams, *The Country and the City*, pp. 195–214.
75 Williams, *The Country and the City*, pp. 201–202.
76 K. D. M. Snell, *Annals of the Labouring Poor: Social Change and Agrarian England, 1660–1900* (Cambridge: Cambridge University Press, 1985), pp. 387–388, 396–397.
77 T. Hardy, 'Preface to *Far from the Maddening Crowd*' (1874), in Orel (ed), *Thomas Hardy's Personal Writings,* p. 9; Williams, *The Country and the City*, p. 207; Snell, *Annals of the Labouring Poor*, pp. 379, 410.
78 Pooley and Turnbull, *Migration and Mobility in Britain since the Eighteenth Century*, pp. 69, 84, 94–98, 103, 117–119, 130; Whyte, *Migration and Society in Britain*, pp. 142, 147, 151, 173.
79 Hardy, 'The Dorsetshire Labourer' (1883), p. 180; J. Barrell, 'Geographies of Hardy's Wessex', in K. D. M. Snell (ed), *The Regional Novel in Britain and Ireland, 1800–1990* (Cambridge: Cambridge University Press, 1998), pp. 100–101.
80 V. Turner, *The Ritual Process: Structure and Anti-Structure* (1969; Ithaca: Cornell University Press, 1977), pp. 94–130.

11   Pip at the fingerpost

Nineteenth-century urban–rural
relations and the reception of
Dickens's *Great Expectations*,
1860–1885

Mary Hammond

Charles Dickens's *Great Expectations* (1860–1861) is set in the first turbulent quarter of the nineteenth century, but it is implicitly concerned with the related social changes taking place almost half a century later. [1] The tensions between city and country are much more than a convenient backdrop to this conceptual parallel: comparative urban–rural experiences are in fact a key part not only of its structure but also of its cultural affect, informing the development of its main protagonist Philip ('Pip') Pirrip and simultaneously reflecting on a segmented and at times antagonistic mid-century Victorian body politic.

The novel is divided into three sections representing the three stages of Pip's 'expectations': Stage 1, set in the rural marshes of Kent; Stage 2, set in London; and Stage 3, moving restlessly between London and Kent and also squeezing in an offstage decade in Egypt, a well-used Victorian literary trope which gives Pip the chance to affirm his mature masculinity in the colonies. It is something of a critical commonplace now that this structure has a Miltonian feel: Pip's innocence comes to an end in Stage 1 when he meets and falls in love with Estella, his social better, in the neglected but (to Pip) idyllic Kent garden of her guardian, Miss Havisham. Wicked London is the setting for his 'fall' in Stage 2 as he is educated for a gentleman and becomes a profligate snob. Stage 3 drives him relentlessly back and forth between the urban and rural worlds until he learns to mend his ways – and simultaneously realises that, for him, the price of social mobility is that while he can live anywhere, he belongs nowhere.[2] A pivotal moment in the novel occurs at the end of Stage 1 as Pip leaves his village for the first time and pauses in distress by the fingerpost pointing the way to London and his new future:

> the village was very peaceful and quiet, and the light mists were solemnly rising as if to show me the world, and I had been so innocent and little there, and all beyond was so unknown and great, that in a moment with a strong heave and sob I broke into tears. It was by the finger-post at the end of the village, and I laid my hand upon it, and said, 'Good-by, O my dear, dear friend!'[3]

This moment clearly signals the end of 'innocent' country Pip prior to his plunge into the great urban unknown which will become only too familiar to him in the next decade of his life, and will change him forever. But the common critical focus on this bildungsroman as a modern *Paradise Lost* and its obsessive return to the 'garden' of the Kent countryside 'as an index to character, as a metonymic *mise-en-scène*, or as a metaphoric reflection of an ethical code' is in some respects insufficient when we consider the range of contexts in which *Great Expectations* first appeared, examine some of the different incarnations in which it has been reproduced over time and explore the different responses it has engendered in different regions.[4] Viewed from this wider perspective it becomes clear that the metaphorical implications of the novel's 'garden' were not interpreted in the same way by all readers, illustrators or publishers, and that the metaphor offers very different horizons of interpretation in different reception contexts.

This chapter aims to read some of the different cultural appearances of *Great Expectations* as important sources of evidence for the plurality and mutability of nineteenth-century rural–urban encounters. My claim that there is an intimate relationship between literature and urban-rural identities is not original, of course; Ian Dyck is not strictly accurate when he claims that 'micro-study of the town-country relationship [has been left to] demographers, geographers and economic historians, who understandably have focused on population shifts, trading networks and service exchanges rather than the cultural dimensions of the contrast'.[5] Raymond Williams is only the most famous of those who have studied the concept from a cultural dimension, proving that literature, too, can offer rich material for micro-studies.[6] But, mindful of the interdisciplinary spirit of this book, here I move away somewhat from traditional text-based readings of the urban–rural interface in *Great Expectations*. Instead, like the other chapters in this section, I use Victorian print culture as a lens through which to examine the inherent dynamism of the interrelationships between physical migration, regional identity and cultural change in nineteenth-century Britain. I argue here that a consideration of the reception contexts of reissued, reillustrated and pirated versions of this text over a period of years can aid in our understanding of changing social mores. The significance of Pip's emotional moment of stasis at the fingerpost – poised between innocence and experience, emotional integrity and moral dissipation, country and city, and the working and the upper middle classes – is thus less a metaphor in my account than it is a cultural barometer. It is a moment, as we shall see, which carries lasting significance and which reveals changing attitudes to urbanisation in the twenty years following the novel's first appearance.

Great Expectations, the city and the country in the 1860s

In the autumn of 1860, commuting regularly between his new country house in Kent and the London offices of his new periodical, *All the Year Round*, Dickens was a worried and exhausted man. The current serial in his magazine, *A Day's Ride: A Life's Romance* (18 August 1860–23 March 1861), written by his friend Charles Lever, had precipitated a plunge in circulation which he could ill afford, since for complicated reasons he was at that moment responsible for the upkeep not only of his own large house and nine children but also of three additional separate establishments (those of his estranged wife; his mother and recently bereaved sister-in-law and her five young children; and – secretly – his mistress Nelly Ternan and her family). Performing in his reading tours, running the new magazine in an increasingly competitive literary marketplace and writing for it a series of clever, reflective articles called the *Uncommercial Traveller* took up most of his creative energy, but in light of incipient financial difficulty he had no choice but to 'strike in', as he put it to his friend Forster, and take over the leading serial himself at a time when writing a new novel was the last thing he felt like doing.[7] *Great Expectations* is the extraordinary result. Ironic and at times comical as only vintage Dickens can be, it is nonetheless bursting with the unresolved fragments of its author's troubled past and current lives, situating them against a restless emotional pendulum of alternating urban–rural longings, neither of which is ever wholly resolved. In this sense it is undoubtedly far more 'about' the 1860s than it is 'about' the 1820s; and, as I will show, it can tell us as much about Dickens's cultural moment (and indeed some of the key moments that came after him) as about the author himself.

The novel's early publication history is well documented: weekly serialisation (unillustrated) in *All the Year Round* in Britain and simultaneously (illustrated) in *Harper's Weekly* in the USA between December 1860 and August 1861; a three-volume unillustrated edition published by Chapman and Hall (London) and T.B. Peterson's (Philadelphia) in 1861; a one-volume illustrated edition in 1862, and numerous further editions (both illustrated and unillustrated) both within and beyond Dickens's lifetime. I will return later to the significance of some of these illustrations and the interesting cultural changes which they signal. But first I want to explore in greater detail the early reception history of the unillustrated UK versions, since it is slightly more complicated (and more interesting) than this official story suggests. Thanks to recent developments in digital technology, we can now trace more fully than ever before its lesser known and in some cases illegitimate twists and turns through rural as well as urban contexts.

Chapman and Hall and Peterson's, like most other large publishers in this period, were based in conurbations and they understandably served and indeed depended on large urban readerships. This sense of new novels emerging from the city and predominantly serving the city reader was apparently bolstered by contemporary reviewing practices; as befits the appearance of a new Dickens novel, reviews in the major urban magazines and newspapers were numerous and substantial. The *Daily News* (edited by Dickens's friend, John Forster), the *Literary Examiner*, the *Saturday Review*, the *Spectator*, the *Morning Post*, and *The Times* were all based in London. *Blackwood's Magazine* was based in Edinburgh, the *Dublin University Magazine* in Dublin and the *Daily Tribune*, the *Times* and the *Atlantic Monthly* in New York. All these publications – as a number of modern analyses of the novel's critical reception have pointed out – devoted several pages to reviews upon its volume release in summer 1861.[8] But this does not mean that discussion of *Great Expectations* in 1860–1 was largely an urban phenomenon; indeed, this is an assumption that has tended to be constructed and perpetuated by modern critics. Discussions or passing mentions of *Great*

Expectations which appeared in rural or small-town newspapers have seldom, if ever, made it into scholarly discussions of Dickens's novels, but they are quite numerous and well worth examining. Not only do they give us a much better sense of the reach of one of Dickens's major late works, but they demonstrate a very particular and – for social geographers – interesting type of engagement with the text. A comparative analysis of the position which each type of publication adopted in relation to Dickens's representation of urban (upper-class) moral vacuity versus rural (lower-class) moral integrity reveals that a strikingly different type of self-identification existed in urban and rural journalism in this period.

Many of the urban reviewers praise the novel's lower-class characters and criticise its middle-class ones, attacking above all Dickens's poor sense of the difference. It is significant that Wemmick (the lower-middle-class city employee with a self-constructed rural retreat in Walworth) comes in for much praise, while Miss Havisham (rural dwelling but upper-middle class and patently unbalanced) comes in for particular criticism. The *Morning Post*, for example, calls Miss Havisham 'the prime and chief monstrosity of the story', spluttering: 'This woman's character has no redeeming trait; she is such a foolish, senseless, fantastical, impossible humbug.'[9] The London *Guardian* called both her and Estella 'utterly unnatural',[10] and *The Times* described her as one of 'Mr Dickens's worst mannerisms'.[11] The *Morning Post* admits grudgingly that 'Pip himself is not badly drawn, allowing for the limited space of three volumes in which the blacksmith's boy has to become a gentleman and go through various adventures, and allowing for the extraordinary absence of comprehension of class distinctions for which Mr. Dickens is remarkable.'[12] The *Dublin University Magazine* agrees, putting Pip's waning appeal for readers down to 'time and good fortune, combined with the weakness that mars all Mr. Dickens's attempts at painting the social life of the more polished classes'.[13] The *Spectator* also attributes the novel's failure to Dickens's blindness to class differences:

> The cause which renders Mr. Dickens's great genius so comparatively impotent in the more cultivated sphere of life and sentiment which he sometimes essays to paint, is not far to find. In the uneducated classes character is far more characteristically expressed, if we may use the expression, than in the higher. The effect of cultivation is to draw a certain thin semi-transparent medium over the whole surface of human nature, so that the effects of individual differences of character, though by no means hidden, are softened and disguised, and require, not so much a subtle discrimination to discern, as a subtler artistic faculty to delineate without falsification.[14]

When we consider the trajectory of Pip's journey from blacksmith's boy to gentleman, so closely mapped by Dickens onto a physical and emotional migration from country to city, from simple, rural, familial pleasures to selfish and sometimes even illegal urban entanglements, the class issue mentioned by so many of these reviewers can be seen as implicitly connected to these relative geographies. Dickens is famous for his portraits of the urban working classes, but *Great Expectations* is different. In this novel, Dickens's focus when he moves Pip to the city is not on happy working-class slum dwellers but on middle-class corruption, and the negative criticism which the shift engendered is surely at least partly a result of the juxtaposition of the different moral connotations inscribed in its settings. In fact these urban reviews contribute significantly to a sense that city dwellers in this period considered themselves intrinsically different from country people – superior, smoother, more civilised. And they felt that in painting city dwellers as morally dissipated – in giving them 'character' (especially bad character) – Dickens has got something both ethically and aesthetically wrong. This presents a curious contrast to the pastoral Romantic tradition which had dominated just a few decades earlier (even in the popular early works of Dickens such as *The Pickwick Papers*, serialised 1836–7) and which yearned nostalgically for the countryside as the industrial cities began their inexorable sprawl. This sea change was becoming increasingly evident in the work of other authors. Even Elizabeth Gaskell, who in the 1840s and early 1850s had painted dire pictures of urban poverty and demonised the coming of the railways, later softened her view: in 1855 in *North and South* she marries her 'civilised' rural Southern gentlewoman Margaret Hale off to a brusque Northern industrialist and, after revising their respective prejudices, settles them happily in a mill town in Darkshire. In *Great Expectations* Dickens was in some ways writing against the cultural and literary tide.

The urban-rural rivalry we see here is not new; as Ian Dyck notes:

> Good-natured teasing between rural and urban people has a long history in England but the Restoration period sees the beginning of gratuitous and mean-spirited stereotypes, especially of rural workers ... An urban identity is negatively distilled from the anti-countryman literature and more positively from close exploration of the distinctiveness of urban, particularly London culture.[15]

In the nineteenth century the relationship between town and country was, perhaps, even less stable than it had been during the Restoration and what we seem to be seeing now, in 1860, is a backlash against the demonising of the city that had dominated from the 1820s to the 1850s. This could be a result of the fact that urbanisation had reached a tipping point: as Eric Hobsbawm points out, 'Townsmen outnumbered countrymen for the first time in 1851.'[16] But the literary scales were also shifting: the urban reception of Dickens's return to the pastoral in *Great Expectations* suggests that this, his thirteenth novel, was born into a very different world from *Pickwick*. It was a world still happy to romanticise the simple pleasures of the countryside but far less inclined to accept relentlessly negative depictions of the city and its inhabitants.

The subtle self-identification apparent in these urban reviews is significant in itself, but equally significant is the tenor of the references to the novel which appeared in smaller regional papers with considerable rural readerships. They often reprint extracts of the longer metropolitan reviews, of course, as part of the common Victorian practice of sharing news stories, but they also frequently publish original reviews and these repay close critical study. Not all these papers liked the story; in fact one, the *Hereford Journal*, shared the urban papers' opinion of Dickens's struggle to delineate social differences, opining: 'The humour is more forced and exaggerated than ever, and it labours under a manifest difficulty in depicting the feelings and observations of a youth in an inferior position, from his mouth when he is a man, and in a higher station of life.'[17] But by far the greater number are enthusiastic. After the first instalments the *Northampton Mercury* felt: 'It has all the vivid originality of his writings, and promises to be a great attraction. The mingled yarn of comic and tragic incident of which the web of his tales is constituted, is manifest in the earliest instalments.'[18] And in direct contrast to the urban reviewers, the *Chester Chronicle* picked out Dickens's characterisations for particular praise: 'The whole of the characters are depicted in the clever, truthful, easy, and happy manner for which Mr Dickens is so justly celebrated, and the materials are thrown together in such an interesting form that no-one can help reading "Great Expectations" with avidity.'[19] In reviewing the novel in its entirety, the *Derby Mercury* agreed: '[Here] we have a score of characters as original, as artistically drawn, and more elaborately developed, than any our well-beloved author has before contributed to the world of literature.'[20]

Such reviews are, however, only a fraction of the interest these regional newspapers provide to the literary or cultural historian. Several of them also reprint short verbatim extracts from the novel, and they do so in ways that work far beyond the customary Victorian reviewing practice of printing lengthy quotations to prove a point or whet the reader's appetite. These extracts are not reviews at all, as they appear quite out of context and they make no comment whatsoever on the rest of the novel. In fact they are clearly piracies: there is nothing in Dickens's correspondence to indicate that permission for reprinting them was received from him (though we know he was a keen copyright watcher), and the records of his earnings with his publishers contain no clear evidence that he was paid for them.[21] Understandably, perhaps, since they need to work as stand-alone segments, they often focus on the humorous episodes. For example, the *Leeds Times* of 6 April 1861, p. 3, reprints the scene in which Mr Wopsle plays Hamlet; the section on Wemmick's marriage to Miss Skiffins entitled 'An Impromptu Wedding' was reprinted in the *Worcestershire Chronicle* on Wednesday 31 July 1861, p. 4; the section in which Pip and Estella have tea together after her arrival in London appears as 'Tea at an Hotel' in the *Salisbury and Winchester Journal*, Saturday 24 August 1861, p. 3, and also in the *Bath Chronicle and Weekly Gazette* on Thursday 1 August 1861, p. 6. There are many other examples: reprinting bits of a popular novel without permission was common practice and undoubtedly good publicity for the authors concerned.

A closer look at some of these extracts pays further dividends, though, beyond the evidence they provide of widespread readership, and they should be of particular interest to historians interested in urban–rural relations since they are frequently adopted in the service of the quietly proud entrenchment of regional, and specifically non-London, identities. Judging by their contents, regional newspapers were clearly well aware by this period that most of their readers were interested in and profoundly affected by London, whether through the nationally significant decisions made in Westminster or the unarguable importance of the nation's capital as the centre of trade, commerce and art. Almost all the regional papers I have examined carry a section on the arts and politics by a 'London Correspondent' along with news on the London law courts and the stock markets. But necessity does not breed respect or envy in rural and small-town newspapers – far from it. Their use of *Great Expectations* in the 1860s serves to highlight the negotiations between the strategic importance of metropolitan news and the entrenchment of a subtly oppositional rural identity in which they were engaged in this period.

The *Hampshire Advertiser* is an interesting case in point. It prints the 'Tea at an Hotel' extract on the same page as articles which implicitly pick up on its critique of urban practices. In the novel, Dickens uses the episode to underscore through humour Pip's painful sense of his inadequacy and powerlessness in all his dealings with Estella:

> I rang for the tea, and the waiter, reappearing with his magic clue, brought in by degrees some fifty adjuncts to that refreshment but of tea not a glimpse. A teaboard, cups and saucers, plates, knives and forks (including carvers), spoons (various), saltcellars, a meek little muffin confined with the utmost precaution under a strong iron cover, Moses in the bullrushes typified by a soft bit of butter in a quantity of parsley, a pale loaf with a powdered head, two proof impressions of the bars of the kitchen fire-place on triangular bits of bread, and ultimately a fat family urn: which the waiter staggered in with, expressing in his countenance burden and suffering. After a prolonged absence at this stage of the entertainment, he at length came back with a casket of precious appearance containing twigs. These I steeped in hot water, and so from the whole of these appliances extracted one cup of I don't know what, for Estella.
>
> The bill paid, and the waiter remembered, and the ostler not forgotten, and the chambermaid taken into consideration – in a word, the whole house bribed into a state of contempt and animosity, and Estella's purse much lightened – we got into our post– coach and drove away. Turning into Cheapside and rattling up Newgate-street, we were soon under the walls of which I was so ashamed.[22]

In the *Hampshire Advertiser*, however, this extract is part of a subtle mosaic of inter-cultural references ranging from gentle jibes to xenophobia which help to constitute the paper's regionally focused address to its readers. One article appearing on the same page called 'Capital, Credit and Advertising' claims that 'We of the people are not very fond of Dukes; but we'd all like to be Dukes well enough ourselves', and is an ironic mock-manual on 'getting on' in society which serves to expose the vacuity of such ambitions. Another which also appeared alongside the Dickens extract is titled 'The Secret of Charming Manners'. Here we are loftily told, equally tongue-in-cheek, that 'There are people who do excellently well in the country, who astonish us by a general air of unfitness and failure in London society', and (without attribution to Dickens) honest Joe Gargery is held up as an example of an urban social failure. There is no doubt here that the *Advertiser*'s sympathies lie with Joe. This is just as Dickens intended, of course, but the paper's championing of honest rural simplicity is in stark contrast to the discomfort and disapproval with which the urban reviewers greeted his harsh judgement of London snobbery.

Other articles unrelated to Dickens further entrench this proud sense of a rural English identity. 'Tea At An Hotel' is immediately followed by an extract called 'The Cowardly Frenchman' taken from the *Autobiography* of Sir J. McGrigor, Bart, late director-general of the Army Medical Department, which tells the story of a treacherous French soldier who turned on and killed his rescuer. Immediately following this comes 'Londoners and Their Appreciation of Natural Beauties' by the unreformed urbanite Edmund Yates, reprinted from *Temple Bar Magazine*. This extract makes an impassioned case for greater understanding by rural-dwellers of the special place Londoners hold in their hearts for 'that solemn stillness, that peaceful quiet, which above all is so entrancing to the man in populous city pent, whose ear is accustomed to rattle of the cabs, the roar of the steam-engine, and the hum of the many-footed multitude'... '[T]he man with a country-house and pleasant grounds in a lovely situation', Yates claims, 'has very little real appreciation of their delight, but, as it were, acts as steward of them for us, his hardworking city friends.' This naive idealisation of the countryside as some sort of spiritual playground accords with Michael Bunce's observation that the construction says far more about urban self-definition than about real country life:

> the affection for the countryside may reflect fundamental human values and psychological needs which can be traced to a basic human desire for harmony with land and nature, for a sense of community and place and for simplicity of lifestyle. With the rise of urban-industrial society these needs have been magnified and projected on to a countryside redefined as the symbolic antithesis of the city; a place for reconnecting to natural processes and ancestral roots. Yet the idealisation of the countryside is intricately bound up in the development of modern urban civilization.[23]

All very well for the urbanite, perhaps; but it is not difficult to imagine the combination of laughter and derision with which Yates's patronising and idealised view of country life must have been greeted by those who actually lived and worked there. Surrounded by these other clearly carefully selected extracts which demonstrate a profound lack of understanding of country life on the part of urbanites, the 'Tea at an Hotel' extract thus takes on a connotation very different from Dickens's original intentions for it. Here, utterly divorced from its original context, it serves purely to poke fun at the London practice of serving inadequate and absurdly expensive teas; embedded in this mosaic of other pieces of similar 'evidence', it becomes further proof of urban chicanery.[24]

This juxtaposition of country and metropolis on almost every page of the provincial newspapers clearly provides an important backdrop for Pip's journeys between two worlds for these readers, and the *Hampshire Advertiser* is by no means an isolated example. I have written at length elsewhere about the particular relevance which *Great Expectations* extracts may have had for Dickens' real-life neighbours in Kent when they appeared in this period in the *Kentish Chronicle*.[25] Although I do not have room to rehearse these arguments here, two further brief examples will serve to bring home the point. *Trewman's Exeter Flying Post* printed the 'Tea at an Hotel' extract on 14 August 1861 (p.6) and surrounded it with snippets of gossip, among them stories about drunken London women coming to a bad end, a long commentary on the poor quality of the serialised fiction in *Temple Bar* magazine which glorified urban dissipation, and the exorbitant cost of opening the Houses of Parliament (£500 a time into the Lord Chancellor's pocket). In a related vein, the *Belfast Morning News* used *Great Expectations*, not to point up the contrast between rural and urban life, but to highlight the iniquities of the English judicial system: the sad story of Magwitch's childhood spent 'in jail and out of jail, in jail and out of jail' is reprinted under the title 'An English Jail-Bird's Story', and is surrounded by other stories of English violence.[26]

It is clear, then, that *Great Expectations*, the story of a boy's journey into urban disillusionment, was vilified by many a metropolitan paper made uncomfortable by its message of intrinsic urban immorality. The regional papers generally not only liked it much better but clearly saw it as an opportunity, carving it into chunks and serving it up as part of the tapestry of their print identities. It is tempting to speculate, as Fischler does, on what the response from both urban and regional papers might have been had Dickens stuck to his original unhappy ending set in Piccadilly, where the end of Pip's hopes is signalled only too clearly through the reality of working for a living and his final farewell to Estella: 'Implicitly, in preferring the urban setting of Piccadilly for his [original] finale', Fischler suggests, 'Dickens puts himself in accord with Tennyson's belief that salvation cannot be achieved in a postlapsarian garden; explicitly, Dickens differs from Tennyson in that the vision of salvation this ending offers is severely limited in its joy and is not transferred from earth to Heaven.'[27] It is not difficult to imagine what the regional papers would have made of this proof that, as Thomas Hardy would put it a few years later in 1874, 'the devil had gone with the world to town.'[28]

Great Expectations in a changing world, 1862–1885

The next twenty-five years in the cultural life of *Great Expectations* are, as Hardy's comment above indicates, as illuminating as its first reception in terms of changing urban-rural relations. Bunce argues that by mid-century idealisation of the countryside, and horror at the city, were both alive and well: 'In 1866 Ruskin described London as "that great foul city … rattling, growling, smoking, stinking – a ghastly heap of fermenting brickwork, pouring out poison at every pore."'[29] But Ruskin is probably atypical, given his famously vehement proto-environmentalist beliefs. Fischler provides us with a more nuanced model, perhaps, mapping changes in the pastoral mood through different examples in literature:

> Romantic love, in a garden setting, is featured prominently in three works of the period: Alfred, Lord Tennyson's *Maud*, completed in 1855; Charles

Dickens's *Great Expectations*, serialized from 1860 to 1861; and W. S. Gilbert's play *Sweethearts*, produced in 1874. And, by the end of the brief nineteen years that separate the first from the last of these, neither love nor the garden is assigned the same spiritual significance as it was before.[30]

This sort of pastoral idealisation through which Nature, love and spirituality are intertwined certainly wore many faces across the century. By the time Thomas Hardy began publishing in 1871, the Elysian world depicted in most pastoral literature was seen as under serious threat: Hardy's early novels are notable examples of the use of urban infiltrators to disrupt traditional rural ways of life. But the parallel existence of depictions of city (and particularly middle-class) life as superior to rural life is also worthy of our attention. *Great Expectations'* incarnations after the death of its author in 1870, produced and illustrated as they were by urban professionals and appearing roughly contemporaneously with Hardy's novels, shed light on the opposite end of the urban-rural dialectic. These illustrated editions tend to shift the ground from romanticisation to mockery of the rural, and simultaneously soften the contours of Dickens's urban critique.

The illustrated editions that first appeared in the 1860s offer marked differences in terms of their target readerships. In Britain, readers got no illustrations until the 1862 Chapman and Hall 'Library Edition' with eight plates by Marcus Stone which portray the novel's central rural character, Joe, as a noble rustic. In the United States, however, the first serialisation in *Harper's Weekly* was copiously illustrated with forty plates by John McLenan in which comic caricatures of Joe, Pumblechook, the Aged, the Pocket family and others abound, with little distinction apparent between classes or urban versus rural environments. For American readers, clearly, British 'character' was universal and Dickens was meant to be funny. These two sets of illustrations did sterling service in new editions for some years.

Beyond the 1860s, however, new illustrations in Britain began to indicate an altered balance between rural and urban, working- and middle-class characters. Miss Havisham becomes increasingly gothic. In 1862 and 1875 she was depicted by Marcus Stone and F.A. Fraser respectively as a normal, attractive if slightly odd woman, dressed inappropriately in a wedding dress but still capable of playing a genteel round of cards. By 1885, in F.W. Pailthorpe's plates for the Robson & Kerslake edition, she was an elderly, rather grim eccentric; but by 1910, in the hands of Harry Furniss in the 'Charles Dickens Library Edition', she was a Gothic monstrosity (no doubt as befits a middle-class woman of means who has incarcerated herself in the country). Equally, while in 1862 Joe is depicted by Stone as tall, manly and dignified as he says farewell to the newly wealthy Pip, by 1875 he is depicted by Fraser as a soft-hearted, slow-witted buffoon wonderingly spelling out the letters of his name, and in 1885 in the Robson & Kerslake edition he is a smiling simpleton. He is briefly returned to dignified manliness by Charles Green for the 1898 Gadshill Edition, but then all ten of these plates are marked by the artist's penchant for crisp, almost photographic realism, long on authentic detail but short on Dickensian 'character'. By 1910, again in the hands of Furniss, Joe is a hirsute, bumbling giant.

The change which seems to have taken place in the thirteen years which separate the Stone and the Fraser editions – like the shift in the spiritual significance of the garden in Fischler's three examples of the pastoral between 1855 and 1874 – is subtle but significant. Only two of Stone's eight 1862 plates depict London and he is content to use darkness as an effect in both settings, frequently illustrating night-time scenes to highlight the novel's most dramatic moments. Fraser's 1875 illustrations, however, depict eleven London scenes out of a total of twenty-eight plates, and they show the city – along with all middle-class interiors – as well lit, clean and ordered, all darkness now reserved for the rural marshes. Picking up on Fraser's lead, the 1910 edition takes it in a whole new direction. All Furniss's country and working-class scenes are chaotic, dark, riotous and heavily theatrical, forming a stark contrast with his noble, romanticised depictions of all the novel's middle-class characters (barring Miss Havisham, whom it was clearly felt deserved to share the Dantean fate of her country neighbours). There is a clear rural–urban – working–middle class divide evident in these images, the more noteworthy, perhaps, in light of Furniss's long career as a satirical illustrator for *Punch* during which he became famous for his cartoons of politicians, and his many illustrations for other Dickens works in which the divide is far less apparent. The early urban reviewers of *Great Expectations* would no doubt have been gratified by the contrast Furniss provided here, that patently endorsed their view of superior urban middle-class polish.[31]

These shifting aesthetic fashions in illustrated editions of *Great Expectations* signal important if subtle changes in rural–urban relations across the second half of the nineteenth century. But this novel's print history also contains scraps of evidence about changing attitudes to rural émigrés. In 1902, H. Rider Haggard was to despair of these young hopefuls:

> Everywhere the young men and women are leaving the villages where they were born and flocking into the towns ... as a consequence the character of Englishmen appears to be changing, not ... entirely for the better... those cities whither they go are full of misery.[32]

This anxiety was already well established some twenty years earlier among those who, like Hardy, were not persuaded by burgeoning notions of urban polish and superiority; his tragic novel, *The Mayor of Casterbridge* (1886), revolves around the futile struggles of a rural traditionalist to adapt to the modern, rapidly expanding, urban capitalist world. So it is probably no coincidence that a year earlier, in 1885, Pip's emotional prelapsarian moment at the fingerpost appeared for the first time in an illustrated edition of *Great Expectations*; as Hobsbawm notes, 'The 1870s and 1880s were an age of universal catastrophe for agriculture', and simultaneously London had grown by almost three million people between 1841 and 1881.[33] The stakes, however, were higher than ever, and the risks of failure ever greater: bankruptcies might be relatively rare, but dire poverty was still a reality for many émigrés. So pivotal and topical was this moment of rural–urban transition now seen to be, in fact, that F.W. Pailthorpe made it the frontispiece to the whole novel, the first thing readers encountered when they opened Dickens's book (see Figure 11.1).

Figure 11.1 'Pip leaves the village.' Title-page of 1885 edition, illustrated by F.W. Pailthorpe (London: Robson and Kerslake). Scanned image by Philip V. Allingham, courtesy of the Victorian Web.

Figure 11.2 'Pip leaves the village.' Unpublished sketch by F.W. Pailthorpe (c. 1885). Reproduced by kind permission of Commander Mark Dickens of the Charles Dickens Estate, and the Henry W. and Albert A. Berg Collection of English and American Literature, The New York Public Library, Astor, Lenox and Tilden Foundations.

Dickens's tortured critique of personal ambition mapped onto the rural–urban divide is foregrounded by the prominent position accorded to this image: now, in 1885, this is a book explicitly about a country labouring boy going to London, with all the complexities – discussed more fully in Barry Sloan's chapter – which that action implied. But the thoughtful and quite resolute Pip depicted here as already on the road did not emerge fully formed. In an earlier incarnation, not used by the artist or perhaps rejected by the publisher, Pip was more akin to the emotional figure Dickens intended (see Figure 11.2).

We cannot now be sure why this version was rejected or by whom, but the change might be of some significance: it was obviously felt that the depiction of a country boy dissolving into tears over leaving his home would not hit its mark with audiences in the 1880s as it had done in the 1860s. Part of this is certainly attributable to changing social attitudes and an increasing impatience with sentimental literature. But at least some of the shift can surely be attributed to an increasing perception that urban immigration was largely unstoppable and hugely problematic, and its use here suggests also that the phenomenon was capable of exposing inherent (usually bad) characteristics in the rural émigré. In terms of the available meanings generated by Dickens's story, the change is profound. If in Figure 11.2 Pip is a reluctant dreamer reflective of Dickens's innocent Stage 1 child, in Figure 11.1 he clearly has a harder heart and a somewhat stronger appetite for leaving. Appearing as it does before the first page is read, this powerful sense of Pip's self-interest colours the whole novel, shifting it just a few degrees from the Miltonian tragedy Dickens probably intended towards a harsher social realism much more suited to the end of the century.

In analysing some of this canonical novel's many reincarnations over a twenty-five year period I have attempted to show that literature is subtly and differently embedded in different regional cultures at different times, and thus potentially provides us with a rich source of evidence through which we might map changes in the relationships between the rural and the urban, the regional and the national, the traditional and the modern. As Dyck suggests, 'we have tended to study urban and rural people in separate spheres. And in some ways this is warranted, but there are moments in England's past where contemporaries experience and perceive town–country dichotomies.'[34] The reception history of *Great Expectations* captures some of these key moments.

Notes

1 Using internal textual evidence, Mary Edminson has calculated that the novel takes place between around 1807 and 1826. Quoted in A. Sadrin, *Great Expectations* (London: Unwin Hyman, 1988), p. 37.

2 See, for example, A. Fischler, 'Love in the Garden: *Maud, Great Expectations*, and W. S. Gilbert's Sweethearts', *Studies in English Literature, 1500–1900*, 37:4, Nineteenth Century (Autumn,1997), pp. 763–781, particularly p. 775. Also G. Finney, 'Garden Paradigms in 19th-Century Fiction', *Comparative Literature*, 36:1 (Winter, 1984), pp. 20–33.

3 C. Dickens, *Great Expectations*, edited by Edgar Rosenberg (New York: Wm Norton, 1998), p. 124.

4 Finney, pp. 21–2.

5 I. Dyck, 'The Town and Country Divide in English History', in M. Chase and I. Dyck (eds) *Living and Learning: Essays in Honour of J.F.C. Harrison* (Aldershot: Scolar Press, 1996), pp. 81–102 (esp. pp. 82–3).
6 See R. Williams, *The Country and the City* (Oxford: Oxford University Press, 1975).
7 Letter to John Forster, 4 October 1860, *Letters of Charles Dickens*, Vol. 9, K. Tillotson and G. Storey (eds) (Oxford: Clarendon Press, 1965–1997), p. 321.
8 P. Collins, *Charles Dickens: the Critical Heritage* (Abingdon and New York: Routledge, 1986); G. Ford, *Dickens and His Readers: Aspects of Novel Criticism since 1836* (New York: W.W. Norton, 1965).
9 'GREAT EXPECTATIONS', *Morning Post*, Wednesday 31 July 1861, p. 3.
10 Re-printed in the *Leeds Times*, Saturday 21 September 1861, p. 6.
11 Unsigned review by E.S. Dallas, *The Times*, 17 October 1861, p. 6.
12 'GREAT EXPECTATIONS', *Morning Post*, Wednesday 31 July, 1861, p. 3.
13 'Mr Dickens's Last Novel', *Dublin University Magazine*, December 1861, pp. 685–93.
14 *Spectator*, 20 July 1861, pp. 784–5.
15 Dyck, pp. 90–91.
16 E. Hobsbawm, *Industry and Empire: The Penguin Economic History of Britain, Vol 3* (London: Penguin, 1968), p. 157.
17 *Hereford Journal*, Wednesday 13 March 1861, p. 5.
18 'Literary Memoranda', *Northampton Mercury*, Saturday 8 December 1860, p. 7.
19 'All the Year Round – London: Chapman and Hall', *Chester Chronicle*, Saturday 9 February 1861, p. 5.
20 *Derby Mercury*, Wednesday 24 July 1861, p. 6.
21 *Accounts of sales of the works of Charles Dickens: Chapman and Hall*, Vol. 2, National Arts Library, Victoria and Albert Museum, F.D. 18.3. See also R. L. Patten, *Charles Dickens and His Publishers* (Oxford: Oxford University Press, 1978).
22 C. Dickens, *Great Expectations* (1860–61; Oxford: Oxford University Press, 1993), p. 245.
23 M. Bunce, *The Countryside Ideal: Anglo–American Images of Landscape* (London and New York: Routledge, 1994) , p. 2.
24 All these extracts are taken from the *Hampshire Advertiser*, Saturday 10 August 1861, p. 7.
25 M. Hammond, *Charles Dickens's Great Expectations: A Cultural Life, 1860–2012* (Burlington, VT: Ashgate, 2015).
26 *Belfast Morning News*, Thursday 27 June 1861, p. 4.
27 Fischler, p. 773.
28 T. Hardy, *Far From the Madding Crowd* (1874: London: Macmillan, 1965), p. 162.
29 Bunce, p. 15.
30 Fischler, pp. 765–66.
31 Full sets of illustrations for all these editions of *Great Expectations* can be found on the Victorian Web (http://www.victorianweb.org/authors/dickens/ge/artov.html).
32 H. Rider Haggard, *Rural England: Being an Account of Agricultural and Social Researches Carried Out in the Years 1901 & 1902*, Vol. 2 (1902; Boston, 2001), pp. 539–42.
33 Hobsbawm, *Industry and Empire*, pp. 158; 198.
34 Dyck, p. 95.

12 Country bumpkin or backbone of the nation?

The urbanisation of the agricultural labourer and the 'unmanning' of the English in the later nineteenth century

Barry Sloan

The vivid description of rural sights and sounds in Green Heys Fields may seem an unexpected start to Elizabeth Gaskell's *Mary Barton* (1848), a novel subtitled 'A Tale of Manchester Life', but it is an immediate reminder of the close proximity of the city and countryside in the nineteenth century. The fields are the popular destination of industrial workers on their occasional holidays, a location they can walk to from the city in half an hour. To people like John Barton, who was born and bred in Manchester, country life and work are unfamiliar curiosities. For his wife, however, who still possesses 'the fresh beauty of the agricultural districts', or the elderly Alice Wilson who collects herbs to prepare the remedies she learnt in her youth in the north country, Green Heys Fields represent the world they left behind when they migrated to the city.[1]

Their experience in particular typifies that of huge numbers of people as the century progressed. It is estimated, for example, that between 1841 and 1901 the rural areas of England and Wales lost more than 4 million people from internal migration, three-quarters of whom moved to towns and cities. The 1851 population census in Britain revealed what has been called 'a watershed event' when 'for the first time in the history of any large nation, more people lived in the towns than in the countryside'.[2] Although Britain was at the forefront of mass urbanisation, and England is the focus for this chapter, the movement of populations into towns and cities was an increasingly widespread international phenomenon. In the United States where the farm population rose by 50 per cent between 1860 and 1900, town dwellers increased by 400 per cent in the same period. As Philip Bagwell and G.E. Mingay note: 'For every city labourer who took up farming, twenty rural workers flocked to the city, and the city workers who did go west usually did not farm but took up urban jobs or entered mines and factories.'[3] Across Europe, likewise, millions of both internal and external migrants exchanged rural for city environments, leading Eric Hobsbawm to characterise the nineteenth century as 'a gigantic machine for uprooting countrymen'.[4]

The impact of such extensive 'uprooting' was inevitably complex at every level – individual, regional or national. In England, this may be variously demonstrated by evidence from sources as diverse as contemporary periodical journalism, parliamentary reports, individual investigative studies and selected literary and other texts which reveal the contested status of both male and female agricultural workers in the context of educational, social and employment changes, and the opportunities to move and restart life in a different place. Before specifically examining the anxieties aroused by rural depopulation and the rising tide of migration to the towns and cities, it is instructive to consider how such people were represented by some of those who employed them, wrote about them, or claimed to know them. To do so reveals, first, the existing vested social, economic and ideological interests and prejudices centred on the rural labouring class and on their future in this period of change. Those interests and prejudices are subsequently reflected in the alleged negative effects and potential long-term economic, social and moral consequences of the transformation of country dwellers into urban office and factory workers or domestic servants; but, as will be shown, there is also an alternative rhetoric which revalues the male labourer by emphasising his authentic manliness and his place in national history.

As Alun Howkins has shown, although the denomination of the countryman as 'Hodge' extends back to Chaucer, the label did not carry pejorative associations until the mid-eighteenth century, 'and not really before the 1820s does the name Hodge become totally synonymous with backwardness and lack of sophistication'.[5] Thereafter, for all his indispensability to agriculture and the production of the nation's food, Hodge was commonly characterised as a two-legged beast of burden, stereotypically slow-witted, lacking in curiosity or ambition, emotionally stunted and irremediably parochial. From the mid-nineteenth century, numerous writers offer essentially the same allegedly typical account of the labourer's circumscribed life: after childhood fieldwork, he is described as passing quickly into employment; his youthful marriage is followed by numerous children and inevitable economic hardship. Then, a brief interval of greater prosperity when the eldest members of his family have begun to earn is succeeded by decline into premature ageing and impoverishment as his capacity for work diminishes and the young adults move on with their lives. To some observers, this life cycle is evidence of the lower or alien nature of the labouring class which justifies existing power relations; for others, it was at least in part a troubling consequence of the way those same power relations operated to the continual disadvantage of the labourer. John Eddowes reflects this dilemma in a pamphlet purporting to represent *The Agricultural Labourer as He Really Is* (1854). Although his principal concern is the immorality and drunkenness associated with hiring fairs, he sets this in a context of wider and increasing degradation and regression. 'So very far are [the labourers] below their fellow men in mental culture', he claims, 'that it has been confidently suggested by a medical man intimate with their condition, that there is a positive defect in their intellectual powers, which have been gradually deteriorating through many ages of continued neglect, each generation being mentally weaker than the one preceding it.'[6] Eddowes does not question the need for authority to be exercised over the lives of agricultural labourers, but his Christian responsibility as a clergyman leads him to challenge the circumstances that leave his parishioners living in worse conditions than animals. Other philanthropically minded commentators urged the indispensability of the labourer developing self-discipline to improve his situation:

Hodge must exercise the kind of economies and financial prudence that were alien and impossible for him in equal measure, and which were recommended in middle-class publications he would never read. T.E. Kebbel's pompous claim in *Cornhill Magazine* in 1873 typifies this perspective:

> Out of their present wages, what the better class of agricultural labourers contrive to save is often quite enough to enable them, after twenty years' service, to take a small farm of ten or twelve acres, without imprudence. ... An agricultural labourer, from forty to forty-five years of age, of tried skill, probity and sobriety, with 200*l* in his pocket, is a made man. True, he has had to forego the luxury of marriage: but so have his betters.[7]

For all his experience of agricultural matters, Kebbel simply ignores the realities of labourers' lives here and appeals to the morality of his middle-class readers through the implication that a failure of character and self-control alone will stand in the way of a man becoming a small tenant farmer. Others are forthrightly defensive of the interests of landowners and farmers forced by the provisions of the amended Poor Law of 1834 to subsidise the alleged improvidence and opportunism of feckless labourers. Thus, writing in *Cornhill Magazine* in 1864, J.Y. Stratton declares:

> the peasant should have one privilege immediately conceded to him, for good and substantial reasons – that of paying his fair share of the poor-rate. He would thus become guarantee that the fund is not imposed upon by unscrupulous members of his class, who are accustomed to consider it a provision purposely made for them, as soon and as often as they can advance a claim to it. The principle of self-help is much talked of, but little developed among the peasantry.[8]

Significantly, too, Stratton attacks the Poor Law for eroding 'the notion of independence' the labourer has 'manfully struggled for' by encouraging him to seek relief from the parish or a place in the workhouse.[9] His notion of the emasculating effects of relief given without obligation is a further suggestion that the contemporary labourer is increasingly enfeebled in comparison with earlier generations. The positions taken in these examples may differ, but they have a common judgemental note, and imply that Hodge and his kind need to be managed and told what to do, if not actually compelled to do it. The articles urge the need for moral reform to mitigate the social and economic problems associated with labourers, but they do not question the continuing subservience of the workforce or consider that individuals may have ambitions of their own. The tone and vocabulary project the labourer as a socially, intellectually and morally inferior being, even when the writer is motivated by humane concern or shame at the conditions in which he lives. In both these respects, the articles represent many discussions from the 1850s onwards.

A number of factors contributed to the debate. These include the impact of government commissioned reports in the late 1860s on the conditions of rural employment, particularly of children and women, which were held up as an affront to England's standing in the world and a disgrace in a purportedly Christian country.

Revelations of the practices of so-called gang masters who ran agricultural labour teams, especially in Norfolk, aroused public concern not only about the conditions in which women and children were housed and the nature of their work, but also about the moral dangers and corruption to which they were exposed. Thus an article in *All the Year Round* responding to the Sixth Report of the Children's Employment Commission in 1867 appeared under the stark heading, 'Slavery in England', and the *Quarterly Review* drew on the same rhetoric when it likened the gang leaders to 'slave-driver[s]' and the predicament of their workers to 'negro bondage'.[10] Yet although those caught up in gangs were seen as victims, there was also anxiety that, to the detriment of society, the 'precocious independence' of children so employed would preclude them from becoming the biddable, deferential adult workers upon which the rural economy depended, while the women's immodesty and coarseness of speech violated every measure of female decency and respectability.[11]

The formation of the National Agricultural Labourers Union (NALU) in 1872 to campaign for wage increases was another source of controversy. Although its achievements were uneven and faltering, it meant that agricultural workers were no longer a wholly disparate and largely voiceless section of the community, and the scale of its initial appeal and impact alarmed landowners and farmers alike. This is seen in a three-part article, 'Peasantry of the South of England', attributed to George Jennings Davies, published in *Fraser's Magazine* in 1873. Davies advances numerous claims and arguments which cannot be considered here, but his view of the labourer reveals some telling contradictions. On the one hand, he mocks the gullibility of readers of the NALU newspaper, *The Labourers' Chronicle*, whose 'illogical mind[s]' fail to question the reliability of the 'facts' they are given and who are ignorant of 'the other side of the questions argued'.[12] 'Hodge' is belittled and union spokesmen and the newspaper are accused of deliberately 'warm[ing]' him with weekly 'stimulants' which incite him to hate his own country, believe that he could live in luxury and free from squires and parsons in Australia or elsewhere and forget that 'an industrious man can live in England and that a lazy one cannot live out of it'.[13] Yet having developed this figure of a 'scarecrow, tatterdemalion Hodge', Davies dismisses him as 'a caricature of his race' – a phrase which casts agricultural labourers as a separate species – in favour of 'the true, respected, cheerful labourer – *his country's pride*', whose relationship with his employer is harmonious and whose economic position is much better than NALU claims.[14] The equivocation is striking: Davies' apparent esteem for the 'true' labourer is contingent upon his compliance with a specific subservient role in the hierarchy of country life. Even this is subsequently qualified by the author's hope that 'the present agitation' will rouse 'the thinking powers of the peasant' so that the next generation will be 'more thrifty' and 'place themselves in an independent position before taking a wife'.[15] But the labourer who attempts to engage in union business exposes only his own underlying stupidity, and if he believes himself the victim of injustice, it is implied that he is also lazy, greedy and unpatriotic. From this perspective, therefore, he will only be 'his country's pride' as long as he also remains a country bumpkin.

A similar paradox characterises some reactions to the introduction of the Elementary Education Act of 1870 and the subsequent legislation which defined and strengthened arrangements for compulsory schooling. While the advantages of widening individuals' horizons, increasing their aspirations and desire for greater personal freedom, and giving them access to new and better rewarded forms of employment through education might seem self-evident, not everyone agreed. There were parents who resented the loss of income when their children had to attend school, farmers who claimed education was a disruptive nuisance and many others who regarded it both as irrelevant to a future workforce and destructive of children's relationship to the land and the natural world. Ironically, however, migration was frequently the result of advances in mechanisation, the widespread shift from arable to animal farming and the increasing use of labourers on short contracts or as casual employees – all strategies used by farmers to save money during the depressed years of the 1880s and early 1890s. Nevertheless, as late as the turn of the century, Henry Rider Haggard's interviews with landowners and farmers conducted for his monumental study of contemporary agriculture, *Rural England* (1902), contain repeated complaints that education had led to a shortage of labourers and the loss of the most skilled and able from the land. For example, one Hampshire farmer told Haggard: 'Education, in his opinion, had much to do with [labourers leaving the countryside], as its result was to inspire boys with a repugnance for work on the land, or even to learn the more remunerative labour of thatching and hurdle-making.'[16] More unexpectedly, perhaps, in 'The Dorsetshire Labourer' (1883), Thomas Hardy complained that children were reduced to a 'transitional state' with 'a composite language without rule or harmony' as a consequence of education which discouraged their use of native dialect.[17] Such responses suggest that insofar as education facilitated social mobility, urban employment, material aspiration, a desire for greater personal freedom and cultural sophistication, it might be associated with various kinds of loss. For the farmer this was the decline of a ready supply of biddable labourers with traditional rural skills; for Hardy it was the erosion of the past, of custom, history and regional characteristics which previously had been perpetuated by lack of change across generations.[18] These kinds of loss increasingly came to be associated with a threat to Englishness itself and encouraged a retrospective valorisation of the labourer as its most authentic embodiment.

This alternative projection of the agricultural labourer, not as the drudge of the nation but as its backbone and as the embodiment of a kind of quintessential Englishness, is anticipated in William Howitt's *The Rural Life of England* (1838). Howitt claimed that 'it is in rural life that the superiority of England is, perhaps, more striking than in any other respect'.[19] Rural life, he maintains, has 'raised millions of frames strong and muscular and combatant, and enduring as the oaks of its rocky hills; ... it has nerved those frames to the contempt alike of danger and effeminacy; and has quickened them with hearts full of godlike aspirations after a virtuous glory'.[20] For a nationalist like Howitt, therefore, England's greatness, its moral ascendancy, cultural sophistication and exemplary status originate in the countryside and are developed in the nation's leaders and artists through the specific inspirational effect of 'living amongst our manly and high-minded peasantry – the hardy sons and bold defenders of their natal soil, – the strong-hearted old fathers, – the fair and modest daughters of uncorrupted England'.[21] This contrasts sharply with the view of the labourer as an inferior or degenerating species proposed by Eddowes, Davies and Stratton. Howitt's labourers not only cultivate the land but are credited with its defence and with the preservation of its integrity against the taint of foreign influence. A similar association reappears in a very different context in 1878 when the founder of the National Agricultural Labourers' Union, Joseph Arch, argued that the right to vote, which had already been granted to town workers in the Second Reform Act of 1867, should be extended to the countryside. Arch refuses to indulge in special pleading and ignores the popular image of countrymen as ignorant boors. Rather, he recasts them as the descendants of those who defended the nation and secured its liberties. Are 'the sons of sires who fought at Cressy and Waterloo, and struck for freedom at Naseby and Dunbar' likely to exercise the right to vote in a way that would damage their country? he asks.[22] Arch responds to those inclined to dismiss the suitability of rural workers as voters by condemning *them* for displaying the very 'stupidity and ignorance' they ascribe to the Hodge stereotype which he has already rejected. This promotion of the countryman as soldier and servant of the empire and defender of the nation is carried forward variously in other late nineteenth-century texts. In 'The Wiltshire Labourer', for example, Richard Jefferies writes of 'a race of men of the sturdiest order, the true and natural countrymen; men standing upright in the face of all, without one particle of servility'.[23] Drawing on military imagery, he characterises them as 'our last line of defence – the reserve, the rampart of the nation', but notes the irony that they are 'despised' at home, while their worth is 'estimated at its true value in the colonies'.[24] Yet in this same essay, which was commissioned by *Longman's Magazine* to follow Hardy's contribution on 'The Dorsetshire Labourer', Jefferies takes the radical view that for men whose 'labour' is their 'capital', urban migration in pursuit of greater security of employment and housing than are available in the country is both inevitable and understandable. The result is that 'Our last line at present is all unsettled and broken up, and has lost its firm and settled front.'[25] Herein lies the real danger in Jefferies' opinion, and this sense of national vulnerability receives even stronger endorsement towards the end of the century, as we will see.

The honour due for the commitment and sacrifices of countrymen in military service overseas on behalf of the empire provides the focus for A.E. Housman's poem, '1887', where again the intimate connection between the character of the dead soldiers and the rural environment which formed them is foregrounded:

> To skies that knit their heartstrings right,
> To fields that bred them brave,
> The saviours come not home tonight
> Themselves they could not save.
>
> It dawns in Asia, tombstones show
> And Shropshire names are read;
> And the Nile spills his overflow
> Beside the Severn's dead.[26]

And in his poem, 'Drummer Hodge' (1899), Hardy elegises the young soldier 'Fresh from his Wessex home' who has fallen in the Boer War and whose remains will 'for ever be' a 'portion of that unknown plain' in Africa – an idea that provides a clear precursor for Rupert Brooke's 1914 sonnet, 'The Soldier'.[27] Both these works project the consoling fantasy that in spite of their death and burial far from home, these common soldiers from humble country backgrounds somehow remain unassimilated into the foreign soil, their Englishness outlasting their mortal bodies. However, perhaps Hamo Thorneycroft's sculpture, 'The Mower' (1894), gives the trope of the heroic labourer its most complex resonances. Here, while the half-naked figure exhibits idealised male strength and beauty, his clothing is ambiguously suggestive not only of a farm worker but of a soldier in colonial service. Similarly, the shaft of the mower's definitive work implement, the scythe, projects from his side, resembling the barrel of a soldier's weapon, while the blade is relatively concealed behind his legs. From the viewer's perspective, the agricultural and military signifiers merge so fluidly that they are ultimately indistinguishable and, even more explicitly than in the poems, here Hodge the country bumpkin reaches his apotheosis as the representative of archetypal English manliness.

Such wishful recasting of the old stereotype in a more heroic mould coincides with the growth of obvious practical concerns about rural depopulation in the period. Haggard's informants not only deplored the shortage of agricultural labourers but also the fact that those left were commonly the elderly and least capable – people Haggard himself calls 'the dullards, the vicious, or the wastrels' who 'are unfitted for any other life'.[28] His additional observation that 'it is this indifferent remnant who will be the parents of the next generation of rural Englishmen' highlights another anxiety that surfaces throughout *Rural England*: namely, the degeneration of the race which is now predicted as a direct consequence of urbanisation.[29] Haggard's book begins on a note reminiscent of Howitt, referring to the land as 'the true mother of our race' and suggesting that without a strong connection to it, the race 'would soon dwindle into littleness'.[30] After questioning whether it 'can … be denied that the national temperament is undergoing modifications, subtle perhaps, but nonetheless profound', he continues:

> Moreover, the physique deteriorates. This was a fact that came home to any who, after the countrybred yeomen were exhausted, took the trouble to compare them with the crowds of town-reared men that presented themselves at the London recruiting offices to volunteer for service in South Africa. The intelligence too is changed; it is apt no longer to consider or appreciate natural things, but by preference dwells on and occupies itself with those more artificial joys and needs which are the creation of civilised, money and pleasure-seeking man.[31]

These words are laden with implication and echoes: they reiterate the association between countryman and soldier and his place in national history, and condemn urban life and work as corrosive and debilitating, both physically and mentally. The city is not held up as the cornerstone of national prosperity and the epitome

Figure 12.1 'The Mower' (1888–90) by Sir Hamo Thorneycroft (1850–1925). Bronze sculpture. © Tate, London, 2015.

of advanced civilisation but as the nemesis of English character and manliness, not least because it promotes false values.

Paradoxically, however, if the countryman's physical attributes once taken as evidence of his animal nature now appear as marks of distinction and are no longer incompatible with intelligence, Haggard's declaration that 'the greatness of the nation' will decline with the loss of 'a continually renewed supply of men and women, healthy in mind and body' barely disguises a reductive view of them as prime breeding stock. In the appendix to *A Farmer's Year* (1899), Haggard reproduces a speech he gave to the Norfolk Chamber of Agriculture on 'the rural exodus'. Here his views on racial degeneration and anti-urbanism are even more explicit. He invites his audience to:

> look at the pure-bred Cockney – I mean the little fellow that you see running in and out of offices in the City, and whose forefathers have for the last two generations dwelt within a two-mile radius of Charing Cross. And then look at an average young labourer coming home from his day's field work, and I think you will admit that the city breeds one stamp of human beings, and that the country breeds another. They may be a little sharper in the towns, but after all it is not mere sharpness that has made Great Britain what she is, it is the thews and sinews of her sons which are the foundation of everything, and even, healthy minds that dwell in healthy bodies. Take the people away from their natural breeding and growing grounds, thereby sapping their health and strength in cities such as nature never intended to be the permanent homes of men, and the decay of this country becomes only a matter of time.[32]

Neither the *sang-froid* of class conscious snobbery nor the functional vocabulary of animal husbandry disguises Haggard's alarmist note: his concern extends far beyond the state of agriculture and the shortage of labourers to the future of the empire itself in a context of growing economic, political, and, potentially, military challenges to Britain's international position. The implication may be extreme, but it is not unique. The journalist and social investigator, Peter Anderson Graham, for example, writing in 1892, comments that without 'the infusion of new blood' from the countryside, 'the urban population would languish and become enfeebled', and Haggard quotes Rev. J. Frome Wilkinson's opinion that 'the exodus from the country was not only serious, but vital, and that involved in it, was nothing less than the fate of the manhood of the nation'.[33] Such views are complemented in General Booth's correspondence with Haggard where he argues the importance of providing incentives to dissuade people from coming to the cities where many of them are corrupted by urban squalor. Rural migration, therefore, is blamed not only for creating a labour problem, which might be critical if imported food was cut off in a national emergency – another of Haggard's concerns; it is also interpreted as a threat to essential qualities in the national character of the English and the virility of the race which are embedded in the country population.

Although the emphasis in these writings is primarily on the threat to English manhood, town life is also blamed for encouraging vanity and materialism in women at the cost of their sentimentally imagined country innocence and virtue. According to Rev. Augustus Jessopp: 'The girls find places in the towns as domestic servants, and come back to us for a few days' holiday with the manners of gentlewomen (not merely *lyedies*), and become eloquent propagandists of the abominable doctrine that there is nothing like life in the towns.'[34] Similarly, Hardy claims that as country people become what he calls 'inter-social citizens', the 'humorous simplicity' of the men, and the 'unsophisticated modesty' of the women are 'rapidly disappearing or lessening, under the constant attrition of lives mildly approximating to those of workers in a manufacturing town'.[35] The women in particular, he adds disapprovingly, have 'acquired the rollicking air of factory hands'.[36] Paradoxically, neither Jessopp nor Hardy imagines that labourers will ever return to the circumscribed, parochial lives of previous generations, that the impact of education could – or should – be halted, or that urban opportunities, freedoms and markets will cease to attract the rural population; rather, they read the changing situation principally in terms of effects they deplore rather than of the progress and opportunities it offers others. It is therefore ironic that Jessopp's prescriptions for stabilising the rural population rely heavily on bringing to village life many of the amenities and resources associated with the towns, such as better medical provision, recreational facilities and the support of housing organisations like the Peabody Fund and the Guinness Trust. Without such improvements, Jessopp imagines an apocalyptic scene of rural desolation with 'this dear land of ours, that was once called Merry England, becoming spotted with huge cankerous ulcers of pampas or prairie – with never a sound of a human voice to stir the echoes and never a happy human face to make the sunshine glad in heaven'.[37] His image is curiously close to one used by Rider Haggard in the same year, 1899, in his Christmas Day reflection in *A Farmer's Year*:

> When travelling in the United States of America I have seen a mule and cow harnessed to a plough, which was being directed by a woman across a great expanse of plain studded with tree stumps, and roughly fenced with their tops dragged into a kind of zariba. Is that a possible future to which our agriculture may look forward?[38]

Yet as far back as 1873, Richard Jefferies predicted that pressures on traditional agriculture would produce greater changes than in the previous fifty years, and turn farming into 'a commercial speculation' organised differently and operated with less labour and more machinery.[39] He also projected a necessary alternative future for the labourer who, he expects, will be employed by an agricultural company in conditions more akin to those of an industrial worker than to previous generations of ploughmen or cowherds, which will dignify his skills with new status:

> Like the great factories and manufactures [sic], companies such as these would run up a small street or so of four-roomed houses for their own artisan – they will scarcely be called labourers in the future. Men to drive the steam-plough, to manage the valuable stalls of cattle, to work the various and

complicated machinery of such an establishment, will require to exhibit intelligence hitherto lacking – lacking, perhaps, principally for want of mental exercise. Such artisans must receive higher pay, in all probability about, or nearly equal, to the wages paid in factories...[40]

Not only is this upbeat anticipation in marked contrast to Jessopp and Haggard's pessimistic end-of-century visions of the potential fate of the depopulated countryside which reflects their underlying desire to perpetuate old structures and relationships. Their despondency is also a measure of how far change had already affected both farming and the rural population. Jessopp's nostalgic reference to 'Merry England', an imagined, ahistorical Arcadia unsullied by nineteenth-century modernity, seems particularly whimsical, but it invokes a trope that found resonances in the cities and their suburbs to which so many families had migrated, and from which some now wished to escape back to the country either permanently or for recreation and restoration from the stresses of the urban environment.

One such was Edward Thomas who was born in London but spent most of his adult life trying to flee the city and immersing himself in rural life and the natural world. His prose work, *The South Country* (1909), includes a number of parables about alienated countrymen in London, one of which tells of a Welsh villager whose father, like Thomas's own, moved to the city for a better-paid job. As a child, he was frequently taken into the countryside, and his father read to him from Walton, Borrow, Wordsworth, Thoreau and Gilbert White; but as an adult, after his father's death and his mother's return to Wales, he temporarily succumbed to the attitudes of his fellow urban commuters, affecting their 'horrible, cowardly scorn for those who were poor or outlandish, and for all things that were not like those in their own houses or in those of the richer people of their acquaintance or envy'.[41] The man's story exemplifies Thoreau's notion of a life of 'quiet desperation', because he despises his own servitude to work and urban culture.[42] In a passage which echoes Richard Jefferies' spiritual exhilaration on Liddington Hill recorded in *The Story of My Heart* (1883), and Blake's poem, 'The Garden of Love', the man recognises his irresistible need to reconnect to the countryside after returning to 'the field, the golden field where I used to lie among the buttercups and be alone with the blue sky', only to discover that it has been enclosed as a cemetery with a chapel 'for all the unknown herd, strange to one another, strange to everyone else, that filled the new houses spreading over the land'.[43] He starts going into the country as often as possible, and after the hopeless pursuit of love with a much younger cousin, he begins saving money from his London employment in the winter, and resigning it to do casual work on the land in the summer months. There he is free to 'dream' himself 'no longer one of the mob-led mob'.[44] Ironically, although the man's London boss has exhorted him to believe that he is playing a part in 'the sublime machine of modern civilization', *this* is the work he regards as slavery, not rural labouring. However, the tragedy is that he knows his freedom is only a dream, and that he will forever be displaced: 'I realise that I belong to the suburbs still', he tells his interlocutor; 'I belong to no class or race, and have no traditions. We of the suburbs are a muddy, confused, hesitating mass, of small courage though much endurance.'[45] This sorry conclusion therefore proposes another version of degeneration as the consequence of city life on rural migrants: not only are they changed and weakened by urban life but they may end up, like this exemplary figure, socially and mentally isolated, distanced from their country origins without becoming assimilated into city culture, pining for a lost, increasingly idealised past and estranged from circumstantial realities.

Thomas's story may be an idiosyncratic fiction, but it suggests some of the tension, dislocation, fears and hopes associated with migration from the country to the city found in other contexts. Christopher Ferguson has shown how, earlier in the century, James Carter moved to and fro between London and Essex, never able, perhaps, to feel fully at home in either location, and in *Mary Barton*, Elizabeth Gaskell hints at the disappointment of Alice Wilson who dies without fulfilling her wish to revisit her rural home. In the early twentieth century, Margaret Penn, the illegitimate child of an unknown 'gentleman' who had been raised from infancy in a labourer's family after the death her mother, records how her youthful ambition to commute fourteen miles from the village of Hollins Green to Manchester to train as a court dressmaker caused great anxiety: even with a convenient rail connection, Manchester remained all but unknown to the villagers, and was feared as a place of moral corruption and wickedness.[46] (Although Penn's foster family remained distant from the city, their story is another example of change: Mr Winstanley left agricultural labour for better pay and conditions as a council road mender. This enabled the family to move to a larger house. One of his sons worked in a local iron foundry, although the other was a farm labourer.) When, later, rather as in *Great Expectations*, Margaret is summoned to London by previously unknown relatives, she becomes 'an object of unparalleled interest and curiosity'; and when she departs from Manchester station with her newly discovered Aunt Mildred, her foster father's emotion, confusion and anxiety recall Dickens's representation of Joe Gargery's reactions when Pip is told he must go to the city.[47] Whether necessity, opportunity or ambition prompted their departure, those leaving the country for the city knew – and usually hoped – that their lives would change, although they could never be sure of the extent or nature of this or of how it would affect their relationships. What this chapter proposes, however, is that rural migration was much more than a private and personal matter. Rather, it had significant social, structural and cultural implications which are reflected in the flourishing discussion and representation of the lives of the rural labouring population, especially from the 1860s onwards. In the following decades, government reports and journalistic investigations into rural life prompted public responses and articles in some of the leading periodicals of the day. Particular issues were repeatedly examined: how to improve the labourer's lot, usually within the existing paternalistic and hierarchical social structures; how to counteract his perceived improvidence and the allegedly debilitating effects of the Poor Law arrangements; how to instil in him the doctrine of self-help; and how to remove those aspects of his treatment that affronted the Christian and civilised values of the most powerful nation in the world. The gradual, and often grudging, acceptance of the irresistibility of the rural labourer's rising social, economic and legal demands and aspirations, and of his expectation of parity with urban workers, raised the stakes on such questions. These were further heightened, on the one hand, by the increasing accessibility and attractions of urban life to the rural population, and, on the other, by mounting economic pressures on land owners and tenant farmers, and by changes to the traditional practices of agriculture, which led to job reductions and insecurity of employment and housing. Anxieties about the practical consequences of rural depopulation for agriculture mutated into fears informed by contemporary theories of degeneration that the cities associated with wealth, prestige and power would also be the seedbed of national destruction because of the rapidly unmanning effects of urban life. It was in this context that the rural migrant became such a focus of interest, not just as a labourer, but as an iconic figure in the story of England, as F.E. Green's rhetorical description of the ploughman as 'the figure of Destiny, in whose rhythmic stride and noble sweep of the arm lies the hope of Britain' so vividly claims.[48] Where previously he had often been dismissed as a bumpkin or member of an alien species, the agricultural labourer was now identified as the residual source of uncompromised, authentic English manhood just when his numbers were decreasing. And with complementary irony, too, as rural poverty continued to boost the urban population, the increasingly depopulated countryside became the repository of nostalgic ideals and imaginings of the past and of a better and more wholesome way of life than that of the cities and their suburbs.

Notes

1 E. Gaskell, *Mary Barton* (1848; Harmondsworth: Penguin, 1970; rptd 1985), p. 41.
2 J. Long, 'Rural–Urban Migration and Socioeconomic Mobility in Victorian Britain', *The Journal of Economic History*, 65:1 (March 2005), pp. 1–35, on pp. 1–2.
3 P. S. Bagwell and G. E. Mingay, *Britain and America 1850–1939: a study of economic change* (London: Routledge Kegan and Paul, 1970; rptd 1987), p. 85.
4 E. Hobsbawm, *The Age of Capital 1848–1875* (London: Weidenfeld and Nicholson, 1975; reissued 1995), p. 196.
5 A. Howkins, 'From Hodge to Lob: reconstructing the English farm labourer, 1870–1914', in M. Chase and I. Dyck (eds), *Living and Learning: Essays in Honour of J.F.C. Harrison* (Aldershot: Scholar Press, 1996), pp. 218–235, on p. 218. Of related interest, see also Mark Freeman, 'The agricultural labourer and the "Hodge" stereotype', *Agricultural History Review*, 49:II (2001), pp. 172–186.
6 J. Eddowes, *The Agricultural Labourer as He Really Is, or Village Morals in 1854*, in Mark Freeman (ed.), *The English Rural Poor 1850–1914* (London: Pickering and Chatto, 2005), vol. 1, pp. 5–26, on p. 18.
7 T.K. Kebbel, 'The Agricultural Labourer', *Cornhill Magazine*, 27:159 (March 1873), pp. 307–319, on p. 315.
8 J.Y. Stratton, 'The Life of a Farm Labourer', *Cornhill Magazine*, 9:50 (February 1864), pp. 178–186, on p. 178.
9 Stratton, 'The Life of a Farm Labourer', p. 184.
10 Unsigned review, 'Slavery in England', *All the Year Round, A Weekly Journal Conducted by Charles Dickens, With Which is Incorporated Household Words*, 15 June 1867, p. 585. 'ART.VII – 1. *Sixth Report of the Commissioners of the Children's Employment Commission. 1867. – 2. Seventh Report of the Medical Officer of the Privy Council with Appendix. (1864)*', *Quarterly Review*, 145:245 (July 1867), pp. 173–190, on p.178.

11 'ART.VII', p. 182.

12 G. J. Davies, 'Peasantry of thc South of England', *Fraser's Magazine*, 7:41 (May 1873), pp. 542–558, on p. 544.

13 Davies, 'Peasantry of the South of England', p. 545.

14 Davies, 'Peasantry of the South of England,', p. 547. The italics are in the original.

15 Davies, 'Peasantry of the South of England', p. 550.

16 H. Rider Haggard, *Rural England* (London: Longmans, Green and Co., 2 vols, 1902), vol. 1, p. 64.

17 T. Hardy, 'The Dorsetshire Labourer', *Longman's Magazine*, 2:9 (July 1883), pp. 252–269, on p. 254.

18 The tension between educated middle class contempt for the ignorance of the rural working class and concern at the loss of the traditional culture of the countryside with the spread of education was noted elsewhere, too. In 1856, a newspaper in Mantua noted: 'The prejudice which used to operate against all the popular classes still exists against the peasants. They do not receive the education of the middle class: hence their differences, the lack of esteem for the countryman, his vigorous desire to escape from the oppression of this contempt. Hence the decadence of old customs, the corruption and deterioration of our race.' Cited in Hobsbawm, *The Age of Capital*, p. 173.

19 W. Howitt, *The Rural Life of England* (1838; 2nd ed. London: Longman, Orme, Brown, Green & Longman, 1842), p. 3.

20 Howitt, *The Rural Life of England*, p. 3 and p. 4.

21 Howitt, *The Rural Life of England*, p. 329.

22 J. Arch, 'The Labourers and the Vote', *Nineteenth Century* 3:11 (January 1878), pp. 48–52, on p. 49.

23 R. Jefferies, 'The Wiltshire Labourer', *Longman's Magazine*, 3:13 (November 1883), pp. 52–65, on p. 63.

24 Jefferies, 'The Wiltshire Labourer', p. 64.

25 Jefferies, 'The Wiltshire Labourer', p. 64.

26 A. E. Housman, *Collected Poems* (Harmondsworth: Penguin, 1956; rpt 1961), p. 21.

27 T. Hardy, *The Works of Thomas Hardy* (Ware, Herts: Wordsworth, 1994), p. 83.

28 Rider Haggard, *Rural England*, vol. 2, p. 539.

29 Rider Haggard, *Rural England*, vol. 2, p. 539.

30 Rider Haggard, *Rural England*, vol. 1, p. 2.

31 Rider Haggard, *Rural England*, vol. 2, p. 568.

32 H. Rider Haggard, *A Farmer's Year* (London: Longman's, Green and Co., 1899), p. 466.

33 P. G. Anderson, *The Rural Exodus* (London: Methuen and Co., 1892), p. 2 and Haggard, *Rural England*, vol. 1, p. 573.

34 A. Jessopp, 'The Cry of the Villages', *Nineteenth Century: a monthly review*, 45,268 (June 1899), pp. 865–879, on p. 867.

35 Hardy, 'The Dorsetshire Labourer', p. 262.

36 Hardy, 'The Dorsetshire Labourer', p. 262.

37 Jessopp, 'The Cry of the Villages', pp. 868–869.

38 Haggard, *A Farmer's Year*, p. 440.

39 R. Jefferies, 'The Future of Farming', *Fraser's Magazine* 8:48 (December 1873), pp. 687–697, on p. 692.

40 Jefferies, 'The Future of Farming', p. 693.

41 E. Thomas, *The South Country* (Wimborne Minster, Dorset: Little Toller Books, 2009), p. 80.

42 H.D. Thoreau, *Walden* (New York: Signet Classics New American Library of World Literature Inc., 1964), p. 10.

43 Thomas, *The South Country*, p. 81. Thomas was a great admirer of Jefferies and published a study of his work in 1909. It is notable that animal imagery so often linked to rural workers is used here to denote the debased lives of urban dwellers.

44 Thomas, *The South Country*, p. 84.

45 Thomas, *The South Country*, p. 85.

46 M. Penn, *Manchester Fourteen Miles* (1947; Firle, Sussex: Caliban Books, 1979). In her autobiography, Penn calls herself Hilda Winstanley, and refers to her childhood home as Moss Ferry.

47 Penn, *Manchester Fourteen Miles*, p. 235. See also Charles Dickens, *Great Expectations* (1861; Harmondsworth: Penguin Classic, 1985), chapter 18.

48 F. E. Green, *A History of the English Agricultural Labourer 1870–1920* (London: P. S. King and Son, 1920), p. 5.

Bibliography

Introduction

Bunce, M. *The Countryside Ideal* (London: Routledge, 1994).

Burns, S. *Pastoral Inventions: Rural Life in Nineteenth-Century Life and Culture* (Philadelphia: Temple University Press, 1989).

Dyck, I. 'The Town and Country Divide in English History', in M. Chase and I. Dyck (eds), *Living and Learning: Essays in Honour of J.F.C. Harrison* (Aldershot: Scolar Press, 1996).

Hobsbawm, E. *The Age of Capital 1848–1875* (London: Weidenfeld and Nicolson, 1975).

Howkins, A. 'Rurality and English Identity', in D. Morely and K. Robbins (eds), *British Cultural Studies: Geography, Nationality, and Identity* (Oxford: OUP, 2001).

Lee, B. and Reinders, R. 'The Loss of Innocence: 1880–1914', in M. Bradbury and H. Temperley (eds), *Introduction to American Studies* (London: Longman, 1981; 3rd ed. 1998).

Light, A. *Common People* (London: Penguin Books, 2014).

MacRaild, D.M. and Martin, D.E. *Labour in British Society, 1830–1914* (London: Palgrave Macmillan, 2000).

Marshall, N. 'Rural Experience and the Development of the Middle Class: The Power of Culture and Tangible Improvements', *American Nineteenth-Century History*, 8:1 (2007).

Marx, K. and Engels, F. *The Manifesto of the Communist Party* (1848) at http://www.marxists.org/archive/marx/works/download/pdf/Manifesto.pdf

Nye, D.E. *America as Second Creation* (Cambridge, MA: MIT Press, 2004).

Williams, R. *The Country and the City* (London: Chatto and Windus, 1973).

Woods, M. *Rural* (London: Routledge, 2011).

Chapter 1: Lincoln's April Fair: renegotiating rural and urban relations in a small city, *c.*1820–1910

Primary sources

Fairs and markets committee of Lincoln Corporation, minutes at Lincolnshire Archives (L1/1/20/1-3).

Grantham Journal, 13 April 1878.

Lincolnshire Chronicle, 29 April 1842; 28 April 1848; 29 April 1859; 29 April 1864; 30 April 1864; 30 April 1869; 8 March 1878; 26 April 1878; 28 April 1882; 27 April 1883; 24 April 1885; 30 April 1886; 29 April 1892; 6 May 1898; 28 April 1899; 24 April 1903.

Lincolnshire Echo, 28 April 1893; 21 April 1894; 16 May 1894; 16 May 1895; 21 April 1897.

Police Officers' Journals and Pocket Books at Lincolnshire Archives (CONSTAB 2/1/2/2/1).

Hardy, T. *The Mayor of Casterbridge* (1886), edited by M. Seymour-Smith (Harmondsworth: Penguin, 1978).

Rider Haggard, H. *Rural England Being an Account of Agricultural and Social Researches Carried Out in the Years 1901 and 1902, Vol. 2* (Cambridge: Cambridge University Press, 1902).

Stamford Mercury, 27 April 1821; 26 April 1822; 24 April 1829; 27 April 1832; 3 May 1844; 22 April 1864.

Secondary sources

Burchardt, J. *Paradise Lost: Rural Idyll and Social Change Since 1800* (London: I.B. Tauris, 2002).

Bushaway, B. *By Rite: Custom, Ceremony and Community in England, 1700–1880* (London: Junction Books, 1982).

Davey, B. *Lawless and Immoral: Policing a Country Town, 1838–1857* (Leicester: Leicester University Press, 1983).

Dobraszczyk, P. 'Victorian Market Halls, Ornamental Iron and Civic Interest', *Architectural History*, 55 (2012).

Elvin, L. 'The May Hirings', *Fireside Magazine*, 4 (1967).

Elvin L. *Lincoln As It Was* (London: Hendon Publishing Company, 1974).

Freeman, M. 'The Agricultural Labourer and the Hodge Stereotype, c. 1850–1914', *Agricultural History Review*, 49 (2001).

Hill, F. *Victorian Lincoln* (Cambridge: Cambridge University Press, 1974).

Joyce, P. *The Rule of Freedom: Liberalism and the Modern City* (London: Verso, 2003).

MacCarthy, F. *William Morris* (London: Faber & Faber, 1994).

Mills, D. 'Population, 1801–1901', in A. Walker, (ed.), *Monks Road: Lincoln's East End Through Time* (Lincoln: The Survey of Lincoln, 2006).

Moses G. 'Rustic and Rude: Hiring Fairs and their Critics in East Yorkshire, c.1850–1875', *Rural History*, 7 (1996).

Moses, G. 'Passive and Impoverished? A Discussion of Rural Popular Culture in the Mid-Victorian Years', *Rural History*, 22 (2011).

Reay, B. *Rural Englands: Labouring Lives in the Nineteenth Century* (Basingstoke: Palgrave Macmillan, 2004).

Royle, S. 'The Development of Small Towns in Britain, in P. Clark (ed.), *The Cambridge Urban History of Britain, Volume III, 1840–1950* (Cambridge: Cambridge University Press, 2000).

Schmiechen, J. 'The Nineteenth-Century Townscape and the Return of the Marketplace in Victorian History', in T. Larson and M. Shirley (eds), *Splendidly Victorian: Essays in Nineteenth- and Twentieth-Century British History in Honour of Walter L. Arnstein* (London: Ashgate, 2001).

Thompson, E.P. *Customs in Common* (London: Merlin Press, 1991).

Wiener, M. *English Culture and the Decline of the Industrial Spirit, 1850–1980* (Cambridge: Cambridge University Press, 1981).

Wilson, C. *Lincolnshire's Farm Animals* (Lincoln: Society for Lincolnshire History and Archaeology, 2012).

Wright, N. *Lincolnshire Towns and Industry, 1700–1914* (Lincoln: History of Lincolnshire Committee, 1982).

Chapter 2: Policing Brough Hill Fair, 1856–1910: protecting Westmorland from urban criminals

Primary sources

Appleby Petty Sessions, court minute books, WTPS/A, 1851–1903.

Appleby Petty Sessions, Court Registers, WTPS/AA/AB 1880–1886.

Bulmer, T.F. *History, Topography and Directory of Westmoreland* (Manchester: Bulmer, 1885).

Clarke, T., Rev., Bowness, W. and Southey, R. *Specimens of the Westmorland Dialect, Reprinted from the Westmorland Gazette* (Kendal: Atkinson & Pollitt, 1870).

Descriptions of persons appointed, Cumberland Police, SCons 2/7, 1865–1884.

Garnett, F.W. *Westmorland Agriculture 1800–1900* (Kendal: Titus Wilson, 1912).

General Orders from the Chief Constable: 1857–1897, SCons 1/14; *1888–1897*, SCons 1/114.

Green, W. *The Life and Adventures of a Cheap Jack* (London, 1876).

Gregg, B.M. *A Police Constable's Guide to his Daily Work* (London: Effingham Wilson, 1919).

Kendal Mercury, 24 October, 1852; 1 October, 1859; 5 October, 1861.

Kendal Police, record book of policemen, WS/Cons 10/1, 1860–1947.

Kirkby Lonsdale Police Occurrence Book, WS/Cons 2/8, 1897–1922.

Kirkby Stephen Police Occurrence Books, WS/Cons 4/1 1857–1880; WS/Cons 4/2, 1883–1894; WS/Cons 4/3, 1894–1902.

Kirkby Stephen Police Charge Books, WS/Cons 4/10 1874–1888; WS/Cons 4/11, 1888–1915.

Kirkby Stephen Petty Sessions Court Registers, WTPS/KS no.1, 1880–1894.

Lancashire Evening Post, 2 October 1901.

Lancaster Gazette, 16 April 1861; 17 October 1863.

Leland, C.G. *The Gypsies* (Boston: Houghton, Mifflin and Co., 1886).

Loisan, R. *Confessions of Robert Loisan, alias Rambling Rob* (No publisher cited, c.1870), at East Riding Archives and Local Studies Service, Beverley, Yorkshire.

Manchester Courier and Advertiser, 29 September, 1896.

Morning Post, 12 October, 1857.

Maryport Police Station, Correspondence, CAC SCons 4/75, 1877–1881.

Morton, J.C. *A Cyclopedia of Agriculture, Practical and Scientific, by Upwards of Fifty of the Most Eminent Practical and Scientific Men of the Day*, vol. 2 (London, 1855).

Nash-Stephenson, R. 'On Statute Fairs: their Evils and their Remedy', *Transactions of the National Association for the Promotion of Social Science* (1858).

Newcastle Courant, 22 October 1852.

North Eastern Daily Gazette, 12 October 1888.

Northern Echo, 1 October 1870; 2 October 1893.

Nottinghamshire Guardian, 10 October 1850.

Page, J. *The story of the Manchester Fairs* (Manchester: Heywood, 1887).

Prisoners tried at Quarter Sessions and Assizes, Cumberland and Westmorland. Record of persons brought before Quarter Sessions and Assizes. Metropolitan Police, PCOM 2/451, 14 October 1907.

Returns of the distribution and constitution of staff, Cumberland Police, SCons 2/19, 1866–1873. 2/20; 1874–1890; 2/21, 1891–1901.

Sanger, G. *Seventy Years a Showman*. (New York, E.P. Dutton, 1927).

Tremenheere, H.S. *Commission on the Employment of Children, Young Persons, and Women in Agriculture (1867). Second Report of the Commissioners, with appendix part I* (London: H. M. Stationery Office, 1868).

Royal Commission on Market Rights and Tolls. Minutes of evidence, Vol. VII. With appendices. Parliamentary Papers, C.6268-I: p. 288.
Westmorland Gazette, 9 October, 1858; 8 October, 1870; 5 October, 1878; 6 October, 1878; 5 October, 1894.
Westmorland Quarter Sessions Minute Book, WQ/M/32, 1859–1875.
York Herald, 28 October 1882; 6 January 1883.
Yorkshire Post and Leeds Intelligencer, 5 November, 1884.
Yorkshire Weekly Post, 10 October, 1908.

Secondary sources

Addison, W. *English Fairs and Markets* (London: Batsford, 1953).
Alexander, S. *St. Giles's Fair, 1830–1914 Popular Culture and the Industrial Revolution in 19th Century Oxford* (Oxford: Ruskin College, History Workshop, 1970).
Anderson, B.R.O. *Imagined Communities: Reflections on the Origin and Spread of Nationalism* (London: Verso, 2006).
Bailey, P. *Leisure and Class in Victorian England* (London: Methuen, 1978).
Becker, H.S. *Outsiders: Studies in the Sociology of Deviance* (New York: The Free Press, 1963).
Beckett, J.V. *Coal and Tobacco: the Lowthers and the Economic Development of West Cumberland, 1660–1760* (Cambridge: Cambridge University Press, 1981).
Cameron, D.K. *The English Fair* (Stroud: Sutton Publishing, 1998).
Catt, J. *Northern Hiring Fairs* (Chorley: Countryside Publications, 1986).
Caunce, S. 'The Hiring Fairs of Northern England, 1890–1930: A Regional Analysis of Commercial and Social Networking in Agriculture', *Past and Present*, 217:1 (2012).
Cohen, A.P. *Belonging: Identity and Social Organisation in British Rural Cultures* (Manchester: Manchester University Press, 1982).
Critchley, T.A. *A History of Police in England and Wales* (Montclair, NJ: Patterson Smith, 1972).
Crone, R. *Violent Victorians: Popular Entertainment in Nineteenth-Century London* (Manchester: Manchester University Press, 2012).
Cunningham, H. 'The Metropolitan Fairs' in A.P. Donajgrodzki (ed.), *Social Control in Nineteenth Century Britain* (London: Croom Helm, 1977).
Emsley, C. *The English Police: a Political and Social History* (London: Longman, 1996).
Emsley, C. *Crime and Society in England, 1750–190* (London: Pearson Longman, 2005).
Emsley, C. *The Great British Bobby* (London: Quercus, 2009).
Fiske, J. *Understanding Popular Culture* (Boston: Unwin Hyman, 1989).
Gatrell, V.A.C., Lenman, B. and Parker, G. *Crime and the Law: the Social History of Crime in Western Europe since 1500* (London: Europa, 1980).
Giddens, A. *Modernity and Self-identity* (Cambridge: Polity Press, 1991).
Giddens, A. *A Contemporary Critique of Historical Materialism, vol.2: Nation and Violence* (Cambridge: Polity Press, 1985).
Harries-Jenkins, G. 'The Development of Professionalism in the Victorian Army', *Armed Forces & Society* 1:4 (1975).
Harrison, B. 'Religion and Recreation in Nineteenth-Century England', *Past and Present*, 38 (1967).
Jones, D.J.V. *Crime in Nineteenth-Century Wales* (Cardiff: University of Wales Press, 1992).
Judd, M. '"The Oddest Combination of Town and Country": Popular Culture and the London Fairs', in J.K. Walton and J. Walvin (eds), *Leisure in Britain, 1780–1939* (Manchester: Manchester University Press, 1983).

Malcolmson, R.W. *Popular Recreations in English society, 1700–1850* (Cambridge: Cambridge University Press, 1973).

Moses, G. '"Rustic and Rude": Hiring Fairs and their Critics in East Yorkshire *c.*1850–1875', *Rural History,* 7:2 (1996).

Moses, G. 'Reshaping rural culture? The Church of England and hiring fairs in the East Riding of Yorkshire c. 1850–1880', *Rural History*, 13:1 (2002).

Neocleous, M. *The Fabrication of Social Order; a Critical Theory of Police Power* (London: Pluto Press, 2000).

Novak, S.'Professionalism and Bureaucracy: English Doctors and the Victorian Public Health Administration', *Journal of Social History*, 6:4 (1973).

Perren, R. 'The Marketing of Agricultural Products from Farm Gates to Retail Store,' in: E.J.T. Collins (ed.), *Agrarian history of England and Wales* (Cambridge: Cambridge University Press, 2000).

Philips, D. *Crime and Authority in Victorian England: the Black Country, 1835–1860* (London: Croom Helm, 1977).

Radzinowicz, L. 'Towards a National Standard of Police' in M. Fitzgerald, G. McLennan and J. Pawson (eds), *Crime and Society Readings in History and Theory* (London: Routledge and K.P. with Open University Press, 1981).

Roberts, M.J.D. *Making English Morals: Voluntary Association and Moral Reform in England, 1787–1888* (Cambridge: Cambridge University Press, 2004).

Shepherd, M.E. *From Hellgill to Bridge End: Aspects of Economic and Social Change in the Upper Eden Valley 1840–95* (Hatfield: University of Hertfordshire Press, 2003).

Sowerby, R.R. *Kirkby Stephen and District* (Kendal: Wilson, 1948).

Starsmore, I. *English Fairs* (London:Thames and Hudson, 1975).

Taylor, D. *The New Police in Nineteenth-century England: Crime, Conflict and Control* (Manchester: Manchester University Press, 1997).

Westmorland Federation of Women's Institutes, *Some Westmorland Villages* (Kendal: Westmorland Federation of Women's Institutes, 1957).

Wiener, M.J. *Reconstructing the Criminal: Culture, Law, and Policy in England, 1830–1914* (Cambridge University Press, 1990).

Williams, K. *The English Newspaper* (London: Springwood Books, 1977).

Woolnough, G. *Policing Petty Crime in Victorian Cumbria* (PhD dissertation, Keele University, 2013).

Chapter 3: Urban Unitarians vs. rural Trinitarians: town liberals in a planter culture

Primary sources

Channing, W.E. *Slavery* (Boston: James Munroe and Co, 1835).

Channing, W.E. *The Works of William E. Channing, D.D.* (Boston: American Unitarian Association, 1882).

Clapp, D. 'Letter on the Religious Conditions of Slaves,' *Monthly Religious Magazine* 3 (May 1846).

Clapp, T. 'A Thanksgiving Sermon, Delivered in the First Congregational Church, New Orleans, 19 December 1850', *Daily Picayune*, 22 December 1850.

Christian Register, 10 April 1841.

Gilman, S. *The Old and the New: Discourses and Proceedings at the Dedication of the Re-Modeled Unitarian Church* (Charleston: Samuel G. Courtenay, 1854).

Gilman, S. *A Sermon on the Introduction to the Gospel of St. John* (Charleston: Unitarian Book and Tract Society, 1825).

Joseph Gales Papers, Southern Historical Collection, University of North Carolina, Chapel Hill.

Henkel, D. *Against the Unitarians: A Treatise on the Person and Incarnation of Jesus Christ, In Which Some of the Principal Arguments of the Unitarians are Examined* (New Market, Va: 1830).

Logan, G.W. et al. *Annual Reports Rendered by the Managers of the Charleston Unitarian Book and Tract Society On the Occasion of Its Thirty-Sixth Anniversary, Sunday, August 9, 1857* (Charleston: Walker, Evans & Co., 1857).

Miller, S. *Letters on Unitarianism Addressed to the Members of the First Presbyterian Church of Baltimore* (Trenton, N.J.: George Sherman, 1821).

Richard D. Arnold Papers, Southern Historical Collection, Wilson Library, University of North Carolina, Chapel Hill.

Whitridge, J.B. *Calling Things by Their Right Names: A Brief Reply To An Article Under That Title, In the Southern Watchman of May 19, 1837. By a Layman* (Charleston: Walker and James, 1937).

Secondary sources

Adams, R. *The Charleston Unitarianism Gilman Began With*, in K.B. Murdock (ed.) (Cambridge: Harvard University Library, 1952).

Alhstrom, S.E. *A Religious History of the American People* (New Haven: Yale University Press, 1972).

Brooks, A.A. *A History of Unitarianism in the Southern Churches: Charleston, New Orleans, Louisville, Richmond* (Boston: American Unitarian Association, [n.d.].

Conkin, P.K. *American Originals: Homemade Varieties of Christianity* (Chapel Hill: University of North Carolina Press, 1997).

Duffy, J. (ed.), *Parson Clapp of the Strangers' Church of New Orleans* (Baton Rouge: Louisiana State University Press, 1957).

Eaton, C. *Freedom of Thought Struggle in the Old South* (New York: Harper and Row, 1964).

Gibson, G.H. "Unitarian Congregations in the Antebellum South" in *Proceedings of the Unitarian Historical Society* 12:2 (1959).

Gibson, G.H. 'Unitarian Congregations in Ante-Bellum Georgia' *Georgia Historical Quarterly* 54 (1970).

Gohdes, C. 'Some Notes on the Unitarian Church in the Ante-Bellum South: A Contribution to the History of Southern Liberalism' in: D.K. Jackson (ed.) *American Studies in Honor of William Kenneth Boyd by Members of The Americana Club of Duke University* (Durham: Duke University Press, 1968).

Howe, D.W. 'A Massachusetts Yankee in Senator Calhoun's Court: Samuel Gilman in South Carolina', *New England Quarterly* 44 (1971).

Macaulay, J.A. *Unitarianism in the Antebellum South: The Other Invisible Institution* (Tuscaloosa: University of Alabama Press, 2001).

Moltke-Hansen, D. 'The Expansion of Intellectual Life: A Prospectus,' in M. O'Brien and D. Moltke-Hansen (eds) (Knoxville: University of Tennessee Press, 1986).

O'Brien, M. and Moltke-Hansen, D. (eds) *Intellectual Life in Antebellum Charleston* (Knoxville: University of Tennessee Press, 1986).

Pease, W.H. and Pease, J.H. *The Web of Progress: Private Values and Public Styles in Boston and Charleston, 1828–1843* (Athens and London: The University of Georgia Press, 1991).

Rugemer, E. *The Problem of Emancipation: The Caribbean Roots of the American Civil War* (Baton Rouge: Louisiana State University, 2009).

Stange, D.C. *Patterns of Antislavery among American Unitarians, 1831–1860* (Rutherford: Fairleigh Dickinson University Press, 1977).

Wells, J. *The Origins of the Southern Middle Class, 1800–1861* (Chapel Hill: University of North Carolina Press, 2004).

Wilbur, E.M. *A History of Unitarianism in Transylvania, England and America* (Boston: Harvard University Press, 1952).

Wright, C. *The Beginnings of Unitarianism in America* (Boston: Starr King Press, 1955).

Wright, C. *The Liberal Christians: Essays on American Unitarian History* (Boston: Beacon Press, 1970).

Chapter 4: Country butchers and the city in the Exe Valley, 1840–1900

Primary sources

Exeter and Plymouth Gazette [from 1884 the *Devon and Exeter Gazette*], 26 Dec 1835; 22 Mar 1841; 11 Feb 1843; 24 Dec 1847; 5 Jan 1850; 15 Sept 1855; 12 Sept 1857; 22 Jun 1866; 23 Sept 1882; 9 Jan 1886.

General Purpose and Markets Committee Minutes, 1840–1900, Exeter City Archive.

Royal Commission on Markets and Tolls (1889) Vol III, London: HMSO.

Trewman's Exeter Flying Post, 13 June 1844; 25 Dec 1845; 12 July 1849; 14 Feb 1858; 16 Dec 1863; 23 Dec 1863; 14 Dec 1870; 28 Dec 1870; 5 July 1871; 2 Dec 1874; 11 Oct 1876; 19 Dec 1877; 25 Sept 1883.

Western Times, 18 Apr 1840; 6 Nov 1841; 20 Dec 1845; 25 Dec 1852; 11 Jan 1862; 11 Oct 1862; 13 Dec 1863; 20 Dec 1863; 16 Jan 1863; 6 Jan 1865; 12 Feb 1867.

White, W. *History, Gazetteer and Directory of Devonshire* (London: White's, 1850).

Secondary sources

Alexander, N. and Akehurst, G. 'The emergence of modern retailing, 1750–1950', *Business History*, 40, 4 (1998).

Benson, J. and Shaw, G. (eds). *The Evolution of Retail Systems, c.1880–1914* (Leicester: Leicester University Press, 1992).

Brown, J. *The English Market Town: A Social and Economic History 1750–1914* (Marlborough: Crowood Press, 1986).

Burnett, J. *Plenty and Want: A Social History of Diet in England* (London: Nelson, 1966).

Collins, E.J. (ed.) *Agrarian History of England and Wales, Vol. VII, 1850–1914* (Cambridge: Cambridge University Press, 2000).

Jeffreys, J.B. *Retail Trading in Britain, 1850–1950* (Cambridge: Cambridge University Press, 1954).

Newton, R. *Victorian Exeter* (Leicester: Leicester University Press, 1968).

Perren, R. *The Meat Trade in Britain, 1840–1914* (London: Routledge & Keegan Paul, 1978).

Phillips, M. 'The Evolution of Markets and Shops in Britain', in Benson and Shaw, *Evolution of Retail Systems, c.1880–1914* (Leicester: Leicester University Press, 1992).

Schmiechen, J. and Carls, K. *The British Market Hall: a Social and Architectural History* (New Haven: Yale University Press, 1999).

Scola, R. 'Food Markets and Shops in Manchester, 1770–1870', *Journal of Historical Geography*, 1:2 (1975).

Shaw, G. 'The Study of Retail Development' in J. Benson and G. Shaw (eds), *The Evolution of Retail Systems, c.1880–1914* (Leicester: Leicester University Press, 1992).

Chapter 5: Doncaster and its environs: town and countryside – a reciprocal relationship?

Primary sources

Baines, E. *Directory of Yorkshire*, 1822, Vol. 1 (Leeds, 1822).

Doncaster Archives, AB2/2/3, *Council Minutes*, 11 March 1840; 9 May 1843; Feb 1842; AB2/2/5, 9 May 1860; DD/BW/E11/126, Battie-Wrightson Miscellaneous Papers, Doncaster Agricultural Society Leaflets.

Doncaster Chronicle, 18 Oct 1844; 30 Jan 1863; 15 Feb 1867; 7 Mar 1873; 18 Apr 1873, supplement.

Doncaster Gazette, 28 Feb 1840; 5 May 1844; 17 May 1844; 2 Feb 1849; 12 Jun 1863, p. 5; 9 May 1873.

Farmer's Magazine, Vol. 1, May to December (1834).

The Farmer's Guide to Scientific and Practical Agriculture (Vol. 2, 1862).

The Journal of the Royal Agricultural Society of England (Vol. 2, 1841).

The New York Farmer and American Gardener's Magazine (Vol. 9, 1836; Vol. 10, 1837).

White, W. History, *Gazetteer and Directory of the West Riding, 1837* (Sheffield, n.p., 1837).

Secondary sources

Berend, I. *Economic History of Nineteenth Century Europe* (Cambridge University Press, Cambridge, 2013).

Briggs, A. *Victorian Cities* (London: Odhams, 1965).

Brown, D. 'The Rise of Industrial Society and the End of the Self-Contained Village, 1760–1900?' in C. Dyer (ed.), *The Self-Contained Village?: The Social History of Rural Communities 1250–1900* (Hatfield: University of Hertfordshire, 2007).

Brown, J. *The English Market Town: A Social and Economic History 1750–1914* (Marlborough: Crowood Press, 1986).

Chalklin, C. *The Rise of the English Country Town, 1650–1850* (Cambridge: Cambridge University Press, 2001).

Chalklin, C.W. 'Country Towns' in G.E. Mingay (ed.), *The Victorian Countryside* (London: Routledge and Kegan Paul, 1981).

Cherry, G.E. and Sheail, J. 'Town and Country: An Overview' in E.J.T. Collins (ed.), *The Agrarian History of England and Wales, Vol. VII, 1850–1914*, Part II (Cambridge: Cambridge University Press, 2000).

Girouard, M. *The English Town: A History of Urban Life* (Yale: Yale University Press, 1990).

Holland, D and E.M. *A Yorkshire Town: The Making of Doncaster* (iBook edition, 2012).

Holland, S. 'The Evolution of a Northern Corn Market: Doncaster 1843–1873', *Northern History*, 51, 2 (September 2015).

Holland, S. 'Contrasting Rural Communities: The Experience of South Yorkshire in the Mid-Nineteenth Century', Unpublished PhD Thesis, Sheffield Hallam University, 2013.

Howe, A. *Free Trade and Liberal England 1846–1946* (Oxford: Clarendon Press, 1997).

Jones, P. *The Sociology of Architecture: Constructing Identities* (Liverpool: Liverpool University Press, 2011).

Marshall, J.D. 'The Rise and Transformation of the Cumbrian Market Town, 1600–1900', *Northern History*, Vol. 19 (1983).

Miskell, L. 'Puttting on a Show: the Royal Agricultural Society of England and the Market Town, *c.*1840–1876', *Agricultural History Review*, 60:1 (2012).

Perren, R. 'The Marketing of Agricultural Products: Farm Gate to Retail Store' in E.J.T. Collins (ed.), *The Agrarian History of England and Wales, Vol. VII, 1850–1914, Part II* (Cambridge: Cambridge University Press, 2000).

Schonhardt-Bailey, C. *From the Corn Laws to Free Trade: Interests, Ideas and Institutions in Historical Perspective* (Massachusetts Institute of Technology Press, MA, 2006).

Smart, P. 'Corn for Sale! The Markets and Corn Exchanges in Reading and Wokingham', *Berkshire Old and New*, 30 (2013).

Chapter 6: 'Following the tools': migration networks among the stone workers of Purbeck in the nineteenth century

Primary sources

Letter from Jn Bishop, 10 June 1771, Dorset Record Office D-RWR/E/107.

The National Archive [hereafter NA]: census enumerators' books for Langton Matravers, Dorset 1841 (NA HO 107/278/2), 1851 (NA HO 107/1856), 1861 (NA RG 9/1343), 1871 (NA RG 10/1992), 1881 (NA RG 11/2098) and 1891 (NA RG 12/1641); and Sheldon, Derbyshire 1851 (NA HO 107/2149), 1861 (NA RG 9/2539) and 1871 (NA RG 10/3627).

K. Schürer, *1881 Census for England and Wales, the Channel Islands and the Isle of Man* (study number 4177) (Colchester: UK Data Archive, 2000).

Secondary sources

Anderson, M. *Family Structure in Nineteenth-Century Lancashire* (Cambridge: Cambridge University Press, 1971).

Bailey, C. '"I'd Heard It Was such a Grand Place": Mid-19th Century Internal Migration to London', *Family and Community History*, 14 (2011).

Benfield, E. *Purbeck Shop: a Stone Worker's Story of Stone* (Cambridge: Cambridge University Press, 1940).

Bryant, D. 'Demographic Trends in South Devon in the Mid Nineteenth Century', in K.J. Gregory and W.L.D. Ravenhill (eds), *Exeter Essays in Geography in Honour of Arthur Davies* (Exeter: Exeter University Press, 1971).

Caird, J. *English Agriculture in 1850–51*, 2nd edn (London: Longman, Brown, Green and Longmans, 1852).

Crickland, M.M. and Vellacott, C.H. 'Industries', in W. Page (ed.), *The Victoria History of the County of Dorset* (London: Archibald Constable, 1908).

Drury, G.D. 'The Use of Purbeck Marble in Medieval Times', *Proceedings of the Dorset Natural History and Archaeological Society*, 70 (1948).

Edgar, M. and Hinde, A. 'The stone workers of Purbeck', *Rural History*, 10 (1999).

French, C. 'Persistence in a Local Community: Kingston Upon Thames 1851–1891', *Local Population Studies*, 81 (2008).

Fripp, J. 'Mobility in Victorian Dorset', *Proceedings of the Dorset Natural History and Archaeological Society*, 129 (2009).

Gant, R. 'School Records, Family Migration and Community History: Insights from Sudbrook and the Construction of the Severn Tunnel', *Family and Community History*, 11 (2008).

Hinde, A., Davies, H.R. and Kirkby, 'D.M. Hampshire Village Populations in the Nineteenth Century', *Southern History*, 15 (1993).

Hinde, P.R.A. 'The Population of a Wiltshire Village in the Nineteenth Century: a Reconstitution Study of Berwick St James, 1841–71', *Annals of Human Biology*, 14 (1987).

Hutchins's History and Antiquities of the County of Dorset, edited by W. Shipp and J.W. Hodson, 3rd edn, 4 vols (Westminster, 1861–70).

Howard, P.D. 'An analysis of migration in rural northern Hampshire 1841–1861' (MA dissertation, University of Southampton, 1996).

John Mowlem's Swanage Diary, 1845–1851, edited by D. Lewer (Dorchester: Dorset Publishing Co., 1990).

Jones, M. 'Combining Estate Records with Census Enumerators' Books to Study Nineteenth-Century Communities: the Case of the Tankersley Ironstone Miners, *c.* 1850', in D. Mills and K. Schürer (eds), *Local Communities in the Census Enumerators' Books* (Oxford: Leopard's Head Press, 1996).

Kerr, B. 'The Dorset Agricultural Labourer 1750–1850', *Proceedings of the Dorset Natural History and Archaeological Society*, 84 (1962).

Kerr, B. *Bound to the Soil: a Social History of Dorset 1750–1918* (London: John Baker, 1968).

Leivers, C. 'The Modern Ishmaels? Navvy Communities in the High Peak', *Family and Community History*, 9 (2006).

Moore, M. 'Stone Quarrying in the Isle of Purbeck: an Oral History' (MA dissertation, University of Leicester, 1992).

Nair, G. and Poyner, D. 'The Flight from the Land: Rural Migration in South-East Shropshire in the Late Nineteenth Century', *Rural History*, 17 (2006).

Pooley, C. and Turnbull, J. *Migration and Mobility in Britain since the Eighteenth Century* (London: University College London Press, 1998).

Razzell, P.E. and Wainwright, R.W. (eds), *The Victorian Working Class: Selections From Letters to the Morning Chronicle* (London: Cass, 1973).

Robin, J. *Elmdon: Continuity and Change in a North-West Essex Village 1861–1964* (Cambridge: Cambridge University Press, 1980).

Saville, J. *Rural Depopulation in England and Wales, 1851–1951* (London: Routledge and Kegan Paul, 1957).

Saville, R.J. *Langton's Stone Quarries*, 2nd edn (Langton Matravers: Langton Matravers Local History and Preservation Society, 1986).

Southall, 'H.R. The Tramping Artisan Revisits: Labour Mobility and Economic Distress in Early Victorian England', *Economic History Review*, 44 (1991).

Wojciechowska, B. 'Brenchley: a Study of Migratory Movements in a Mid Nineteenth Century Rural Parish', *Local Population Studies*, 41 (1988).

Chapter 7: 'Life in our villages is practically no life at all': sketching the rural–urban shift in nineteenth-century depictions of Wales

Primary sources

'Aunt Maria's Diary of the Doings Round the Towns', *South Wales Star*, 24 March 1893; 7 April, 1893; 28 July 1893.

Beale, A. *The Vale of the Towey; or, Sketches in South Wales* (London: Longman, Brown, Green & Longman, 1844).

'Electric Tramway to Barry Island', *Evening Express*, 14 October 1892.

Lane, A. *Sketches of Wales and the Welsh* (London: Hamilton & Adams, 1847).

Reports of the Commissioners of Inquiry into the State of Education in Wales, Part II: Report on the Counties of Brecknock, Cardigan, Radnor, and Monmouth (London: HMSO, 1847).

'Round the Towns [by Mr Gadabout]', *South Wales Star*, 10 February 1893.

'Rural Life', *Cardiff Times*, 20 August 1887.

'Rural Life', *South Wales Star: Barry, Cadoxton and Penarth Edition*, 28 September 1891.

Saunders, S.M. 'The Courtship of Edward and Nancy', *Young Wales*, 1897.

Sinclair, C. *Hill and Valley; or, Hours in England and Wales* (New York: Robert Carter, 1838).

'Sketches from the Country', *Aberystwyth Observer*, 9 February 1889.

'Sketches of Welsh Life: God's Poor', *Llangollen Advertiser*, 28 December 1894.

'Tales and Sketches of Wales: A Welsh Heroine', *Pembrokeshire Herald*, 10 December 1869.

Secondary sources

Aaron, J. 'Introduction: Chartism, Nationalism and Language Politics', in J. Aaron and U. Masson (eds), *The Very Salt of Life* (Dinas Powys: Honno, 2007).

Eliot, S. 'From Few and Expensive to Many and Cheap: The British Book Market 1800–1890', in S. Eliot and J. Rose (eds), *A Companion to the History of the Book* (Chichester: Wiley-Blackwell, 2009).

Kinsley, Z. *Women Writing the Home Tour, 1682–1812* (Aldershot: Ashgate, 2008).

Pratt, M. *Imperial Eyes: Travel Writing and Transculturation* (London: Routledge, 1992).

Schensul, J.J. and Lecompte, M.D. *Designing and Conducting Ethnographic Research* (Walnut Creek, California: AltaMira, 1999).

Smith, D. 'Barry: A Town out of Time', *Morgannwg*, 29 (1985).

Williams, J. 'Artegall, or Remarks on the Reports of the Commissioners of Inquiry into the State of Education in Wales', in J. Aaron and U. Masson (eds), *The Very Salt of Life* (Dinas Powys: Honno, 2007).

Zagarell, S.A. 'Narrative of Community: The Identification of a Genre', *Signs*, 13, 3 (Spring, 1988).

Online sources

Welsh Newspapers Online, National Library of Wales (2013). Available at: http://welshnewspapers.llgc.org.uk/en/home

Welsh Journals Online, National Library of Wales (2009). Available at: http://welshjournals.llgc.org.uk/

Chapter 8: The early popular press and its common readers in nineteenth-century *fin de siècle* Prague

Primary sources

Illustrirtes Prager Extrablatt, 1879, 1881.

Národní listy, 28 February 1880.

Národní politika, 28 October 1896.

Pochodeň, 14 July 1914.
Pražský illustrovaný kurýr, 1893–1918.

Secondary sources

Anderson, P. *The Printed Image and the Transformation of Popular Culture: 1790–1860* (Oxford: Oxford University Press, 1991).
Boháč, A. *Hlavní město Praha: Studie o obyvatelstvu* (Praha: Státní úřad statistický, 1923).
Burke, P. *Lidová kultura v raně novověké Evropě* (Praha: Argo, 2005).
de Certeau, M. *The Practice of Everyday Life* (Berkeley, L.A.: University of California Press, 1984).
Chlad, B. 'Jak jsem ilustroval "Kurýra"', *Humoristické Listy*, 67:11 (1924).
Cohen, G.B. 'Society and Culture in Prague, Vienna, and Budapest in the Late Nineteenth Century', *East European Quarterly*, 20:4 (1986).
Conboy, M. *The Press and Popular Culture* (London: Sage, 2002).
Dorčáková, J. 'Počátky senzacechtivého tisku v českých zemích' (MA Dissertation, Charles University, Prague, 2010).
Fialová, L. et al. *Dějiny obyvatelstva českých zemí* (Praha: Mladá Fronta, 1996).
Fritzche, P. *Reading Berlin 1900* (Cambridge, MA/London: Harvard University Press, 1996).
Horská, P., Maur, E. and Musil, J. *Zrod Velkoměsta: Urbanizace českých zemí a Evropa* (Praha, Litomyšl: Paseka, 2002).
Kodetová, O. *Prameny k revolučnímu hnutí a ohlasu ruské revoluce, sv.I., Rok 1905* (Praha: Nakladatelství ČSAV, 1959).
Machačová, J. and Matějček, J. *Nástin sociálního vývoje českých zemí 1780–1914* (Opava: Slezské zemské muzeum, 2002).
Machek, J. 'Pražský illustrovaný kurýr. Masový tisk jako obraz světa obyčejných lidí'(PhD Dissertation, Charles University in Prague, 2012).
Sekera, M. 'Podíl Grégrů na rozvoji novinářství a politické publicistiky', in M. Řepa and P. Vošahlíková (eds), *Bratři Grégrové a česká společnost v druhé polovině 19. století* (Praha: Eduard Grégr a syn, 1997).
Wood, N.D. 'Urban self-identification in East Central Europe before the Great War: Cracow's Popular Press and the Case of Cracow', *East Central Europe/L'Europe du Centre*, 33:1–2 (2006).

Chapter 9: Reorienting the Piney Woods: rural and urban change in south Mississippi, 1830–1910

Primary sources

Annual Reports of the War Department: for the Fiscal Year Ended June 30, 1899: Report of the Chief Engineers Part II (Washington, DC: United States Government Printing Office, 1899).
Claiborne, J.F.H. 'A Trip Through the Piney Woods', in Franklin Riley (ed.), *Publications of The Mississippi Historical Society* (Volume IX, Oxford, MS: Mississippi Historical Society, 1907).
Gulf and Ship Island Minute Book, 1887–1907, Hattiesburg, MS, University of Southern Mississippi Special Collections.
Hattiesburg American, 24 May 1918.

Hilgard, E.W. *Report on the Geology and Agriculture of Mississippi* (Jackson, MS: E. Barksdale, 1860).

National Archives of the United States, Washington, DC, *World War I Selective Service Registration Cards, 1917–18*, M1509.

Report of Mississippi State Board of Centennial Managers (Jackson, MS: Clarion Steam Printing Establishment, 1877).

Thomasville Echo, 19 June 1902.

United States Department of Commerce, Bureau of the Census, *Thirteenth Census of the Unites States, 1910*.

Vasseulus, P. Oral History Interview quoted in O.B. Caudill (ed.), *Hattiesburg: the First Hundred Years An Oral History* (Hattiesburg, MS: The Mississippi Oral History Program, 1982).

Secondary sources

Adkins, H. G. 'The Historical Geography of Extinct Towns', in P. W. Prenshaw and J. O. McKee (eds), *Sense of Place: Mississippi* (Jackson, MS: University Press of Mississippi, 1979).

Adkins, H.G. 'The Geographic Base of Urban Retardation in Mississippi, 1800–1840'. *Studies in the Social Sciences*, 12 (1973).

Adkins, H.G. 'The Historical Geography of Extinct Towns', in P.W. Prenshaw and J.O. McKee (eds), *Sense of Place: Mississippi* (Jackson, MS: University Press of Mississippi, 1979).

Ayers, E. *The Promise of the New South: Life After Reconstruction* (Oxford: Oxford University Press, 1992).

Blevins, B. *Cattle in the Cotton Fields: A History of Cattle Raising in Alabama* (Tuscaloosa, AL: University of Alabama Press, 1998).

Bond, B.G. (ed.) *Mississippi: A Documentary History* (Jackson, MS: University Press of Mississippi, 2003).

Bond, B.G. 'Herders, Farmers and Markets on the Inner Frontier: The Mississippi Piney Woods, 1850–1860', in S.C Hyde (ed.), *Plain Folk of the South Revisited* (Baton Rouge: Louisiana State University Press, 1997).

Braudel, F. 'Histoire et sciences sociales: La longue durée', *Annales E.S.C.*, XIII, 4, (1958).

Cowdrey, A. *This Land, This South* (Lexington, NY: University Press of Kentucky, 1983).

Danbom, D. *Born in the Country: A History of Rural America*, 2nd ed. (Baltimore, MD: Johns Hopkins University Press, 2006).

Davis, B.*The Southern Railway: Road of Innovators* (Chapel Hill, NC: University of North Carolina Press, 1985).

Early L.S. *Looking for Longleaf: The Fall and Rise of an American Forest* (Chapel Hill, NC: University of North Carolina Press, 2004).

English, A. *All Off For Gordon's Station: A History of the Early Hattiesburg, Mississippi Area* (Baltimore, MD: Gateway Press, Inc., 2000).

Flores, D. 'Place: An Argument for Bioregional History', *Environmental History Review*, 18:4 (Winter 1994).

Geddes, P. 'Civics: As Applied Sociology, Part 1', *Sociological Papers, 1904* (London, 1905).

Goldfield, D. *Region, Race and Cities: Interpreting the Urban South* (Baton Rouge, LA: Louisiana State University Press, 1997).

Gregory, J. *The Southern Diaspora: How the Great Migrations of Black and White Southerners Transformed America* (Chapel Hill: University of North Carolina Press, 2005).

Guice, J.D.W. 'Cattle Raisers of the Old Southwest: A Reinterpretation', *Western Historical Quarterly*, 8:2 (Apr.,1977).

Hardy, T. *No Compromise With Principle: Autobiography and Biography of William Harris Hardy* (New York: American Book-Stratford Press, Inc., 1942).

Hattiesburg News, 29 November 1912.

Herring, M.R. *Way Station to Space: A History of the John C. Stennis Space Center* (Washington, DC: National Aeronautics and Space Administration, 1997).

King, Jr, J.C. 'The Closing of the Southern Range: An Exploratory Study', *The Journal of Southern History*, 48: 1 (February 1982).

Kirby, J.T *Poquosin: A Study of Rural Landscape and Society* (Chapel Hill, NC: University of North Carolina Press, 1995).

Mackay, B. 'End or Peak of Civilization?' *Survey Graphic*, LXVII, (October 1932).

McKee, J.O. 'The Residential Patterns of Blacks in Natchez and Hattiesburg and Other Mississippi Cities' (PhD Dissertation, Michigan State University, 1972).

McMillen, N.R. *Dark Journey: Black Mississippians in the Age of Jim Crow* (Urbana, IL: University of Illinois Press, 1989).

Moore, J.H. *Agriculture in Ante-Bellum Mississippi* (Columbia, SC: University of South Carolina Press, reprint edition, 2010).

Napier III, J.H. 'The Gilded Pearl: From Settlers to Sawmill Hands', *Gulf South Historical Review* 10:1 (Fall 1994).

Noe, K.W. *Southwest Virginia's Railroad: Modernization and the Sectional Crisis in the Civil War Era* (Urbana, IL: University of Illinois Press, 1994).

Nye, D.E. *America as a Second Creation: Technology and Narrative of New Beginnings* (Cambridge, MA: MIT Press, 2003).

Odum, H.W. *Southern Regions of the United States* (Chapel Hill, NC: University of North Carolina Press, 1936).

Owsley, F.L. *Plain Folk of the Old South* (Baton Rouge: Louisiana State University Press, reprint 2008).

Phythian-Adams, C. in: *Societies, Cultures and Kinship, 1580–1850* (London: Leicester University Press, 1993).

Reay, B. *Rural Englands* (New York: Palgrave Macmillan, 2004).

Richards, J. and Mackenzie, J.M. *The Railway Station: A Social History* (Oxford: Oxford University Press, 1986).

Rowe, M. *Captain Jones: Biography of a Builder* (Hamilton, Ohio: The Hill-Brown Printing Company, 1942).

Rowland, D. *Mississippi: Comprising Sketches of Counties, Towns, Events, Institutions, and Persons, Arranged in Cyclopedic Form* Volumes I and II (Jackson, MS: Mississippi Department of Archives and History, 1907: reprint, Spartanburg, SC: The Reprint Company Publishers, 1976).

Saikku, M. *This Delta, This Land: An Environmental History of the Yazoo-Mississippi Floodplain* (Athens, GA: University of Georgia Press, 2005).

Schivelbusch, W. *The Railway Journey: The Industrialization of Time and Space in the 19th Century* (Berkeley: University of California Press, 1986).

Skates, J.R. 'Hattiesburg: The Early Years,' in K.G. McCarty (ed.), *Hattiesburg: A Pictorial History* (Jackson, MS: University Press of Mississippi, 1982).

Stover, J.F. *Railroads of the South: A Study in Finance and Control* (Chapel Hill, NC: University of North Carolina Press, 1955).

Thigpen, S.G. *A Boy in Rural Mississippi* (Picayune, MS: S.G. Thigpen, 1966).

Trachtenberg, A. 'Foreword', in W. Schivelbusch, *The Railway Journey: The Industrialization of Time and Space in the 19th Century* (Berkeley: University of California Press, 1986).

Wetheringtron, M.V. *New South Comes to Wiregrass Georgia, 1860–1910* (Knoxville, TN: University of Tennessee Press, 1994).

Vance, R.B. *Human Geography of the South* (Chapel Hill, NC: University of North Carolina Press, 1932).

Young, A.L. and Kidd, R.S. 'Some Eight to Ten Miserable Tenements: Archeological Investigations at Old Augusta, Perry County, Mississippi', *Mississippi Archeology*, 33, 1 (1998).

Chapter 10: The urbanisation of James Carter: autobiography, migration and the rural–urban divide in nineteenth-century Britain

Primary sources

Archives of the Royal Literary Fund, *Registered Case File, vol. 25, no. 813: Mr. James Carter, a Tailor of Colchester*, British Library Add MS RLF 1/813/1-60.

Baudelaire, C. *The Painter of Modern Life and Other Essays*, trans. J. Mayne (New York: Phaidon Publishing, 1964).

Boase, F. *Modern English Biography: Containing Many Thousand Concise Memoirs of Persons Who have Died since the Year 1850* (Truro: Netherton and Worth, 1892).

Carter, J. *Continuation of the Memoirs of a Working Man* (London: Charles Cox, 1850).

Carter, J. *Memoirs of a Working Man* (London: Charles Knight, 1845).

Carter, J. *Thoughts on Several Subjects* (London: Charles Cox, 1852).

'The Countryman in London', in *The Universal Songster; or the Museum of Mirth*, vol. 1 (London: John Fairburn, 1825).

Cowper, W. *The Poems of William Cowper: Volume II, 1782–1785*, edited by J.D. Baird and C. Ryskamp (Oxford: Clarendon Press, 1995).

Cruikshank, G. *The Countryman in London* (London: R. Harrild, [1814]).

Cruikshank, G. 'Picture of London', in *The Metropolis of England Displayed; or, A Pilot Thro' London* (London: G. Smeeton, n. d.).

Cruikshank, G. *Looby Lump's Life in London* (London: George Humphrey, 1822).

Egan, P. *Life in London* (London: Sherwood, Neely and Jones, 1822).

Grant, J. *The Great Metropolis*. 2 vols (London: Saunders and Otley, 1837).

Hardy, T. 'The Dorsetshire Labourer', 1883, in Hardy, *Personal Writings: Prefaces, Literary Opinions, Reminiscences*, (ed.) H. Orel (Lawrence: University of Kansas Press, 1966).

Hardy, T. 'Preface to *Far from the Madding Crowd*', 1874, in Hardy, *Personal Writings. Prefaces, Literary Opinions, Reminiscences*, (ed.) H. Orel (Lawrence: University of Kansas Press, 1966).

Hardy, T. *Thomas Hardy's Personal Writings: Prefaces, Literary Opinions, Reminiscences*, (ed.) H. Orel (Lawrence: University of Kansas Press, 1966).

London Metropolitan Archives, *Saint Paul, Covent Garden, Westminster, Transcript of Baptisms, Marriages and Burials, 1819 Jan–1819 Dec*, no.158, LMA 098/018.

The Metropolis of England Displayed; or, A Pilot Thro' London (London: G. Smeeton, n. d.).

'Obituary: Mr. James Carter', *Gentleman's Magazine*, 49 (1853).

'Review: James Carter, *Two Lectures on Taste*.' *Intellectual Repository and New Jerusalem Magazine* 30, 34 (1853).

Taylor, A. and Taylor, J. *City Scenes; or, A Peep into London for Good Children* (London: Darton and Harvey, 1809).

The Universal Songster; or, Museum of Mirth. 3 vols (London: John Fairburn, 1825).

Wordsworth, W. *The Prelude 1799, 1805, 1850,* (eds) J. Wordsworth, M.H. Abrams and S. Gill (New York: W.W. Norton, 1979).

Secondary sources

Ashton, O. and Roberts, S. *The Victorian Working-Class Writer* (London: Cassell, 1999).

Barrell, J. 'Geographies of Hardy's Wessex', in K.D.M. Snell (ed.), *The Regional Novel in Britain and Ireland, 1800–1990* (Cambridge: Cambridge University Press, 1998).

Bayly, C.A. *The Birth of the Modern World, 1780–1914* (Malden, Mass.: Blackwell, 2004).

Bermingham, A. *Landscape and Ideology: The English Rustic Tradition, 1740–1860* (London: Thames and Hudson, 1987).

Brown, A.F.J. *Essex People, 1750–1900: From Their Diaries, Memoirs and Letters* (Chelmsford: Essex County Council, 1972).

Burnett, J., D. Vincent and D. Mayall (eds), *The Autobiography of the Working Class:An Annotated, Critical Bibliography.* 2 vols. (New York: New York University Press, 1984).

Borsay, J. *The English Urban Renaissance: Culture and Society in the Provincial Town, 1660–1770* (Oxford: Clarendon Press, 1989).

D'Cruze, S. *A Pleasing Prospect: Social Change and Urban Culture in Eighteenth-Century Colchester* (Hatfield: University of Hertfordshire Press, 2008).

Dyck, I. *William Cobbett and Rural Popular Culture* (Cambridge: Cambridge University Press, 1992).

Dyck, I. 'The Town and Country Divide in English History', in M. Chase and I. Dyck (eds), *Living and Learning: Essays in Honour of J. F. C. Harrison* (Aldershot: Scolar Press, 1996).

Ferguson, C. 'Inventing the Modern City: Urban Culture and Ideas in Britain, 1780–1880' (PhD Dissertation, Indiana University, 2008).

George, M.D. *Catalogue of Political and Personal Satires in the British Museum* (London: British Museum, 1978).

Gooder, J. 'Introduction', in H. Adams, *The Education of Henry Adams* (London: Penguin Books, 1995).

Gunn, S. and Vernon, J. (eds), *The Peculiarities of Liberal Modernity in Imperial Britain* (Berkeley: University of California Press, 2011).

Gurney, P. 'Working-Class Writers and the Art of Escapology in Victorian England: The Case of Thomas Frost', *Journal of British Studies*, 45:1 (2006).

Hackett, N. *XIX Century British Working-Class Autobiographies: An Annotated Bibliography* (New York: AMS Press, 1985).

Joyce, P. *Democratic Subjects: The Self and the Social in Nineteenth-Century England* (Cambridge: Cambridge University Press, 1994).

Langton, J. 'Urban Growth and Economic Change from the Seventeenth Century to 1841', in P. Clark (ed.), *The Cambridge Urban History of Britain, 1540–1840* (Cambridge: Cambridge University Press, 2000).

Lawton, R. 'Population Mobility and Urbanization: Nineteenth-Century British Experience', in R. Lawton and R. Lee (eds), *Urban Population Development in Western Europe from the Late-Eighteenth to the Early-Twentieth Century* (Liverpool: Liverpool University Press, 1989).

Mehta, S. *Maximum City: Bombay Lost and Found* (New York: Alfred A. Knopf, 2004).

Mitchell, B.R. *British Historical Statistics* (Cambridge: Cambridge University Press, 1988).

Pooley, C.G. and Turnbull, J. *Migration and Mobility in Britain since the Eighteenth Century* (London: UCL Press, 1998).

Rowe, J.C. *Henry Adams and Henry James: The Emergence of a Modern Consciousness* (Ithaca: Cornell University Press, 1976).

Sharpe, P. 'Population and Society, 1700–1840', in P. Clark (ed.), *Cambridge Urban History of Britain* (Cambridge: Cambridge University Press, 2000).

Snell, K.D.M. *Annals of the Labouring Poor: Social Change and Agrarian England, 1660–1900* (Cambridge: Cambridge University Press, 1985).

Turner, V. *The Ritual Process: Structure and Anti-Structure* (1969; Ithaca: Cornell University Press, 1977).

Vincent, D. *Bread, Knowledge and Freedom: A Study of Nineteenth-Century Working Class Autobiography* (London: Methuen, 1981).

Williams, R. *The Country and the City* (Oxford: Oxford University Press, 1973).

Whyte, I.D. *Migration and Society in Britain, 1550–1830* (Basingstoke: Macmillan, 2000).

Woods, R. *The Population of Britain in the Nineteenth Century* (London: Macmillan, 1992).

Chapter 11: Pip at the fingerpost: nineteenth-century urban–rural relations and the reception of Dickens's *Great Expectations*, 1860–1885

Primary sources

Accounts of sales of the works of Charles Dickens: Chapman and Hall, Vol. 2, National Arts Library, Victoria and Albert Museum, F.D. 18.3.

'All the Year Round – London: Chapman and Hall', *Chester Chronicle*, Saturday 9 February 1861, p. 5.

Belfast Morning News, Thursday 27 June 1861.

Derby Mercury, Wednesday 24 July 1861.

Dickens, C. *Great Expectations*, E. Rosenberg (ed.) (New York: Wm Norton, 1998).

Dickens, C. *Great Expectations* (1860–61; Oxford: Oxford University Press, 1993).

Dickens, C. *Letters of Charles Dickens*, Vol. 9, K. Tillotson and G. Storey (eds) (Oxford: Clarendon Press, 1965–1997).

'GREAT EXPECTATIONS', *Morning Post*, Wednesday 31 July, 1861.

Hampshire Advertiser, Saturday 10 August 1861.

Hardy, T. *Far From the Madding Crowd* (1874; London: Macmillan, 1965).

Hereford Journal, Wednesday 13 March 1861.

Leeds Times, Saturday 21 September 1861.

'Literary Memoranda', *Northampton Mercury*, Saturday 8 December 1860.

'Mr Dickens's Last Novel', *Dublin University Magazine*, December 1861.

Spectator, 20 July 1861.

Rider Haggard, H. *Rural England: Being an Account of Agricultural and Social Researches Carried Out in the Years 1901 & 1902*, Vol. 2 (1902; Boston, 2001).

Unsigned review by E.S. Dallas, *The Times*, 17 October 1861, p. 6.

Secondary sources

Bunce, M. *The Countryside Ideal: Anglo–American Images of Landscape* (London and New York: Routledge, 1994).

Collins, P. *Charles Dickens: the Critical Heritage* (Abingdon and New York: Routledge, 1986).

Dyck, I. 'The Town and Country Divide in English History', in M. Chase and I. Dyck (eds), *Living and Learning: Essays in Honour of J.F.C. Harrison* (Aldershot: Scolar Press, 1996).

Finney, G. 'Garden Paradigms in 19th-Century Fiction', *Comparative Literature*, 36:1 (Winter, 1984).

Fischler, A. 'Love in the Garden: *Maud, Great Expectations*, and W.S. Gilbert's Sweethearts', *Studies in English Literature, 1500–1900*, 37:4 (Autumn, 1997).

Ford, G. *Dickens and His Readers: Aspects of Novel Criticism since 1836* (New York: W.W. Norton, 1965).

Hammond, M. *Charles Dickens's Great Expectations: A Cultural Life, 1860–2012* (Burlington, VT: Ashgate, 2015).

Hobsbawm, E. *Industry and Empire: The Penguin Economic History of Britain, Vol. 3* (London: Penguin, 1968).

Patten, R.L. *Charles Dickens and His Publishers* (Oxford: Oxford University Press, 1978).

Sadrin, A. *Great Expectations* (London: Unwin Hyman, 1988).

Williams, R. *The Country and the City* (Oxford: Oxford University Press, 1975).

Chapter 12: Country bumpkin or backbone of the nation?: the urbanisation of the agricultural labourer and the 'unmanning' of the English in the later nineteenth century

Primary sources

Anderson, P.G. *The Rural Exodus* (London: Methuen and Co., 1892).

Arch, J. 'The Labourers and the Vote', *Nineteenth Century*, 3:11 (January 1878).

'ART.V11-1. *Sixth Report of the Commissioners of the Children's Employment Commission.* 1867. – 2. *Seventh Report of the Medical Officer of the Privy Council with Appendix.* 1864*', *Quarterly Review*, 145:245 (July 1867).

Davies, G.J. 'Peasantry of the South of England', *Fraser's Magazine*, 7:41 (May 1873).

Gaskell, E. *Mary Barton* (1848; Harmondsworth: Penguin, 1970; reprinted 1985).

Green, F.E. *A History of the English Agricultural Labourer 1870–1920* (London: P.S. King and Son, 1920).

Hardy, T. 'The Dorsetshire Labourer', *Longman's Magazine*, 2:9 (July 1883).

Hardy, T. *The Works of Thomas Hardy* (Ware, Herts: Wordsworth, 1994).

Housman, A.E. *Collected Poems* (Harmondsworth: Penguin, 1956; reprinted 1961).

Howitt, W. *The Rural Life of England* (1838; 2nd ed. London: Longman, Orme, Brown, Green & Longman, 1842).

Jefferies, R. 'The Future of Farming', *Fraser's Magazine* 8:48 (December 1873).

Jefferies, R. 'The Wiltshire Labourer', *Longman's Magazine*, 3:13 (November 1883).

Jessopp, A. 'The Cry of the Villages', *Nineteenth Century: a monthly review*, 45:268 (June 1899).

Kebbel, T.K. 'The Agricultural Labourer', *Cornhill Magazine*, 27:159 (March 1873).

Rider Haggard, H. *A Farmer's Year* (London: Longman's Green and Co., 1899).

Rider Haggard, H. *Rural England* 2 vols (London: Longman's, Green and Co., 1902).

Stratton, J.Y. 'The Life of a Farm Labourer', *Cornhill Magazine*, 9:50 (February 1864).

Unsigned Review. 'Slavery in England', *All the Year Round, A Weekly Journal Conducted by Charles Dickens, With Which is Incorporated Household Words*, 15 June 1867.

Secondary sources

Bagwell, P.S. and Mingay, G.E. *Britain and America 1850–1939: a study of economic change* (London: Routledge Kegan and Paul, 1970; reprinted 1987).

Eddowes, J. *The Agricultural Labourer as He Really Is, or Village Morals in 1854*, in M. Freeman (ed.), *The English Rural Poor 1850–1914* (London: Pickering and Chatto, 2005).

Freeman, M. 'The agricultural labourer and the "Hodge" stereotype', *Agricultural History Review*, 49:II (2001).

Hobsbawm, E. *The Age of Capital 1848–1875* (London: Weidenfeld and Nicolson, 1975; reissued 1995).

Howkins, A. 'From Hodge to Lob: reconstructing the English farm labourer, 1870–1914', in M. Chase and I. Dyck (eds), *Living and Learning: Essays in Honour of J.F.C. Harrison* (Aldershot: Scolar Press, 1996).

Long, J. 'Rural–Urban Migration and Socioeconomic Mobility in Victorian Britain', *The Journal of Economic History*, 65:1 (March 2005).

Penn, M. *Manchester Fourteen Miles* (1947; Firle, Sussex: Caliban Books, 1979).

Thomas, E. *The South Country* (Wimborne Minster, Dorset: Little Toller Books, 2009).

Thoreau, H.D. *Walden* (New York: Signet Classics New American Library of World Literature inc., 1964).

Index

For Product Safety Concerns and Information please contact our EU
representative GPSR@taylorandfrancis.com
Taylor & Francis Verlag GmbH, Kaufingerstraße 24, 80331 München, Germany

www.ingramcontent.com/pod-product-compliance
Ingram Content Group UK Ltd.
Pitfield, Milton Keynes, MK11 3LW, UK
UKHW020958180425
457613UK00019B/735